Other books by Dr. Les Carter

The Anger Workbook

Freedom from Depression Workbook

Choosing to Forgive Workbook

People Pleasers

The Worry Workbook

Forthcoming from Jossey-Bass

The Anger Workbook for Christian Parents

THE ANGER TRAP

THE ANGER TRAP

Free Yourself from the Frustrations That Sabotage Your Life

Dr. Les Carter

○

Foreword by Dr. Frank Minirth

Published by Jossey-Bass
A Wiley Imprint
989 Market Street, San Francisco, CA 94103-1741 www.josseybass.com

Jossey-Bass books and products are available through most bookstores. To contact Jossey-Bass directly call our Customer Care Department within the U.S. at 800-956-7739, outside the U.S. at 317-572-3986, or fax 317-572-4002.

Jossey-Bass also publishes its books in a variety of electronic formats. Some content that appears in print may not be available in electronic books.

Library of Congress Cataloging-in-Publication Data

Carter, Les.
The anger trap : free yourself from the frustrations that sabotage your life / Les Carter, Foreword by Frank Minirth.— 1st ed.
p. cm.
ISBN 0-7879-6879-X
1. Anger. 2. Anger—Case studies. I. Minirth, Frank B. II. Title.
BF575.A5C37 2003
152.4'7—dc21

2003006258

Printed in the United States of America
FIRST EDITION
HB Printing 10 9 8 7 6 5 4 3 2 1

CONTENTS

Dedicated with love to Jennifer, Cara, and Megan

FOREWORD

AS YOU MIGHT IMAGINE, I encounter a wide array of symptoms each day as I treat patients in my psychiatric practice. Most commonly, I talk with individuals struggling with depression, anxiety, bipolar disorder, attention deficit, panic disorder, and general mood instability. Each case represents a life that is hurting, and it becomes my privilege to intervene in that hurt with treatment plans designed to eliminate or minimize those difficulties.

In a high percentage of my cases, I hear stories that indicate significant problems with anger. Not all of my patients handle anger in loud and forceful ways, though some do, and these people invariably find that pushy anger does nothing but deepen their woes. Many, thinking that they are avoiding the painful effects of anger, have learned to suppress the emotion, only to discover that it later feeds other unwanted problems like anxiety and depression. Some resort to passive means of handling anger, only to realize later that the anger is not only not resolved, but intensified. I will explain to all these individuals that they can greatly improve their chances of overcoming a variety of emotional strains if they will learn to confront their own anger skillfully. Anger is certainly an emotion that can be understood and managed successfully, but so many people have had such a lack of guidance regarding emotional matters that they need someone to carefully walk them through the steps of appropriately handling anger.

I know of no person who can guide individuals through the maze of anger more effectively than Dr. Les Carter. Throughout our twenty-five-year association, I have known him to be a true student of human emotions. He loves to learn about the things that cause people to respond as they do, and he is a highly skilled communicator who can help the average man or woman clearly comprehend the complex matters of emotional pain. His extensive history of leading anger workshops and counseling individuals through emotional turmoil give him a perspective matched by only a few.

The Anger Trap is a masterfully written book, offering penetrating insights into the factors that can imprison individuals in unwanted patterns of frustration. With his well-developed insights and using case examples,

Les Carter carefully explains how you can change your thinking, your communication, and your behavior as you release yourself from the ravages of anger gone bad.

Read *The Anger Trap* with the anticipation that you will learn many interesting things about yourself. As you couple your willingness to change with Dr. Carter's ability to communicate illuminating truths, there is no reason for you to expect anything less than life-enhancing improvements.

FRANK MINIRTH, M.D.

ACKNOWLEDGMENTS

THROUGHOUT THIS BOOK, I present case studies as a means of illustrating how people can come to terms with the concepts that accompany the process of change. Know that I have carefully altered the identities of those described in each case study to protect confidentiality. The experiences described, however, are quite real. I consider my life as a psychotherapist to be a privilege and I am honored each time individuals choose to work with me in the quest for personal peace.

Many thanks are given to Meagan Nichols for her assistance in preparing the manuscript. Likewise, Vickie Gage and Brian Wade have been most valuable in their assistance as this writing effort unfolded. I am indebted to Bruce Barbour for his efforts in guiding the project to its conclusion; he is a trusted advisor and a true friend. I am fortunate to have him as a mentor.

My work with the people at Jossey-Bass has been nothing short of phenomenal. What a fine team they are! They have a strong sense of purpose as a publishing house, and their infectious passion inspires me to be most conscientious in the work I do with them. Special thanks go to Mark Kerr for leading the editing process. Also, I am grateful for the contributions of Debra Hunter, Sheryl Fullerton, Sandy Siegle, Eric Thrasher, Paul Foster, and Joanne Clapp Fullagar. It has been a true joy to know and work with them and their assistants.

LES CARTER, PH.D.

INTRODUCTION

IT IS NOT UNCOMMON for people to ask why I write and teach about the subject of anger. I wish I could reply that my sole reason is to bring enlightenment to people who, unlike me, have had ongoing problems with anger. Actually I do hope to inspire others to learn how to be most effective in managing this emotion, but I must confess that my interest in the subject has personal roots as well.

I recall as a boy how extended family members seemed to remain stuck in a predictable pattern of agitation, bitterness, or contentiousness. Likewise, in my own family of origin frustration and annoyance seemed to hang on, at times longer than necessary. I can remember being afraid to go to the homes of certain friends because of a dad or brother who was chronically mean. In my own adult life, I have proved capable of responding to frustration in a sour or brash manner, and I have been on the receiving end of the same. Never have I experienced an extended period of time of such peace that there was not someone somewhere in my world capable of mishandling anger.

Being a curious person, I have been unable to let all these observations and experiences of anger pass without looking into the *why* of this emotion's existence. Beginning in my twenties, my quest was to develop as thorough an understanding of the emotion of anger as possible. I am five decades deep into life now, and I have found that examining anger can open a wide door leading to discovery of all sorts of interesting dimensions of the personality. For instance, exploration of anger can lead to discovery about hidden insecurity, fear, misassumption about control, the role of spiritual strength, raw selfishness, and myths that have been accepted as truth. It can prompt us to look deeply into our methods of communication, and it can challenge us to ponder the roles of love, respect, understanding, and forgiveness.

There is a distinct difference between those who are able to find success in taming their anger and those who remain stuck in its clutches. Those trapped by their own anger persistently attempt to force others to meet their demands before they can find peace, whereas those who find release from anger do not. Finding victory over the ravages of anger is contingent upon a powerful willingness to peer into one's own personality, asking such questions as "Why do I feel as I do?" "What do my angry responses say about my most basic guiding beliefs?" "Where does the ability to change come from?" "What adjustments could I make even if my entire world remains as it is?"

As you read *The Anger Trap,* do so with a willingness to confront yourself. In the pages that follow, you are challenged to delineate healthy forms of anger from the unhealthy. You are encouraged to examine carefully some of the most prominent features that keep you imprisoned by the forms of anger that perpetuate pain. And you will be inspired to contemplate how to develop higher priorities that will dissuade you from returning to wearisome behavioral patterns.

Know that I do not write as a lecturing professor who likes to pontificate about the latest theories on anger development. Rather, I am a fellow sojourner who has looked carefully into my own soul and into the souls of many who have entrusted me with personal revelation. The concepts and ideas expressed in these pages are my own reflections, born out of three decades of exploration in the subject.

THE ANGER TRAP

PART ONE

UNDERSTANDING THE NATURE OF ANGER

I

THE CRY BEHIND THE ANGER

THROUGH THE YEARS, as I have counseled with hundreds of people trying to make sense of their anger, I have learned one thing. There is always something more that feeds the anger than what is observed on the surface. Angry people may appear strong, willful, or certain, but be assured that beneath the veneer are fear and loneliness and insecurity and pain. Especially, there is pain. Whether they admit it or not, angry people are hurt people, and they have somehow come to believe that they can resolve their own pain by inflicting pain upon others. Their reasoning is usually subconscious; nonetheless, each time anger is misapplied, it is a reflection of a deep wound that longs to be healed.

As I work with individuals trying to overcome anger's harmful effects, I recognize that they will remain trapped inside their own anger if they do not learn to peer deeply inside their souls to explore the factors that give impetus to their anger. Yes, they will need to learn techniques, if you will, that would represent an improved means of addressing frustration, and they can certainly be expected to learn the difference between healthy and unhealthy forms of anger. They need to recognize, though, that a mere attempt to adjust anger's manifestation without also digging into the matters generating the pain produce superficial change at best.

To be released from the trap of anger, these persons need to identify the cry behind the rage.

Exasperation was written all over Julie's face as she sat in my office with her husband, Steve. "We've been married six years," she explained, "and during that time I've hardly known a moment of peace. When we dated, Steve had been a perfect gentleman. In fact, he was so nice to me and my kids that it almost seemed too good to be true. Well, in the first month of marriage I learned that it *was* too good to be true. This guy has a temper like no one I know." Julie's face turned red and tears watered her eyes as she tried to keep her composure.

"In our first few months of marriage, I learned that he had dozens of do's and don'ts regarding the ways life should unfold. He had rules for everything, and if I or one of my kids broke a rule, the floodgates of anger would burst wide open." Julie went on to explain that Steve could curse easily at her, calling her foul names and making wild accusations. Sometimes he would slam doors, throw things, or punch his fist into a wall. When driving his truck, he would tailgate motorists who drove too slowly and he often made nasty remarks, even though it would do absolutely nothing to move the traffic along more smoothly. Steve had never been fired from his job as a plumbing contractor, but that was because he owned the company. Through the years, he had worn out one employee after another because he could be so moody and belligerent. Anger seemed to be the defining feature of his personality.

When I asked Steve what he thought about the things being related by Julie, he grinned and shrugged, "What can I say? She's right, I've got a temper. But hey, don't most people? It's not like I beat her or anything like that. Yeah, I could probably stand to lighten up a little, but it's not like I'm some sort of criminal."

With that response, Julie heaved a great sigh. "He's impossible, and I don't know if he'll ever get it! His anger is draining me, and I'm not able to handle it much longer. If he's not careful, he's going to get his third divorce because I'm not going to keep putting up with it, just like his first two wives wouldn't."

In my counseling office, I encounter people like Steve who seem to retreat toward anger like an old friend who is not really good for them but is familiar. Despite many damaging experiences, they keep going back to the familiar anger patterns because they know no other way to respond when their world becomes problematic. Family members and friends may plead with them to change tactics, but to no avail. Even after apologies are offered and promises for improvement are made, the ugly forms of anger predictably return. As illogical as it may be, it can seem to outside observers that chronically angry people have a strong commitment to keeping distasteful emotions alive. Certainly they have not made a commitment toward better alternatives.

People like Steve, who have such a ready response of anger, seem to be held captive by their emotional impulses. Though they may openly admit that their anger produces very few positive results, they remain stuck in a nonproductive cycle as if drawn to it like a magnet. This nonproductive anger becomes a trap that keeps them caged inside a life of misery.

Let's acknowledge that no one is entirely free from anger. Whether we want it to be part of our life experience or not, it is natural to each personality. Sometimes we have little control over the possibility of anger being experienced; it can appear quite unannounced. At times it can be triggered by an immediate hurt or frustration, while at other times it is provoked by a memory of past experience. When I counsel angry people, it is not the experience of anger that concerns me; rather, I focus most powerfully on what they do with the emotion and why it can so easily be used nonproductively.

As I continued to speak with Steve about his anger, I learned that this problem had plagued him most of his life. Steve's own father had also lived inside an anger trap. Easily agitated, the father was known for violent outbursts that would seemingly arise from nowhere. "I remember as a grade school boy," Steve recalled, "when my brother and I were bickering in the back seat of the family's station wagon as we were traveling on vacation. Without a word of warning, my dad pulled the car over to the shoulder of the road, then he came around to my door. He opened it with a jerk, yanked me out of the car, then he blistered my bottom *hard*. My little brother started crying and my mother yelled at my dad for being so abrasive, but none of that fazed him. He pushed me back into the car, and still without saying a word, we drove on. That's the kind of guy he was. He was mean and cold. I couldn't begin to count the number of times he took out his anger like that toward either me or my brother."

I probed, "How did that harsh treatment affect you?"

Still trying to act nonchalant, Steve shrugged and said, "I hated it, but I also got used to it. It got to the point where it didn't bother me anymore."

I did not buy that last statement for a second. Receiving such ill treatment *did* bother Steve, and it played a great role in the development of his own adult anger. Throughout his teen years, then through his twenties, thirties, and now his forties, Steve's anger played out in an almost nonstop fashion. That anger did not arise from a vacuum. It had very deep roots that were tied to the pain he never resolved as a boy who lived in fear of his father's next outburst. For him to make improvements in his current management of emotions, he would need to open his mind to great insight and adjustment. Despite his statements to the contrary, I recognized that Steve was a deeply wounded man, and the potency of his current anger was a clear signal that he was not remotely coming to terms with his pain.

The Purpose of Anger

When I hear stories from angry people and those who live with angry people, I learn that the triggering experiences for anger vary widely. Anger may arise, for instance, if a family member speaks in a wrong tone of voice.

It is displayed when a coworker does not produce desired results. Anger is experienced when traffic is unfriendly, when others are argumentative, when bills pile up, when the dog relieves himself indoors, when someone fails to do as promised, when another person is critical, when a child refuses to mind, when one is feeling ignored.

In most of the instances that trigger anger, the emotion is likely to be managed distastefully, usually in insulting, invalidating, or insensitive behavior. That being the case, many will conclude that anger has no positive function. It seems to be the response of a person who is mean-spirited or who has low regard toward those provoking the response.

Anger, though, is not a one-dimensional emotion, and we need not summarily dismiss it as all bad. Although it can certainly be used in an unhealthy or unstable manner, it is not always wrong to feel angry. At the heart of anger is a cry for respect. Though angry persons may not speak these exact words, their emotion may reveal thoughts such as:

"You need to understand that I matter."

"I want to be held in high regard."

"I'm tired of feeling as though life is going to be one extended struggle."

"I deserve better treatment than what I am currently receiving."

"I'm not going to let you get away with ill treatment toward me."

"My opinions are as good as anyone else's. Pay attention to me!"

"Don't look down on me. That's offensive."

When people feel angry, it is a response to a perceived threat or invalidation. The anger taps into a primary desire for self-preservation. In fact, anger can be defined as the emotion of self-preservation. Specifically, angry people wish to preserve personal worth, perceived needs, and heartfelt convictions. Angry people want to feel that they have significance, and they are distressed as they assume that others will not or cannot address them in a way that reinforces personal significance.

Angry people, however, tend to do themselves no favors because the legitimate message of self-preservation can be communicated so distastefully that the receiver of the message hears nothing good. For instance, Steve described to me how his anger could be triggered by Julie's occasional forgetfulness. She might tell him that she would pick up his shirts at the dry cleaner's, but at the end of the day when he asks about the shirts, he will hear, "Oops, I forgot to get them." Likewise, he might ask her to purchase a specific item when she goes grocery shopping, and she could easily pick up a number of items—with the lone exception of the one he had requested. Steve explained to me, "She's been forgetful so many times in our marriage that I can no longer tolerate it. When is it going to occur to her that she needs to be a person whose word can be trusted?"

Was Steve wrong to feel angry? Not necessarily. In fact, it would be reasonable for him to speak openly with Julie about her forgetfulness. Instead of addressing his convictions constructively, though, Steve's communication style resembled a rocket launch. "What's the deal with you?" he would shout. "Why can't you help me with one measly request?" Of course, Julie never received such indignation well, meaning the legitimate portion of his message would be completely lost.

People like Steve can learn to address anger constructively. For instance, requests can be made for appropriate treatment without the request turning into an opportunity to belittle or intimidate. Boundaries and stipulations can be established even as the offending person is treated with dignity. The experience of anger not only does not have to become a springboard for foul treatment, it can actually prompt someone to stand up for needs and convictions in a positive manner.

Those who are caught in the anger trap, however, have not learned to approach anger constructively. Shackled by insecurity, fragile egotism, shame, or distrust, their anger is so raw that it can be displayed in circumstances that may not really warrant anger, and it is commonly displayed in a manner that completely sabotages any possibility for relationship growth or healing.

The Deeper Issue

When people like Steve attempt to make sense of their anger, it is tempting to focus merely on the immediate event that triggers the emotion. For instance, Steve might blame his anger on Julie by saying, "If you had been more responsible, I wouldn't be feeling so tense." Or perhaps he might say, "How else am I supposed to respond when one of the kids talks to me in that smart-aleck tone of voice?" He would not be entirely wrong to link the anger to the immediate circumstance, but in doing so, he could easily ignore the deeper issue.

Angry people are hurting, fragile people. In most cases, they are carrying shame that has gone unresolved for years, perhaps decades. Though the anger may seemingly be a reaction, for instance, to someone's current lack of cooperation, it is also a response that can be traced to pain and rejection in key relationships from years gone by. Though most angry people do not put it in these words, they have concluded that the world is a hostile, often unfriendly place where people cannot fully be trusted. This perception is most commonly formed in the childhood years and expanded during the adult years.

For years, I have met with hundreds of people who attend my anger workshops. As we explore the reasons for the buildup of anger and the options for managing it, I attempt to put their habits into a broad perspective. "How many of you," I ask, "grew up with at least one parent who had problems with anger?" Close to 100 percent of the workshop participants raise their hands. At that point, I emphasize how their current anger is a continuation of the hurt they experienced early in life due to exposure to messages of criticism, condescension, or invalidation. The anger that seemingly is a response to a current frustration is actually being fed by a root system that is drawing upon memories of rejection.

No one was born to become bitterly angry. Our Creator gave each of us life for the purpose of becoming both a recipient and a giver of love. Anger arises from the painful discovery that love is remiss, that judgment, rejection, or abandonment seems more sure. As experiences of antilove mount, the spirit becomes pessimistic, resulting in a sort of free-floating anger that represents a yearning to return to the love that was originally intended by the Creator. In this sense, anger would be considered good, if we could but respond to its promptings constructively. Many, however, use their anger to respond to rejection with rejection, to enmity with enmity, to hatred with hatred. When this occurs often enough, the commitment to goodness is supplanted by persistently dark moods that eventually hold the spirit captive.

If you have had a history of disappointment or relationship friction, you may subconsciously look for "evidence" that perpetuates your pessimistic belief about life. For instance, Steve could recall one episode after another from his childhood when his father would speak belligerently to him. His dad had a quick temper, and the slightest deviation from his preferences could bring a loud and sharp rebuke. If Steve displayed a weary or sluggish spirit while the family ate around the supper table, his father would apparently interpret it as a slight against him, so he might angrily spout, "What's the matter with you? Are you so high and mighty that you can't say anything to the rest of us?" If Steve bickered with his older sister, his dad might shout, "You're so worthless, the only thing you can do good is to make trouble!" Naturally, these words would sting, and Steve stored up feelings of resentment. He repeatedly wished he could have a father who was patient and understanding and supportive.

Now in his forties, Steve no longer had to worry about daily disruptions with his father, but he might occasionally hear words from Julie that reminded him of earlier messages of rejection. Once Julie mentioned that she wished he would be clearer in coordinating his schedule with her so she could be more synchronized with him. She spoke in an even tone of voice, and her request was legitimate. Steve, however, exploded: "Why are you always trying to pin me down? I don't need you to be my nursemaid, telling me when I have to report in to you!" Julie was baffled and shaken because his anger seemed so disproportionate to her request.

What was going on? Steve had assumed a hostile stance toward Julie. Assuming that she was attempting to control or stifle him, he quickly convinced himself that he would *not* allow Julie or anyone else to tell him what to do. Though unaware of it at the moment, he was emotionally drawing upon the hundreds of times his father belittled him and told him how to order his life to suit his own preferences. Using generalized thinking, he assumed that Julie was operating with a similarly hostile agenda. His anger revealed that he could not trust Julie because he had never learned to trust his raging father.

As you try to make sense of your current anger, be willing to examine the emotion within a deep and broad perspective. You inevitably want to preserve your personal dignity as you feel that your world is treating you unfairly, and that can be good. Would you be willing to question why your anger can be too strong or perhaps displaced onto a person who has not merited a sharp rebuke?

Long-Standing Misassumptions

To more fully tap into the origins of your anger, be willing to consider some key misassumptions that tend to accompany anger that is too overpowering or intense.

Misassumption Number One: Conflict Is an Ongoing Reminder That Differences Mean Trouble for the Relationship

When Steve was a boy, he learned that when he had differences with his father, he could expect trouble to follow. If his dad had been more mature or stable, he could have taught Steve that differences are not always wrong or bad, and that they could often become an impetus for personal expansion or growth. In his immaturity, however, the father would treat differences as something to be squelched. To add intensity to this problem, Steve also experienced several key adult relationships (including his two failed marriages) that were defined by poor negotiation of differences. He learned that differentness within those relationships would be accompanied by an attempt to force conformity. Likewise, differentness would draw out a response of defensiveness or invalidation.

Angry people often have such a strong belief that differentness produces pain that they assume a self-preserving stance almost immediately when faced with conflict. The data held inside their "emotional memory chips" alert them to take cover by using any means possible. For instance, angry people might receive another person's expression of differentness with an immediate statement of defensiveness. Perhaps they respond with words of defiance. Sometimes they feel the need to retreat, for the purpose of avoiding the pain that is presumed to be coming.

As an example, Julie approached Steve one Saturday morning to discuss a change in her day's schedule. "We've got a problem regarding our plans to go shopping for the garden supplies," she told him. "Ashley neglected to tell me that she's got to meet some classmates at the library so they could finish a science project. I'm going to have to take care of that before you and I can run our errands."

Steve responded in an irksome tone of voice: "Why is it so predictable that you'll put me on hold when some other matter interferes with our plans? Are you just going to let those kids grow up believing that their priorities will always take precedence over our marriage?"

Julie was stunned. She felt frustrated that her daughter had waited until the last minute to reveal her needs, but she assumed that she could explain her needs clearly to Steve and he would be able to adjust. He had no other pressing matters on his day's schedule. Instead of this simple conflict being handled calmly, though, Steve instinctively assumed that this problem meant trouble. He interpreted Julie's decision to help Ashley as a repudiation of him. He also assumed that the change in schedule would ruin his day.

Why such pessimism? Why was Steve so unwilling to take this minor conflict in stride with the belief that he and Julie could easily find a compromise solution? In his past, Steve learned that when he and a parent or a sibling or a former spouse were at odds regarding schedules, he would be left out. If he tried to negotiate for the purpose of having his needs met, he usually felt rebuffed or misunderstood. A simple request often turned into an ugly tiff that left him feeling that his needs were unmerited, and by the time the conflict ran its course he would be punished, ignored, or scorned.

Misassumption Number Two: Conflict Is a Sure Indication of Rejection

Angry people are pessimists who live with a chronic fear of being deemed unworthy. Many angry people would deny that they suffer from deep insecurity; nonetheless, the ease with which tension rises indicates otherwise. Unable to process conflict with objective criteria, these people immediately assume that problems are directly linked to nonaccepting attitudes of others.

One evening, fourteen-year-old Ashley was clearly in a foul mood. Steve requested that she clean the kitchen, but instead of cooperating Ashley rolled her eyes and huffed as she grumbled about being used as slave labor. About that time, Julie stepped into the picture and immediately sensed trouble, asking "Is there a problem here?" Steve replied to her with an edgy voice, "I'll say there's a problem. Ashley doesn't respect a word I say, and she's got to make a federal case of it every time I ask her to do something." Julie had also had a run-in that day with Ashley, so she responded, "I guess she's in one of her moods again, so we're going to have to be patient."

With that simple response from Julie, Steve swelled up. "Why is it that you can't back me up when Ashley's treating me like dirt?" Julie was once again baffled. Did Steve interpret her simple remark as an invalidation? Later, as she reflected on Steve's tension, she reminded herself that he often turned conflict into a referendum regarding his worth. To her, Steve seemed to be a thin-skinned person who would interpret comments to mean that you were either for him or against him.

Steve's family background instilled a question mark in his mind regarding his inherent worth. His dad was not without positive traits, as evidenced by the fact that he tried to maintain a presence in Steve's life by coaching his baseball teams and teaching him how to work on car engines. Steve recalled, though, that there was a strong emphasis on doing the right thing, and whenever he fell short his father would readily voice displeasure. His mother was not as forceful in her interactions with Steve, but she too had been known to make comments that caused Steve to question his value. "I don't know what I'm going to do with you," she would often complain. "I just wish you could be more cooperative, like your sister."

As an adult looking back on his developmental years, Steve would never say that his parents hated him. He would, however, recall that he felt his acceptance in their sight was tenuous. He knew that if he heard positive words of commendation from them, it would not be long before he would hear sentiments that seemed to imply disfavor. Because his parents did not openly discuss their belief in his inherent value, Steve's feelings of worth came to resemble a yo-yo, up one moment and down the next.

As children develop, adults hold great sway over their impressionable minds. Their words and attitudes have great authority, which means children build their self-concept around adult pronouncements. Children look to their authority figures to answer the question, "Do I matter?" Sometimes parents present a message of affirmation clearly so that even when conflict arises, the child learns to respond with confidence. "I'm valued," the child will learn to reason, "because I'm in the presence of an adult who consistently holds me in high regard."

Angry adults, however, may not be able to recall consistent feelings of safety and security when they were in the presence of an authority figure. I am not suggesting that all angry adults were chronically exposed to harsh abuse and condescension in their early years (though many were). I am suggesting, though, that the message of unconditional love was not fully addressed, leaving a question mark in developing children's minds. Not knowing for certain if their worth was constant, these individuals learned to respond to conflict with an attitude of uncertainty.

Misassumption Number Three: It Is Impossible to Address Self-Preserving Needs with Others Constructively

When I counsel angry adults, I want them to learn that they can stand up for their legitimate needs and convictions in a way that can clear a path for love and cooperation. Often, as I explain how anger does not need to be accompanied by harsh or abrupt methods, I receive words of protest. "You just don't understand what I'm up against," I may hear. "When I become angry with people who give me fits, there is no way that I'll be taken seriously if I just communicate in a soft, friendly tone of voice. I live with stubborn people, and the only way I'm going to be heard is to be strong."

Angry people are often surprised when I explain that calmness and strength are not mutually exclusive traits. In fact, I go on to explain that harsh, forceful communication is not a display of strength, but weakness. Stubborn, abrasive forms of anger are accompanied by an implied message that says, "I'm fearful that you won't respect what I have to say, so I've got to use a power tactic to get your attention." As a contrast, if anger is accompanied by calm confidence, another message is given: "I believe in what I'm saying, and I invite you to believe in me too."

It would certainly be nice if you could count on others to have a cooperative spirit each time you communicate anger with calm confidence. Unfortunately, this is not always going to happen, given the fact that others may not respond to your anger maturely. Despite their lack of proper communication response, you can still choose to manage anger appropriately.

Once Steve spoke with me about a dispute he had with his brother. Because their early years were filled with tension and arguing, they developed a habit as adults of being defensive whenever they needed to discuss differences. On this occasion, they were trying to coordinate plans to get their families together over a holiday, but Steve was frustrated because they had to schedule around the brother's activities as a coach for his son's baseball team. Instead of calmly talking with each other about the times in his schedule that would work, the two men argued forcefully about how the other was never willing to be flexible.

The discussion was very unpleasant, and Steve explained to me, "I've been trying all my life to get through to that bird-brained brother of mine, but I don't suppose we'll ever have any luck with good communication. The only language he understands is bluntness. But even when I shoot straight with him, he'll find a way to turn it into a bad scene."

When I mentioned that he could choose to stand his ground without being drawn into a verbal sparring match, he reacted negatively. "It wouldn't do any good if I somehow could enlist someone like Mother Teresa to negotiate on my behalf. I've never had much success talking about problems with my brother, and I don't expect that to change anytime soon."

Like many angry people, Steve mistakenly assumes that when others handled conflict poorly, his ability to be emotionally calm is lost. In his past, he experienced hundreds, if not thousands, of episodes where he could not be assured of a pleasing outcome. Failing to believe in his own ability to manage anger reasonably when faced with an argumentative person, his emotions took on a negative tone that led him to react poorly.

Individualized Responsibility

A relieved and liberating feeling can come upon people when I talk with them about the truth that their anger may actually have a valid purpose. When people are trained to think of anger in strictly negative terms, it may be a real eye-opener for them to learn that it is both good and necessary to be honest about what is bugging them. Most have mishandled their anger so readily that they have not had many people reinforce the notion that it can be appropriate to preserve personal worth and needs and convictions.

When I work with people trying to make sense of their anger, I emphasize the necessity of separating their emotion from the emotional response of the people who provoke ill feeling. "When you take your cues from others," I explain, "there's no telling where you might go in the expression of your anger. Because the people in your presence may not have taken the time to contemplate their own emotional management, you're setting yourself up for failure when you handle your anger on the basis of the behaviors of those people."

To be released from your anger trap, you need to think in individualized terms. As a boy or girl, you were not mature enough to know how to put emotional distance between yourself and others for the purpose of forging ahead with your own well-devised plans for anger management. In your late teens and early adult years, you may have developed habits of responding poorly to conflict, and those habits may have become the foundation for your current way of responding to friction.

As long as you float through life without a well-conceived plan for anger management and without developing insights regarding your vulnerability to this emotion, you can expect to remain trapped in frequent and ongoing pain. It is a virtual certainty that others will not be able to make you feel calm enough to free you from debilitating anger. The only person who can ultimately make improvements that tame your anger is you. Without an individualized plan for anger management, your emotions resemble the actions of a pinball in an arcade, bouncing from one poorly conceived response to the next.

Steve was at a crossroads in his life. As a middle-aged man who had experienced numerous relationship breakdowns, both in his family life and in business affairs, he knew he did not want the same trend to carry him into his retirement years. Yet because he always tended to point toward others to give evidence for his bad temper, he had made very little headway in emotional maturation.

"Steve, we can proceed with optimism if you will determine that you can lay down your blaming habits and choose to take a long, hard look at your anger management style. The fact that you feel anger so strongly tells me that you're in pain. I'm willing to help you, but it will require that you take full responsibility for your own emotional well-being."

Steve was not sure if he was ready to buy into my line of reasoning, so he replied, "How am I supposed to stop being angry when I am exposed to idiots and I have to put up with foul treatment from so many people? Are you telling me that I've got to turn into some sort of pansy and just let people walk all over me as if I just didn't care? If that's what you have in mind, I can tell you right now that you can count me out."

My response was simple. "Steve, I doubt I'd ever be able to turn you into a pansy, so you can set aside your worries about that. What I'm suggesting is straightforward. You had poor models of anger management when you were growing up, and your anger has so consumed you throughout your adult years that you have known little success in handling conflict. I'm assuming that you'd like to get out of this trap, but it's going to be largely up to you if you can succeed or not. I can help you ferret out the choices you have for handling anger, and I can talk with you about some of the underlying thought patterns that steer anger in the wrong direction. The rest is up to you. This is your life, and ultimately you and you alone are responsible for how it turns out."

Anger is not a mysterious emotion in the sense that it cannot be readily understood. In the pages to follow, we first explore how anger can be expressed, both positively and negatively. We also uncover some of the relational patterns that can keep you stuck in a web of anger, with the understanding that you can choose to be released from unhealthy patterns as you identify better alternatives.

Let me offer you a word of encouragement. When I first met Steve, I did not see many overt signs indicating we could expect a positive outcome from counseling. Initially he was defensive, and he easily minimized the debilitating effects anger had created in his life. Nonetheless, I persuaded him to participate in a six-week anger workshop, and afterward we reconvened for some individual discussion.

In our first meeting after the workshop, Steve remarked, "In all the things we learned in there, one thought stood out above all the others." He paused momentarily, and he then said, "I have choices." Hearing the emphatic way he made that statement, you would have thought that he had just discovered the key to all of life's problems . . . and perhaps he had. Though he had felt bound to his history of poor choices when anger arose, he now saw that he could replace those old maladaptive choices with more appropriate, constructive ones. He had never taken the time previously to contemplate the enormous good that could arise from such a realization.

As the weeks passed, we continued to discuss the changes of thought that were required for him to shift from unhealthy to healthy emotional management. His anger did not go away, but his use of anger changed drastically.

So it can be with you. Consider this simple analogy. Suppose you grew up in a home where English was the only language spoken. If I challenged you today to learn to speak in French, could you do so? *Oui,* but it would be a major effort. You would need special tutoring, and time to learn the new vocabulary and sentence structure. Nonetheless, with persistence it can be done.

The same can be said for restructuring your style of handling anger. Just as learning a new language is no quick and easy task, you cannot expect your anger to be changed overnight. But just as you can incorporate new lingual habits, you can expect to do the same with your emotional habits.

Proceed with the confidence that your awareness and insight can lead you to choose a more productive path. We begin by outlining in the next two chapters the choices that are yours when anger arises. Once you learn to sift out bad choices from good, you will then be ready to delve into the reasons you tend to choose as you do.

○

For Personal Reflection

- ○ What are some common occurrences that trigger your anger? What do you wish to communicate in your anger?
- ○ What is legitimate about your feelings of anger?
- ○ What do you tend to do that causes the legitimate message of your anger to be lost?
- ○ How does your management of anger leave you feeling trapped?
- ○ What painful experiences from your past help keep your current feelings of anger alive?
- ○ Why do you have difficulty accepting the reality that people can be rejecting or insensitive in the midst of conflict?
- ○ How would your management of anger change if you chose to accuse less and assume individual responsibility for your emotional balance?

2

RAW, UNREFINED ANGER

JUST BY LOOKING at Brett, you would never peg him as one prone to strong outbursts of anger. With a medium build and salt-and-pepper hair, he appeared quite pleasant as he engaged easily in friendly conversation. He had a wide circle of friends and acquaintances and was generally well liked. Yet here he was in my office because his wife had asked him to move out of the house. They had engaged in a major argument that resulted in his shouting profanities and pushing her over some furniture. Frightened, she called the police, and Brett was arrested and detained overnight in a holding cell. He was terribly embarrassed as he explained, "This is really out of character for me."

Once we discussed the scenario that was the impetus for him seeking counseling, I probed to learn how he handled anger in general. "I'm not one of those guys who has a short fuse," he told me. "It's not my style to go around raging or making a scene. I guess you can say that I really don't have a lot of anger." Pausing momentarily, he added, "Now my feelings of frustration are a different story. I stay frustrated a lot."

Brett was giving me an opening to educate him a bit regarding the link between anger and frustration, so I chimed in. "You're insinuating that anger is always accompanied by loud shouting or disruptive communication, so if you don't engage in that type of behavior, you are not experiencing anger. I want you to recognize that anger is not so one-dimensional. Sometimes anger *does* result in loud, obnoxious behavior, but it can also be experienced as frustration, irritability, impatience, or futility. It's a very broad emotion that can be manifested in many ways."

"Well, in that case," he replied, "I guess I'd have to say that I've got plenty of anger in me. I didn't realize that frustration is a form of anger."

Anger, being the emotion of self-preservation, can be experienced in many forms. When I talk with people like Brett who want to handle anger successfully, a beginning step is to develop thorough awareness of its manifestations. For instance, Brett previously minimized the awareness of his anger tendency as he assumed that frustration or irritability were not indicators of anger. In our counseling, we were able to identify numerous other behaviors that he had not linked to his anger system. As an example, Brett's wife told me that he tended to pout and withdraw. I explained that a response of that kind indicated anger. Likewise, he sometimes used sarcasm, and he could be critical. Those behaviors too were a response of anger. He could be impatient. He might argue and display easy defensiveness. Sometimes he would be evasive, or he might shut down in his communication with family members. Other times he could be stubborn or unbending in his opinion. He was known to gripe and give advice that others did not want or need. Each of these behaviors could reveal a struggle with unresolved anger.

"Whoa!" he once exclaimed. "I had no idea that so many behaviors could be linked to the one emotion of anger. Looks like I've got some work cut out for me if I'm going to learn how to master it."

You tend to experience anger when you sense that people in your world are unfriendly, uncooperative, rude, ignoring, or disinterested. In the presence of such negative input, your mind can instantly register thoughts of self-preservation: *Why are you doing this to me?* Or *I don't deserve foul treatment.* Or *I'm not putting up with this.* Or *This is ridiculous; I need some relief.* The behavior and the emotional output that can result from such thoughts vary widely, from modest expression of annoyance to wild rage.

I explained to Brett, "If you really want to be released from your anger trap, you've got to be honest regarding the many ways it shows up in your relating patterns. Eventually we'll discuss the reasons your anger gets out of hand, but first you need to be aware of the extent of the problem."

Nonproductive Forms of Anger

When you were a small child, you were not yet sophisticated enough to know how to sift through your options, both good and bad, regarding your use of anger. It is likely that your anger was handled in raw and immature behavior that did little to ease the prevailing atmosphere of conflict. As a child, you could be excused for poor anger management because you did not know any better.

When forced to use logic regarding their choice of anger management, most adults would admit that the raw, childlike forms of anger do not produce good results. They create pain, and they perpetuate problems rather than solving them. Despite this recognition, most adults continue to express anger in a raw, harmful way because they are habituated to childish anger. Though it makes no sense to yell, evade, act defensively, pout, or gripe, adults do these things, well, because that's just the way they have always done them.

Before I can make a breakthrough with people like Brett or Steve, I first help them understand the extent of the options they have regarding how they might handle anger once the feeling registers in their brain. In general, there are three categories of behavior that typify people who are trapped in nonproductive use of anger: suppression of anger, openly aggressive anger, and passive-aggressive anger. Let's break down and examine each one carefully.

Suppression of Anger

Prior to the big scene of rage that prompted Brett to come to my office, he experienced several weeks of seeming calm. His junior high school son was quite preoccupied in a flurry of extracurricular school activities and the beginning of baseball season. Also, Brett had a demanding job with an information technology company, and he lived on edge thanks to the uncertainty of the funding that would keep his job going. During the same period of time, his mother fell and broke her hip. She was a widow and lived nearby, so Brett felt obliged to tend to her medical and financial needs while she recuperated.

Despite the stress and tension created by these obligations, any outside observer would assume that Brett was a calm and cool operator who handled life's demands with ease. He was skilled at keeping a poker face in the midst of tense or excitable circumstances, and whenever anyone queried about how he was handling life, his stock reply was, "No problem." This does not mean, though, that he was experiencing no problems. It only illustrates that he did not expose his feelings often, nor did he seek help or encouragement even when he needed it most. Brett took pride in his iron-man approach to problems.

In a somewhat parallel fashion, his wife, Connie, also kept her feelings locked inside. Her motive was different in that she was a consummate people pleaser. Anyone who knew Connie would agree that she was sweet and friendly, and always available to help people who were struggling. She too had stressors, though few would know that they weighed heavily on her. She was in charge of getting her son to and from his activities. Likewise, she tried to help whenever she could with her mother-in-law's needs, buying groceries and doing her laundry. She sold residential real estate and was in a productive cycle. This was good, but it ate into her time. All the while, she tried to keep up with her friends, and she always had a smile when those friends asked how she juggled so many balls. She would chuckle and say, "You just do what you have to do. My life is never dull!"

Both Brett and Connie were long-time masters in the art of suppressing anger. Brett grew up in a home dominated by fights between his sister and mother, and he vowed early that he would not allow himself to be defined by the bickering and arguing he saw in them. Connie, on the other hand, grew up in a home that saw little open anger. Her parents divorced when she was very young, and she lived alone with her mother. She only occasionally saw her father. Connie's mom was very quiet and efficient in handling her duties, and they rarely discussed emotions or personal matters. They developed a comfortable daily routine that included low friction, so Connie learned to keep her emotions to herself as she would do whatever she was supposed to do with her schoolwork and extra activities. It was always important for her to be liked, so rarely did she engage in any controversial behavior.

The incident that provoked Brett's outburst really was quite innocent. Connie asked him to help with some simple household chores, only to feel that Brett minimized her request and brushed her off. When she pressed harder for his cooperation, that's when he exploded. "Why do you always have to invent things for me to do?" he shouted. "You know I'm not some sort of lazy bum that needs a cattle prod to get into action. I do more things for you than any other husband I know!" Connie did not receive his caustic tone well, and she immediately became defensive, so the bickering began. Once they began airing their ugly feelings, neither could be stopped. Accusations were slung back and forth. Sarcasm spewed forth. Old unresolved hurts were recalled. Then finally Brett decided that he could stand the tension no more; he had to leave the room. Connie was near the doorway, so he pushed her aside and she fell over an ottoman. It was then that the argument went from bad to worse as tears flowed, along with more accusations. Finally Connie called the police, and Brett was escorted, in humiliation, out of his own house in handcuffs.

This ugly scene was caused in large part by weeks of suppressed anger. Small annoyances and aggravations had gone unaddressed. Legitimate needs and desires were not discussed. Leisure time was not budgeted for the purpose of recharging depleted emotional batteries. It might have seemed that Connie and Brett were relatively free from anger, but in reality it had been piling up inside each of them little by little. That's what happens to suppressed anger.

When you suppress anger, you may do so without fully recognizing that you are even feeling angry, or that you are shunning legitimate problems. Suppression is defined as ignoring the need to openly address problematic circumstances because of the assumption that openness will prove to be fruitless or uncomfortable. The decision to suppress is an attempt at pain avoidance. Though there is inevitably a need to preserve personal worth or legitimate needs and convictions, the need is set aside as a false front, portrayed for the purpose of making the hurt go away, even if the effect is only temporary.

There are numerous behaviors that can indicate that you are in the habit of suppressing anger:

- Withdrawal from problems even if it means the problem is left unresolved
- Refusing to expose personal problems or needs
- Being image-conscious to the point of having to appear totally together or above the fray
- Shying away from controversial or troublesome topics
- Making excuses for others' inappropriate behavior or taking responsibility for making others feel good even when they are wronging you
- Easily second-guessing your own good judgment
- Playing the role of the people pleaser; trying to keep others happy
- Letting frustration pass without saying anything
- Refusing to let others help, even when you really need it
- Pretending not to have resentment
- Acting out the role of an encouraging or pleasant person, though you do not really feel that way
- Succumbing to the strong will of others, assuming you have no other option

Surely you have heard the phrase "out of sight, out of mind." Suppressors make the false assumption that if they can cover their real hurt and frustration, it means the anger will just go away. They presume that they have successfully rid themselves of their anger. Time, however, illustrates that the out-of-sight-out-of-mind approach to anger management is only an illusion.

About thirty years ago, a businessman developed a franchise of automobile tune-up shops in our local metroplex. His goal was to lure customers in for the necessary five thousand mile tune-ups required by the cars of that generation. He ran a series of television ads emphasizing how cars would run better and last longer if they received routine maintenance. At the end of each commercial, he was pictured with a wide grin as he would sign off: "See me now or see me later!" He knew that failure to keep up with a car's immediate needs would only mean increased problems for the owner and increased business for him!

When you suppress your anger, you are not solving your problems at all. You are only postponing the inevitable. The anger does not dissolve but is stored (with all its energy) for release at a later time. Sometimes, as in the case of Brett and Connie, it will come out in an explosion of vile and bitter communication. In many cases, suppressed anger returns in the form of depression, anxiety, or panic attack. Often it somaticizes into migraine headaches, backache, ulcers, or heart problems. People who suppress their anger commonly struggle with feelings of futility, disillusionment, and resentment. By not openly and constructively addressing their self-preserving needs, they build upon the pessimistic thought that the world is an unfriendly place that really does not care about their need to be valued.

People who regularly suppress anger can look back upon a personal history that made no allowance for individual uniqueness, especially if uniqueness might prompt them to challenge the status quo or think outside the box. These people learned early that there would be too high a price to pay if they acted upon separate preferences, so they did the only thing their young minds knew how to do: they hid their feelings.

Brett, for instance, could recall how his mother would openly shame his sister for her desire to think or behave in a way that did not meet the mother's approval. He often thought that his sister had legitimate perspectives (as in her ideas about a less-severe curfew), but he also saw how unwilling their mother was to receive her thoughts. He too had points of disagreement with his mother, but seeing how fruitless it would be to discuss them he kept them to himself.

Connie's early lessons in suppression were of a different nature from Brett's. She actually felt very close to her mother and had admired her for the way she worked hard to overcome the potential problems that would come to a single mom. She wanted her mother to be proud of her, and she certainly did not want to be an additional burden, so she was careful as a girl and young adult not to be a nuisance. Since her mom did not talk openly about personal matters, it was easy for Connie to go about her responsibilities with no fanfare and keep her feelings to herself.

Though the reasons for suppressing anger can vary widely, people who suppress operate with the belief that it is not good to express anger. Somewhere along the way they concluded that nothing good can result from emotional transparency, so in the adult years they cringe when potential problems arise. They may actually convince themselves that a stoic or stiff approach to conflict is good. Pain is seemingly averted, yet it is only compounded.

Openly Aggressive Anger

When most people think of anger, it is the image of openly aggressive anger that instantly comes to mind. True to the definition of anger, it is linked to the desire to preserve personal worth, needs, and convictions, but it is communicated in a manner that robs others of personal dignity. Aggressively angry people are so consumed with their self-preservation needs that they cannot or will not factor in the needs of the others involved.

An old Jewish proverb states that "an angry man stirs up strife, and a furious man abounds in aggression." Two and a half millennia after those words were first penned, the same thought holds true today. When anger is managed abrasively or contentiously, it is analogous to swatting a beehive: it only leads to greater agitation, as it is a certainty that nothing good will come of it. Simply put, though anger can have an appropriate message at its foundation, if managed aggressively it never succeeds.

Steve, the man whose wild temper was about to cost him his third marriage, would be a classic example of one whose anger was powerfully aggressive. If Julie had a divergent preference or perspective, he might quickly seek to invalidate her and explain in no uncertain terms that he would not put up with her guff. Although his aggressiveness was born out of self-preservation, it was a fear-based communication that gave a false impression of strength. Like most aggressive people, Steve wanted to send the message that he was an all-powerful, all-important person who had to be taken seriously, and he assumed that a calm communication would be met with disinterest.

Like suppressed anger, openly aggressive anger can be manifested in many ways:

- Loud and forceful communication that allows little room for separate ideas
- Being blunt and opinionated
- Becoming involved in bickering and snippy communication
- Complaining and griping
- Using curse words and insulting speech

- Physical expression of intimidation, such as pushing, hitting, throwing things
- Speaking words of blame and accusation
- Interrupting others in conversation, refusing to listen
- Repeating oneself to emphasize a point; insisting on having the last word
- Being critical or generally pessimistic
- Giving advice that others do not want
- Reacting to others' thoughts with ready defensiveness; rebutting

When people use these forms of anger communication, they are illustrating a deep pessimism toward being accepted if they interact with fair-mindedness or respect. Futility is a defining feature in their personality. Believing that others are incapable of willingly digesting their message, they attempt to force-feed their ideas so there is no question that they will be heard.

Like suppression of anger, using openly aggressive anger only ensures that problems return. Though aggressive people may assume that they have solved their problems once they succeed in their effort to dominate, they are actually working against themselves. For instance, Steve could cite many times in his six-year marriage when he successfully persuaded Julie to do his bidding. Yet even though he had won many battles, he was losing the war because she was beginning to seriously contemplate ending their relationship.

Those who use aggressive anger often have a truly valid message to communicate. Their method of delivery, however, can be so foul that the reasonableness of the message is completely lost. For instance, Steve once became perturbed because his stepdaughter, Ashley, took some of his tools from the garage without returning them. A couple of weeks passed before he discovered that his tools were misplaced, and when he found them he saw they had collected rust from her misuse of them. Steve felt anger welling up inside, and he was unable to let the problem pass without openly addressing it with Ashley.

Did he have a valid reason to feel angry? Yes, Ashley had disrespected him by mishandling his property, so it would be reasonable for him to teach her a needed lesson. When Steve approached Ashley, though, his aggressiveness came through loud and clear. "What's your problem, young lady?" he bellowed. "Do you just think you can do whatever you want with my stuff? Look at how you've ruined my tools. I want an explanation for this, and I want it *now*!"

Of course, Ashley was immediately defensive, and she was unable to respond in any way that would satisfy Steve, so she gave a minimal response and would not look at him. This only infuriated her stepfather so he kept up the loud, verbal bashing until he had made a complete fool of himself. His abusive spirit buried whatever message he needed to convey.

Aggressively angry adults show a strong resemblance to preschool children who have such little self-control that their anger spews out with no regard for the receiver of the outburst. Young children can be excused, however, for such immaturity because they have not yet learned to think about how their response fits in with another's need. In time, they can be taught to use empathy (consideration of others' feelings and perspectives) to handle their emotions in a way that brings satisfaction to themselves even as they illustrate awareness of the communal need for honor.

People like Steve usually have a family history where time was not taken to explore how anger could be managed while also considering the needs of the others involved. Predictably, these people received a shame-based model of anger. Conflict and mistakes were most commonly handled in a condescending or heavy-handed manner. Sometimes family members provoked anger by being excessively pious in their expectations; at other times there may have been no conception at all of common decency. Whatever the case, instead of learning to rein in the impulsiveness that so commonly accompanies childlike anger, their anger remained in its raw state as they imitated the model of anger displayed by parents, siblings, or peers.

Like small children, aggressively angry adults view the world as divided between the haves and the have-nots. Preschoolers learn very quickly that they do not have full power . . . yet. But as conflict is aired in those formative years, they learn to maneuver and manipulate as they witness how loud, forceful people seem to eventually win. In the years leading into adulthood, they do not learn to communicate anger confidently and respectfully. Instead, they come to believe that only forcefulness serves their self-preserving purposes, so they develop forceful and overpowering use of anger.

Rarely do chronically aggressive adults admit that they are bewildered and misguided. Instead of addressing the need to restructure poorly developed emotional responses, they merely point out that others are in need of correction and it is their job to stand for what is right. They continue to bring pain on themselves and others until they recognize that they no longer have to play along with the childlike thinking that is impressed with short bursts of oppression or power.

Passive-Aggressive Anger

Some people have decided there are times when openly aggressive anger only creates more problems than it solves. To their credit, these people can see through the futility of an openly demeaning display of condescension, so they determine not to let themselves get drawn into a war of words. Instead of handling anger constructively or respectfully, however, many of these people manage their anger in a sly, underground way that still indicates low regard toward others. Knowing that loud or obnoxious expression of anger leaves them vulnerable to the rejection of others, they become passive while still engaging adversarially with the person who is the object of their anger.

Staying with our core definition of anger, passive-aggressive people want to preserve personal worth and needs and convictions, but they do so with quiet disdain toward the others involved. They differ from people who use openly aggressive anger in that they choose to belittle others through hidden means and through behavior that leaves them least exposed. They reason that if they do not fully disclose the nature of their anger, others cannot easily control or overpower them. They handle their aggression with a "less is more" philosophy.

Prior to the blowup that caused Brett's wife, Connie, to call the police, he had developed a habit of harboring ill feelings toward her. He did not think Connie was tuned in to the things that brought him satisfaction; instead he viewed her as somewhat self-absorbed and interested in her "woman issues." In years past, he determined that it did no good to talk with her about how they could be more emotionally coordinated. In his opinion, those discussions were of no use, so he held his anger inward.

Just because he grew less vocal when his irritation arose did not mean that his anger went away. It merely changed form and took on a spirit of quiet noncooperation. For instance, Connie once asked him to clear old clothes from the closet as part of a spring-cleaning effort. Brett said he would get to it in a day or so, but he never got around to doing so. Though he did not say it to Connie, he thought to himself how weary he felt as she would direct him to do chores to keep him busy. Didn't she appreciate the many things he already did to keep the household running smoothly? This particular request was seemingly one of many, and his noncompliance was his way of indicating that he was not going to let her or anyone else run his life.

When Brett and I discussed his ways of handling anger, he revealed several other behaviors that indicated he was not willing to openly admit his annoyance even though his actions showed otherwise. He was notorious about not returning phone calls, sometimes for days, because he did not like to be bothered by the requests that might come. Likewise, friends and family learned long ago not to expect him to arrive for an appointment at the agreed time. He had a habit of being consistently late wherever he went. Also, there were times when Connie would want to talk with him about simple family procedures, but he would evade her as he assumed that she just wanted to gripe at him.

The week prior to their blowup, it seemed to Brett that Connie had made more than her usual number of requests. Given the fact that he was already feeling stressed because of his overloaded schedule and his obligation to tend to an ailing mother, it did not take much goading for his anger to turn from passive to destructive.

To get an idea of how anger can be managed in a passive-aggressive form, look over this list of behaviors common to the pattern:

- ❍ Being silent when you know that the other person wants to hear from you
- ❍ Making lame excuses for the purpose of avoiding activities you do not want to do
- ❍ Procrastinating and being chronically forgetful
- ❍ Saying yes even though you are unlikely to follow through with a request
- ❍ Doing tasks in your own manner and at your own time even when you know that it disrupts others
- ❍ Complaining about people behind their back, but rarely face to face
- ❍ Saying whatever the other person wants to hear, and then doing whatever you feel like doing
- ❍ Being evasive for the purpose of indicating that you won't be controlled
- ❍ Putting off responsibility as you choose playful or lazy options instead
- ❍ Repeatedly using the phrase "I don't know" when being asked to explain your choices
- ❍ Giving half-hearted effort

- Having a reputation of general unreliability
- Acting good in front of authority figures or accountability partners, and then acting rebellious when out of their presence
- Being wasteful, even after requests have been made to be more conscientious

As Brett and I talked about the many ways his anger could take on a passive-aggressive quality, he grinned as he acknowledged that this was a common pattern. When asked about the grin, he explained, "When I have to admit that I can be passive-aggressive, it makes me feel like I'm a sneaky kid who has been caught with his hand in the cookie jar."

Brett's description was right on target. Passive-aggressive anger tends to be set up by a deep history of distrust or annoyance owing to the lack of clean emotional exchange in the midst of conflict. Having a history of exposure to controlling or insensitive people, these individuals determined that it was not safe to be open about the things that really bothered them. Yet, also feeling the need to make a statement of self-preservation, they felt compelled to protest in *some* fashion. Passive-aggressive people assumed early in life that their adversaries didn't really want to hear from them, so they decided the best way to thwart others was through noncompliance. Through passive means, they could communicate their displeasure, yet the passivity allowed them to minimize their ultimate vulnerability. Their passive form of communicating displeasure allowed them to feel they were taking a stand of self-preservation, but without having to be emotionally exposed. Accountability regarding their true feelings was something they dearly wanted to avert.

Early in his marriage to Connie, Brett recognized that she wanted to talk things out whenever they had differences. He also learned that she was not a good listener, and whenever he had something important to say she was likely to miss the essence of his message. In time, he became increasingly frustrated with her, but instead of speaking openly about it he was evasive and displayed his frustration via noncooperation. If she ever confronted him about his apparent mood of irritation, he could feign innocence by saying something like, "No, you've got it all wrong. I'm not frustrated, I'm just having a bad day."

Once people enter a pattern of using passive anger, they can feel strongly rewarded for their behavior as it becomes clear that their passivity is far more controlling than openly aggressive anger. They see open aggression as an exposure of neediness, which puts them in a position of feeling greatly disappointed when the desired outcome is not realized. Passivity, however, does not risk such exposure even as it serves the purpose of sending a message to others: "Leave me alone and quit trying to fit me into your mold."

Moving Beyond Futility

Suppression. Open aggression. Passive aggression. These patterns of anger management indicate how futile it can ultimately be to try to make sense of the conflict that accompanies any close, ongoing relationship. The people who consistently handle their anger with one (or all) of these methods often have a legitimate reason to feel that others really do not care about their core needs and convictions. Their life experience has regretfully shown them that fair and reasonable exchange in the midst of conflict does not always happen. Though they may have reasonable concerns to confront, their method of managing their anger can undermine any chance that the anger serves a useful purpose.

Once you reach the adult years, it is possible to make a powerful adjustment to your management of anger so that it does not have to result in ongoing pain and tension. Those who assume they cannot change hold onto a childlike attitude that insists others must change first before they can make any personal improvement. Those who begin the change process recognize that although feelings of anger may be unavoidable, management of that anger can take on a whole new form. They refuse to be held down by behavioral patterns that do not bode well for themselves and those they love.

In the next chapter, we explore the positive alternatives to raw, nonproductive anger; in doing so, you can begin to determine how to channel your anger in a direction that does not leave you feeling emotionally trapped.

For Personal Reflection

- In what circumstances do you feel prompted to suppress your anger?
- What do you fear most about being open with your anger?
- What openly aggressive behaviors are most common for you?
- What are you hoping to accomplish when you use the overpowering approach to anger? Does it work?
- When do you register your anger in a passive-aggressive form? Which behaviors in this category are most common to you?

- What power message are you sending when you are passive with your anger? How does this affect the overall healthiness of your relationships?
- Recognizing that these three forms of anger only perpetuate pain, what would you hope to accomplish by seeking out a healthier form of managing your anger?

3

HEALTHY ANGER OPTIONS

WHEN YOU FEEL ANGRY, there is a strong probability of something legitimate driving the emotion. Even anger that is managed poorly can have a reasonable message at its base. Those who remain trapped by their own anger are unable to articulate the message in a manner that allows them to maintain positive relations. On the other hand, some are able to communicate their anger clearly, and once its usefulness has run its course they can then move on to other lifestyle priorities that are not tied to the anger at all.

I spoke with Steve as he came to my office after yet another angry outburst toward his wife, Julie. This time, he exploded when she extended an invitation to her brother for a weekend dinner at their home. The last such occasion had not gone well because Julie and her brother, Jerome, argued about a difference of opinion related to their deceased father's estate. In Steve's mind, Jerome was a crook who was trying to cheat Julie out of a large portion of her inheritance. So now she was inviting him to return to their home for dinner? It made no sense to him, and he was free in telling his wife so.

Julie had an entirely different perspective on the subject. Though she was frustrated with Jerome's treatment toward her, she was of the opinion that some agreements could be reached, so she was attempting to reach out to her brother with the purpose of creating harmony. As she tried to explain her thoughts to Steve, the conversation went poorly and quickly escalated into an ugly shouting match.

Sitting in my office, Steve took it upon himself to convince me of the correctness of his position. Speaking with the same coercive voice that he used with his wife, he rambled about Jerome's history of manipulation and unreliability. Hearing enough, I put one hand up and stated, "Steve, you can stop now. It's not necessary to convince me of how right you feel."

He protested and returned to his rambling monologue, so again I interrupted and explained, "Steve, my vote doesn't count in this issue. I'm not nearly as interested in deciding if you should host Jerome for dinner as I am in discussing how to handle the anger that so powerfully engulfs you." With that, he ceased his coercive efforts, and we were able to get to the heart of the matter.

Steve's anger was driven by the assumption that Julie cared little about his perspective on an important family matter. Though this assumption was mistaken, he nonetheless assumed that he had to force his opinion on Julie because she might otherwise choose not to listen to him at all. So focused was he in pushing his agenda that he did not consider how his method of communication was working against him. Repeatedly in his history of arguments with Julie, it was evident that his aggressive use of anger always turned her against him, yet despite his lack of success in forcing his agenda, here he was, yet another time, badgering her to agree with him.

When I counsel people like Steve, I attempt to go to the core of the emotional expression to determine what might be viable in the message of anger. In Steve's case, he witnessed how Jerome had a history of treating Julie with disdain, so Steve's anger represented a desire to stand up for the conviction that fairness should be maintained when broaching a sensitive family matter. Not only was he not wrong in this conviction but he would proceed in his communication with his wife knowing that he could lend a perspective that might strengthen her approach to her brother.

Steve's method of communication, however, was so harsh and abrasive that his wife could not discern any loving motive. She felt belittled and insulted to the point that she wanted nothing to do with his ideas. His task was to learn how to match the valid message of anger with a respectable method of communication.

Perhaps the most common mistake made by angry people is communicating a right conviction in an insulting fashion. Angry people can be so intent on making their needs known that they quickly rationalize to themselves that a rude or insensitive approach is both necessary and reasonable. Because it is so highly predictable that this stubborn approach brings only tension, these people become ensnared by their own self-righteousness even as they blame others for making them feel so frustrated.

Establishing a Purpose

To release yourself from the trap of unsuccessful anger, the first step is to establish what you want to do with the emotion. If remaining in the quagmire of distasteful conflict is your goal, the choices described in the last chapter will certainly get you there. You may decide, though, that you are weary of the ugly results of anger gone bad, meaning you are ready to manage your anger in a different, more constructive manner.

Before you can expect to succeed in handling anger well, ask yourself: What do I really want to accomplish when I attempt to convey my feelings? That's the question I posed to Steve in discussing his latest outburst. As I did so, he hesitated and a quizzical look came upon him: "Well, I guess I'm trying to get my point across; is that what you're getting at?"

"That's right. I want you to consider why the anger needs to be expressed in the first place." I knew that Steve was unaccustomed to looking behind the scenes of his emotional expression, so this was an important exercise for him.

"All I know," he said, "is that Julie was asking for trouble when she invited Jerome over for dinner. I was trying to tell her that she'd better watch her backside because he's not a person who can be trusted."

"So you really care about your wife's feelings, and you were in something of a protective mode." He nodded as I paused momentarily. "I'm guessing something happened in the exchange that caused Julie to miss your thoughts of concern."

"No kidding," came his reply. "You'd have thought we were mortal enemies by the way our communication fell apart, but honestly, that's not what I intended to have happen when I first addressed the subject with her."

Ideally, the purpose of anger communication is to establish increased harmony in a relationship. In fact, if handled correctly, healthy anger can enhance the possibility for cohesion and cooperation, and even love. Anger inevitably occurs in the midst of conflict, and its emotional thrust can prompt you to discuss needs and convictions in a way that potentially reduces or eliminates the conflict.

Most people do not experience anger as a harmonizing emotion, and certainly they do not connect anger with love, but that is due to a history of experiencing anger that is purely adversarial. Keeping in mind that most people associate anger with a history of hurt and hostility, it is predictable that they will manage anger with a subconscious pessimism that the current conflict leads nowhere. This pessimism inhibits angry people, then, from using civility in deciding how to proceed, but this does not have to be the case.

Even when anger does not create the desired harmonious effect, it can serve the purpose of establishing self-respect. It can send a message to others that you believe in your own decency, and that you see yourself as one to be considered seriously. Your expression of anger can establish that you believe in the viability of your own convictions. Anger can indicate that you believe strongly in your own core values, and that you wish for others to take you seriously.

There are positive functions of anger:

- Standing firmly for right beliefs
- Expressing caring concern about the poor choices made by others
- Stipulating personal limits and boundaries
- Establishing self-respect
- Holding firmly to personal convictions even as others attempt mind-control maneuvers
- Addressing problems related to irresponsibility or misguided priorities
- Being clear about personal needs
- Demonstrating confidence and inviting others to consider your perspective
- Setting your own course for each day's challenges
- Establishing discipline and coordination in shared efforts

If you are able to tie anger to constructive motives, it is no longer an ensnaring emotion. Instead, anger can become an impetus to propel you to stand for truth and take a proactive approach to conflict resolution. People who choose to mobilize their anger in a manner that leads to appropriate self-preservation are wise enough to recognize that rudeness or condescension does not ultimately lead to good results. Even as they see the necessity of standing firmly for their legitimate needs, they also recognize that life consists of an ongoing series of exchanges that can produce either increased friction or an atmosphere of respect. Their priority is to seek the path toward mutual respect.

Anger with Respect

To be released from the entrapment of your own anger, you need not shun the emotion altogether. You can choose not to give weight to a nonproductive style of anger as you opt instead for assertiveness. This form of anger can be defined as preserving personal worth, needs, and convictions while simultaneously upholding the dignity of the others involved.

Within the past generation, much has been said and written about the subject of assertiveness, to the extent that some have become confused regarding its true meaning or purpose. For instance, when I used the word in a discussion with Steve and Julie, she immediately flinched. "I've always thought of assertive people as being pushy and very forward in driving home their agenda," she explained. "One thing we *don't* need in our home is more encouragement to cram opinions down the other person's throat!"

Steve chimed in: "No one will ever be able to accuse me of not being assertive enough. You don't have to guess my opinions, that's for sure. If you hang out with me long enough, you'll learn that I'm a tell-it-like-it-is person. No sirree, I don't have one bit of a problem being assertive!"

In their comments, it was clear that neither one grasped the true nature of assertiveness. Assertive people are indeed open about their needs and perspectives, but there is no sense of entitlement that accompanies their expression. Likewise, there is no desire to be so strong willed that others feel insignificant or invalidated. Assertive people place great value on the dignity and worth of each person involved in the conflict. They have a belief in their own justifiable feelings and ideas *just as they also* have a high regard for the needs and perspectives of others.

As I explained my understanding of assertiveness to Steve and Julie, each began to recognize that this form of anger was far different from what they typically experienced in their home. Though Steve assumed he was assertive just because he was not bashful about letting his feelings out, he came to understand that he was not at all assertive because he rarely thought about the dignity of the other people involved. His brand of assertiveness was nothing more than loud, insensitive aggression indicating both a deep insecurity and an illusion that he could and should control the minds of those who dared to disagree with him. Julie, on the other hand, began to recognize that assertiveness is not at all pushy but is accompanied by fairness, openness, and care.

Assertiveness can be understood as a combination of directness and self-restraint. Directness is evident in willingness to speak about problems and needs freshly and unambiguously. Self-restraint is evident in the lack of overpowering or harmful action. Assertive anger is practiced when someone chooses to confront conflict with honesty while also treating others consistently with a cooperative spirit. Speaking the truth in love is an apt description of true assertiveness.

Steve, in particular, seemed taken back by my description of assertive anger. In a moment of honest reflection he confessed, "That's not at all how I handle myself when I'm angry. I've always thought of assertiveness as going for the other person's jugular and not letting go once you have his attention."

"Notice how you only create new problems when you use anger as a springboard to attack," I responded. "Not only is the other person harmed by the adversarial approach but you end up being a bully or a condescending communicator. Is that what you really aspire to be?"

By redefining the concept of assertiveness, Steve began the process of becoming disengaged from the anger that had held him captive most of his life. First, he was learning to see anger as an emotion that could have a positive function. Second, he felt challenged to learn how this new attitude about anger could be displayed in his behavior and communication.

How Assertiveness Works

Something distinct comes over angry people as they lay aside the nonproductive use of anger to practice assertiveness. Perhaps the first noticeable adjustment is seen in judiciousness. Rather than responding harshly at the first opportunity, they are willing to confront themselves when anger is felt, asking themselves, *Is it really necessary for me to act upon this emotion?* Sometimes they conclude that the anger has no useful purpose; it may be a reaction to something trivial, or the timing is just not right. Other times, they may determine that it is appropriate to express anger, but with the proper weight or emphasis. By using discretion, they illustrate their willingness to consider how their emotional expression might affect others.

For instance, Steve told me of a small victory related to a matter of frustration with Julie. She asked him to wash her car, so he took the task upon himself because he wanted to be kind toward her. When he opened her car door, he found numerous small items of trash scattered throughout the interior of the vehicle, and because he was much more meticulous in his own car care it created frustration. He explained to me, "In the past I would have gone back inside the house to make a big scene about her sloppy habits. I've been known to hurl insults and make all sorts of sarcastic remarks. This time, though, I decided that I wouldn't say anything right away. I cleaned her car inside and out, then later I made a simple mention of my feelings. When she thanked me for washing her car, I told her I was glad to help her, and that she could help me in the future if she would leave less trash on the floorboard. She got my message, and I didn't even raise my voice or rant and rave!" He was making headway.

Once assertive people determine that their anger is tied to a reasonable cause and that they need to openly express themselves, they determine to do so with an even tone of voice. No pleading, coaxing, or convincing is needed as assertion is expressed. Assertive people are firm in stating their convictions, yet that firmness is accompanied by the realization that others deserve to be given the room to decide for themselves how to respond. Coercion and persuasion are therefore left out of the equation.

Julie once told me she had particular difficulty expressing her frustration toward Steve without also using a form of arm twisting. "In the past, I'd feel like I had to work my way into his brain and make him think the way I wanted him to think. Lately, though, I've felt convicted that forcefulness is a way of disrespecting him. I'd do better if I could simply state what I think or if I would just act upon my convictions, letting him draw his own conclusions." This form of self-restraint was not natural, yet it would represent a great improvement over her old pattern of open aggression and passive aggression.

When assertive people choose not to coerce or persuade, there is no guarantee that the other person will gladly receive what is being said. Sarcasm may be spoken. An invitation to fight might be offered; invalidation may immediately be uttered. What's a person to do in the face of such a poor reception? Arguing or counterinvalidating communication is an option, but such behavior would cross the line from assertiveness to aggressiveness. Staying with the determination to remain respectful, it is possible for assertive people to stand their ground without being rude.

For instance, Julie was once angry with Steve because he overruled a disciplinary decision she made with one of their children. Assertively, she explained to him the rationale for her disciplining the child, and then she had asked him not to correct her in front of the children. At the very least, he should pull her aside to talk it over. As she spoke with him, her tone of voice was firm yet respectful. Instead of receiving her assertion well, Steve took it upon himself to invalidate what she had just said and debate the merits of her discipline practices. Julie was tempted to enter the debate by reexplaining her request, but she realized that it would have lowered her to aggressive interaction. Staying with her calm but firm assertion, she replied, "I know you see this circumstance differently than I do, but that doesn't detract from the request I made. I'd like for you to give strong consideration to what I just said." When he persisted in his argumentative tone, she calmly but firmly stayed the course. "Nonetheless, I'd like for you to consider the validity of what I just told you." Steve still did not want to let go of his aggressive reaction, but at that point, Julie ceased. She had said what needed to be said, and she wisely recognized that additional persuasion would only subtract from the effectiveness of her communication.

Ideally, if you assert your feelings with respect and decency, the others involved will respond with a similar respectfulness. In most relationships, the possibility is only a dream. Despite your attempt to clean up your anger, others may not yet have the maturity and self-restraint to join your efforts. It is at such a time that you can choose to remain respectful so you do not get pulled off track.

Assertive people recognize that their communication of anger is not an attempt to conquer the ones generating the frustration. They refrain from any attempt to win in the battle of wills. In fact, if the other person feels the need to win, he or she will simply step away from one-up, one-down communication altogether. An adult-to-adult form of interaction is maintained, as opposed to a parent-to-child manner or that of a prosecuting attorney. This means assertive people do not fall into the habit of chronic repetition of the main point. They say what needs to be said and then quietly hold firm. They do not attempt to bolster their argument by bringing in extra subjects to discuss. Instead, they stick to the issue at hand. Likewise, assertive people know when to cease. They make the points they feel are appropriate, and then they are wise enough to know when to draw the confrontation to a close.

All the while that assertive people are openly communicating their convictions, there is a recognition that no matter how wrong others may be, dignity can still be maintained. Behavior can be focused; talk can be direct. Yet the value of all involved is recognized. Decisiveness and directness are understood to be valuable traits, but they are not used at the expense of another person's self-esteem. Let's summarize how assertiveness differs from aggressiveness:

ASSERTIVENESS	AGGRESSIVENESS
Discretion regarding the necessity of anger	Anger perhaps tied to unnecessary subjects
Even tone of voice	Pleading or coercion prioritized
Respect consistently maintained	Respect summarily disregarded
Succinct	Can seem unending
Keeping other person's needs in perspective	Others' needs ignored as self takes center stage
Open to all alternatives	Rigid and demanding
Guided by constructive motives	Destructive in nature
Responds to resistance with calm firmness	Responds to resistance with harshness

Releasing Anger

There are times when you have an opportunity to be assertive, yet the situation is not served by an open statement of confrontation. For instance, marital partners learn that sometimes it is wiser not to engage in discussion about differences, knowing that nothing good will come. Parents, too, can recognize that there are circumstances when it is better not to address a problem because doing so would put the child into an emotionally overloaded mind-set. Likewise, fellow employees, friends, or extended family members can conclude that although assertion has its place in a relationship, there are moments when the relationship is harmed if negatives are brought out into the open. Sometimes it makes sense to refrain from addressing a problem or difference.

When you choose to keep the positive qualities of a relationship alive by refraining from engaging in anger, you practice releasing anger. You acknowledge that although anger can have a positive function, there are times when other personality traits can be given priority. Discretion can be used as you determine that you will set aside the need for self-preservation to respond most appropriately to the needs of the persons in your immediate presence.

Releasing anger can be displayed in numerous ways:

- Showing genuine tolerance for others' flaws or weaknesses
- Recognizing when not to press an issue
- Being fair in your expectations of others
- Choosing to set aside a critical spirit, becoming fair-minded
- Giving priority to forgiveness
- Choosing kindness, even if others have not earned it
- Staying out of fruitless debate or discussion
- Accepting the truth that you cannot expect life to give you everything you want
- Allowing another to make a mistake
- Dropping the requirement that others should line up to your ideal standards

In choosing to release your anger, you recognize that you are a limited person who is not able to force life to unfold just as you would please. You can recognize the inevitability of human error, and instead of making it your task to force others to cease being imperfect you can accept fallibility. By choosing to release your anger, you indicate that you place a premium on qualities such as self-restraint, humility, and acceptance.

As a simple illustration, let's suppose you are at a large extended-family gathering, and you are bothered because your sister-in-law seems bossy and critical. You would like to correct her, but then you remind yourself that your sister-in-law has been bossy for as long as you have known her, and besides, she's really pretty harmless. You can choose to accept her quirks and move on without letting anger take root in your personality.

Let's look, though, at a more difficult illustration. Suppose at that same family gathering you encounter a cousin who engaged in sexually inappropriate behavior with you many years ago when you were a preteen. You have already confronted him as an adult, though he did not receive it well. You deeply disrespect him now because you know that he has cheated on his wife and he still treats women with contempt. What do you do with the anger you feel whenever you are in his presence?

In a case like this, you can practice assertion by keeping up good personal boundaries. You can choose not to engage with him on any serious level, and it is even appropriate to instruct your children to keep a safe distance from him. You may also decide not to attend other gatherings where he is present. Once you become satisfied that you are maintaining an appropriate stance of self-preservation, you can choose not to indulge thoughts of hatred or bitterness. You can release yourself from the illusion that you are the one who can reform him, and instead choose to conduct your life without letting him play a role in deciding whether you can feel content.

When I spoke with Julie and Steve about the option of releasing their anger, they each balked, but for different reasons. Steve spoke first: "Are you trying to tell me that I'm just supposed to turn my head and not notice when people do things that are obviously wrong? I'll tell you one thing, I'm nobody's doormat, and I'm not going to turn into some sort of wimp!"

Undaunted, I replied, "Releasing anger is not at all the same as becoming a human doormat. In fact, it's just the opposite. If you communicate anger assertively and then conclude that it's wiser to move on to other priorities, you're displaying genuine maturity. You are indicating that anger is not the defining feature of your personality."

Julie chimed in: "I get the sense that if I let go of my anger it's the same as suppressing it. I've already got a history of holding my anger in, so that's not really going to be a good option for me."

"You're referring to two entirely different means of handling anger," I explained. "On the surface, releasing anger may appear similar to suppressing the emotion, but it's not at all the same. Suppressing anger is a choice motivated by fear, and its goal is to present a false front. Suppression is tied to phoniness. Releasing anger, on the other hand, involves a genuine desire to set the anger aside for the purpose of pursuing higher priorities. People who release anger have decided they're not so committed to their negative emotions that they can't choose to be known as kind, forgiving, or accepting."

Continuing in my explanation, I said, "To be confident that you are truly releasing anger instead of suppressing it, you will need to have a solid track record of being appropriately assertive first. Typically, a suppressor bypasses the opportunity to be direct about feelings because he or she doesn't want to deal with the potential hassles that accompany openness. People who choose to release anger are true to their own self-preservation needs, but they also are wise enough to realize when they've gone far enough in expressing themselves, and they determine that anger has run its course. They know when to move on.

"The anger you feel may come upon you without invitation or warning; if you cling to it for an extended period of time, that is when you become ensnared by it. Knowing, though, that you can exchange the anger for other options, the emotion does not continue to have a hold on you to the extent that it becomes a central feature in your life. Anger is seen for what it is: one dimension among many within your personality."

People who are trapped by their own anger tend to let their emotional direction be determined by instinct or reflex reaction to an undesirable circumstance. Little thought may be given to the purpose of the emotion. All they know is that at the moment they are peeved, and they will do little to put the anger into the larger context of their goals for healthy living. People who can release anger understand their lives are tied to a higher purpose. They recognize that a successful life is accompanied by the need to preserve personal needs and convictions, but they also realize that they cannot achieve success without having a large dose of discernment, diplomacy, and confidence. They understand that anger can play too prominent a role if left unchecked; they choose to exercise caution so it does not overwhelm their personality.

When I talk with people like Steve or Julie or Brett, I emphasize that choice is an ever-present dimension in emotional management. You can choose to suppress your anger, be openly aggressive, or passively display your aggression. You can also choose assertiveness, and you can opt for release of anger. The more inclined you are to consciously deliberate why you feel angry and what you wish to accomplish with it, the more likely you are to manage it in a balanced manner.

In the next several chapters, we explore how other issues in your life that might create instability can influence your use of anger. If you do not understand how insecurity, pridefulness, or fear play a role in your anger, it is likely that it will remain maladaptive. Knowing you have choices, both negative and positive, is a good first step in managing anger. Resolving other underlying tension that can keep anger stirred up is the next step as you learn to get out of the anger trap.

For Personal Reflection

- In what circumstances would it benefit others to hear about your feelings of anger?
- What positive purpose does your anger have? What are you attempting to accomplish with it that is good?
- Assertive anger involves communicating truth while also respecting the others involved. How can you tell that a person is successfully using this balanced approach?
- Assertive people are judicious in knowing when to address a subject and when not to do so. In what circumstances do you need to be more judicious?
- Suppose you are appropriately assertive but the person receiving it attempts to invalidate you. What good options do you have at such a time?
- Releasing anger implies that you have the maturity to know when to move on to other priorities. In what circumstances might you choose to release your anger?
- When is it most difficult to let go of your anger? How would an accepting or forgiving spirit help in those situations?
- How can you know that you are letting go of your anger and not just suppressing it?

4

THE MISSING INGREDIENT

WHEN PEOPLE DESCRIBE their struggle with anger, they often assume that they have no choice in the way it is expressed. They insinuate that anger is a mysterious, uncontrollable reaction. Some suggest that they have a chemical imbalance and as a result are unable to contain their impulses. It is actually true that anger control can be hindered by a depletion of serotonin in the brain, so if an individual has ongoing difficulty with impulsive outbursts of anger, it can be wise to explore a medical cause. Many report that SSRI antidepressants or antiseizure or mood stabilizers result in a remarkable improvement in the intensity of the anger response. Some conclude that the problem with anger is therefore merely biological, and so they should be excused from responsibility if anger flares up. This is stretching the truth about the chemical component too far.

Others dismiss their anger problems by saying, "That's just the way I am." These people see themselves as having a strong inclination toward an opinionated spirit, and they see nothing wrong with it. When irritability, impatience, or abruptness occurs, they later explain it by saying, "Look, this is the way I've been all my life, so you're just going to have to get used to it. I'm never going to be a namby-pamby type of person." In some respects, their argument can be hard to refute because indeed some people are naturally more forceful in presenting their thoughts than others. Yet the implied logic leads to the conclusion that some people, by virtue of inborn temperament, can be excused from handling anger appropriately because anger is simply going to happen. This surely represents poor reasoning.

Still others recognize that their anger can be unruly, but they fall back upon the notion that they are damaged goods, meaning they cannot be expected to monitor their anger well. "If you had experienced the pain that I have," the reasoning goes, "you'd be just as angry. Don't tell me I should get a grip on my anger until you've walked a mile in my shoes." It can seem awkward to suggest to these people that they nonetheless have to balance their anger because such a suggestion might be interpreted as insensitive or invalidating. Yet to assume that anger born out of hurtful experience is unmanageable is to concede that internal strength is not enough to carry a person through tough times.

When people refuse to take full responsibility for how they direct anger, they negate a most essential ingredient involved in emotional management. They overlook *internal focus.*

As soon as Peggy walked into my office, I saw apprehension written all over her face. She was definitely not in a friendly mood, and when she sat down she said, "Let's just cut right to the chase. I didn't want to come here, but I'm sitting in your office because my family basically ganged up on me and twisted my arm until I promised I'd talk to a counselor at least once. I don't really believe in counseling, but I'm here, so we might as well not waste our time."

By no means was Peggy the first person to come into my office under similar circumstances. Family and friends are often the first to recognize a person's need for counseling, and it can take serious nudging before some of them darken my door. In this case, I learned that Peggy was a woman in her late forties who maintained a cynic's disposition and managed to offend almost everyone who tried to love her. She was twice divorced and had two daughters who were out on their own. She had been fired three times in her career as a nurse and she carried a reputation for being moody and unpredictable.

I spoke calmly with her: "I'm sorry that you had to be forced into coming here today, but since you and I are together you might as well tell me what prompted your family to ask you to seek counseling." Being quite verbal, Peggy told me of a deep history of conflict with her parents, siblings, ex-spouses, and two daughters. She admitted to being a brash person who seemed to have a knack for ticking people off, no matter what the circumstance.

"I don't mind saying," she told me, "that I have a very strong personality, and if anger is what happens to come out, then people are just going to have to get used to it." In Peggy's opinion, her greatest problem was the ongoing presence of people who were either indecisive or unreliable. "I'd have a lot less problems if people would just quit getting in my way."

On the surface, people like Peggy merely seem to be rude and obnoxious, with little or no willingness to make the necessary adjustments to tame their anger. Truthfully, some angry people simply do not give up their anger no matter how often others plead with them. Many people, like Peggy, are entrapped by their anger because they have known little else, so because of the raw nature of the emotion it just easily becomes the front-line defense whenever their world is conflicted. When challenged with the possibility, though, of making anger a less-prominent emotion, they can make the necessary changes; they just have to see the possibilities. So despite Peggy's initial display of stubbornness, I decided to see how far I could go in helping her through her anger.

On our second visit (yes, she came back), I said: "Peggy, most people do not really want to live with anger as their primary emotion, and I'm willing to make the assumption that you are not really happy with your history of broken relationships. Am I right in assuming so?"

Still guarded, she nodded her head and replied, "I'll be honest with you. I know there are some people who don't like me, and sometimes even I don't like me. I get tired of being in a bad mood, but I swear, just when I've talked myself into softening up, someone comes along and acts like a real screwball, and before you know it I'm peeved."

"Just out of curiosity," I injected, "when you were a young person growing up, how often did people talk with you about your options regarding your use of anger?" I already knew the answer to the question, but I wanted to make a point.

"Are you kidding? Nobody ever talked with me or anyone else in my family about our emotions. I mean, I was told to shut up a few hundred times, and I was told that I'd better work on my attitude, but I don't think that's the kind of discussion about emotions that you're asking me about."

She was right. I was referring to the truth that everyone needs training in the formative years regarding use of emotions. Telling a child to behave better is not the same as taking the time to develop habits that adequately address inner tension.

Trained Incompetence

When I talk with individuals who routinely struggle with anger, I predictably discover a historical pattern that I call trained incompetence. These people were not given the tools to handle emotional ups and downs; patterns were put into place that virtually ensured that the wrong reaction would become entrenched.

Operating easily upon raw instinct, young children are naturally going to let anger flow in less-than-pleasant ways. What preschooler has *not* thrown a temper tantrum, cried upon being corrected, or pushed to gain a personal advantage? Each of us began with a loose understanding of personal boundaries, and we did not have the presence of mind to blend personal needs and desires with the needs of the surrounding world. During the entire eighteen years or so of childhood development, children look toward the outer world to show them how to negotiate their needs most successfully.

Many parents and influential adults, however, do not know how to guide their young to competence in the delicate task of blending their emotional needs with others. Instead, these adults respond to the young person's anger as a nuisance that has to be eliminated as quickly as possible. Rather than systematically teaching their young to choose healthy patterns of anger instead of unhealthy ones, they communicate so as to virtually guarantee continuation of poor anger management.

Let's look at some of the most common ways children can be trained to remain incompetent in handling anger. As you consider the patterns discussed here, be willing to reflect on your own history of anger training.

"Just Quit Feeling That Way"

When I talk with people like Peggy who have chronic anger, I assume they are almost desperate to push forward in relationships with a message that *will be heard.* A forceful or irritable individual inevitably has a history of contention with key people who did not want to slow down long enough to consider the possibility that she had valid reasons to feel as she did. I once asked Peggy to tell me about her earliest memories of feeling frustrated or angry. Her reply was, "I don't remember very many times when I didn't feel this way."

As I encouraged her to talk openly with me about how her family processed emotions, she became visibly frustrated as the memories flooded her mind. Shaking her head, she recalled, "My dad basically let me and my brother and sister know that we were a bother to him. He was sometimes in a good mood, but that would only happen if everything was going his way. If anyone in the family said or did something that was outside his comfort zone, he took it upon himself to squelch the problem right there on the spot."

"Can you think of an example?"

"Oh, I could come up with hundreds! My sister and I shared a bedroom, so you can imagine our needs would sometimes clash pretty bad. I remember many times when I might be doing homework and she'd want to play the radio. We'd argue about it, of course, like sisters would argue. Dad would step into the scene, and we would each plead our case, but consistently we'd get one type of response from him. He'd start ranting about how he wasn't going to listen to our carping, so we'd just have to shut up and knock off the fussing. When we would press the issue, he'd throw up his hands and shout, 'I don't want to hear any more! Just lay off of each other.' Of course, nothing was ever solved, and my sister and I stayed angry with each other, and we'd resent our father."

Peggy's illustration is representative of many an angry person's memory of "anger training." The message was straight and simple: "Just stop feeling that way—now!" Whenever young people expose their hurt or annoyed feelings, it actually presents a golden opportunity to take the time to discuss the meaning of the emotion and the best way to proceed with it. When Peggy and her sister argued about the radio being on, their father could have gone into a mentoring mode: "I can see that each of you has a preference that is the opposite of the other's. No wonder you feel frustrated. It looks like we'll need to take some time out to determine how we can respond to this problem so you won't remain stuck in your anger."

When I model to counselees how a parent might have spoken calmly about choices, I consistently get the same response. "There's no way anyone would have talked like that in my home. That kind of patient communication would never happen." In fact, my example of the better way can sound so idealistic that it seems naïve.

Idealistic or not, parents really can choose to respond to children's anger calmly and instructively. It requires self-restraint, patience, and creativity, and often parents do not possess the presence of mind to choose such a course. Besides, when they were children, they too were not likely to have had mentoring communication about anger. They were probably told to stop feeling what they felt. Knowing nothing different, they passed on to their children what had been passed on to them.

Recipients of the "stop feeling it" message, like Peggy, enter adulthood without the benefit of knowing how to sift out choices. The anger still remains as it was in its childhood form, until they realize as adults that they can take another path.

"Do as I Say, Not as I Do"

One of the best ways to become competent in any task is through exposure to good modeling. Consider a child who is learning to write the ABCs. An adult can make a big A on a tablet and then turn the pencil over to the child, saying, "Now, I want you to make a letter just like I did." Likewise, a teenager who is learning how to drive a car needs an adult to demonstrate various functions of the automobile and then turn it over to the young person, saying, "I want you to practice what you've seen me do."

Adults can tell their children all sorts of should's and supposed to's regarding how to handle conflict and anger, but ultimately the developing child learns less from the instructions and more from the modeling of the instructor. What models of anger management did you have in your formative years?

That's the question I posed to Peggy. She told me she had many memories of her father being critical, sour, and moody. "He just wasn't a happy person," she told me. "I remember thinking there was something very wrong with him because he could turn any circumstance into an opportunity to gripe. He snapped at us easily, and you never knew when he would go into his next tirade. My goal as a child was to stay as far away from my dad as possible."

"Where was your mother in the midst of all this turbulence?"

"Well, Mom worked in a doctor's office, and it seemed that she would want to stay away from home because it was so unpleasant there. She wasn't a particularly negative person, but I guess the best word to describe her would be 'disengaged.' She took care of her domestic chores, but she didn't really have the know-how or the desire to openly discuss personal issues."

As Peggy talked, I began getting a fuller picture that explained the origins of her own anger. Knowing that anger is linked to the drive to preserve personal worth, I began understanding that she did not feel valued in her home environment. Dad was struggling with his own battles with cynicism and insignificance, and Mom was busy avoiding Dad. Each parent was so preoccupied with personal turmoil that neither was able to address their children's emotional needs. Slowly, Peggy became a young girl who hungered for affirmation, and as she failed to receive sufficient encouragement the roots of her own anger were established.

As young Peggy struggled to determine how she should handle her increasingly volatile moods, she did what any child does. She watched her role models and picked up cues from them. Though her parents would tell her, for instance, not to be argumentative with her brother and sister, she observed her dad being a chronic bickerer, so she did the same. Her mother would silently hold grudges, so Peggy learned to do that too.

As a middle-aged adult, Peggy occasionally had vague notions regarding the proper way to handle anger, but the concept of choices did not often cross her mind. Instead, she remained true to the maladaptive forms of anger that she had learned as a child because those were most familiar to her.

As a simple analogy of the power of modeling, consider how people commonly speak in a regional accent. A person growing up in Boston is going to have a distinctly different accent from someone who grew up in

Macon, Georgia. Likewise, the fellow who spent his youth in Fort Worth sounds different from the one who grew up in Trenton, New Jersey. Why? They had different models. No one sits down with a child and says, "Here is the way our regional accent is spoken." They just speak it and the child imitates it.

"Let's Just Ignore What You Feel"

Imagine being hired by a company that expects you to blend in with fellow workers, participating in fairly complicated procedures. Each new day as you arrive at work, you go to your desk, where a stack of papers awaits you. You're not exactly sure what those papers tell you, and no one has explained what you are supposed to do with them. All you know is that you are supposed to "get it done right," whatever that means. When you make an effort to ask for help, the others in your work area are either too disinterested or too preoccupied to show you the procedures and explain how your work fits into the company's master plan.

Does this illustration seem preposterous? Surely no company would bring on a new employee and then offer no training, ignoring any need for help. Yet that is exactly what happens in many homes, where children are expected to figure out the system despite a complete lack of attentiveness to emotional and relational strategies. Just as an employee with no training will bumble his way through the day's tasks, so might a young person bumble when faced with the task of managing anger and conflict with no training.

When I talked with Peggy about how she struggled as a child to make sense of her anger, I asked if she ever had any curiosity about responding effectively to life's challenges. She shrugged as she said, "I'm not real sure if I ever thought very deeply about things like that. I guess it never dawned on me that I should even have a plan for my emotions. I distinctly remember, however, wishing that someone would talk with me when I felt frustrated or hurt. I wanted to be close to my mother, but she seemed so overwhelmed by my dad's impossible ways that she was largely ineffective when it was time to explore personal matters."

I operate on the assumption that people like Peggy have the competence to choose appropriate ways to handle anger. Ideally, this competence would be drawn out of them in early stages of development, when their emotions are less complex than in the adult years. If emotional matters are ignored, though, the competence does not cease to exist. But just as muscles atrophy if they are not exercised, emotional competence becomes weak if there is no attempt to strengthen the resolve to make wise choices.

"Hurry Up and Finish Feeling That Way"

Most families operate with the assumption that emotional tension, and particularly anger, is a bother. When a young person indicates that she is feeling upset, it is not common for the parents to think, *Oh, good. This will give us a chance to talk about ways to deal with life's complexities.* Instead, it is more common for parents to think, *Here we go again. How many times am I going to have to listen to this trash?*

Imagine that a school-aged child has important homework to complete, but she has one goal in mind as she begins the task: finish as quickly as possible. How likely is it that the work will be satisfactorily completed? As a concerned parent, you would want your child to be more concerned with accuracy and thoroughness than speed.

Adults with anger problems are capable of slowing their thoughts for the purpose of sifting through their choices regarding the best way to proceed. However, if they have a history that did not allow such a luxury, they typically let impulsiveness and bad habits dictate the course of the anger. Careful planning regarding choices in anger management is absent. Because little time was given to exploring options during the formative years, most follow suit by giving little time to the process in the adult years.

Peggy distinctly remembered being told as a girl, "You'd better get a good attitude, and I mean now!" "That was one of my dad's favorite lines," she explained to me. "It didn't matter if I had something valid to say or not, his primary concern was to eliminate my moodiness as quickly as possible. Of course, the more I was told to hurry and get over it, the more powerfully my anger welled up inside me."

Anger is rarely a pleasant experience, for which reason it is understandable if people prefer to move on to something better. Yet the anger is there for a reason; even though there may be discomfort associated with it, the emotion warrants exploration. If it is too hurriedly disposed, the person experiencing the anger misses the opportunity to grapple successfully in an effort to make sense of it.

Contemplative Thinking

The missing ingredient in healthy anger management is internal focus. To make right choices when anger is felt, an individual needs a habit of applying contemplative thinking to the circumstances. Perhaps you would admit: "OK, it's true. During my developmental years I didn't develop the habit of considering all my choices regarding anger. No one ever took the time to help me sort out the pluses and minuses of my feelings. But what can I do about all that at this point in my life?"

Even though it would have been ideal to have been trained, as a child, to contemplate your emotional directions, it is never too late to learn something new. Peggy once complained to me, "I'm almost fifty years old, and I'm pretty set in my ways at this stage in my life. You're suggesting to me that I can suddenly become a new person and just stop being angry, but I'm not sure it'll be that easy. A lot of water has gone under my bridge."

"If you prefer," I replied, "we can assume that you're so stuck in a rut that you're a hopeless case, and you'll just have to live out the rest of your life being angry at the world. That would be an option." She smiled wryly at the suggestion. I continued, "I'm not ready to give up on you at this point. I've heard you tell me that your family history gave you little training to manage your emotions well, and throughout your adult years you've encountered people and circumstances that did not give you reasons to feel optimistic. Nonetheless, today is a new day. If you like, you can choose to begin anew by challenging yourself to rethink your tired old patterns. Are you up to it?"

On numerous occasions, Peggy was told by family and friends that she needed a new attitude, but the proposition had never been put to her quite like this. For the first time in her life, she realized that she could change course in her anger management. But how would it play out? Did she really want to expend the effort? Would her effort lead to any significant improvement? These were the questions floating through her mind.

"So what am I supposed to do, just tell myself to act better?"

"Well, yes, but it's not quite that simplistic," I replied. "First you need to consider if you honestly have what it takes to be a true contemplative thinker. Only if you are convinced that the ability is there will you be able to move forward."

Let's back up momentarily and consider how an angry person's childhood could have been anchored by an entirely different approach. Suppose Peggy became angry with her younger sister because they were bickering over something trivial. Instead of her dad shaming her and telling her to knock it off, he could have taken the time to slow down and uncover the meaning of her irritability. He might have said, "Peggy, I'm assuming you're feeling frustrated because your sister is not showing you the respect you feel you deserve. Let's talk about this." As he would hear her concerns, he could follow it by saying, "I know you don't want to remain angry for the rest of the afternoon, so let's discuss the options you have, both good and bad, to see how you want to proceed from here."

When I described this possibility to her, Peggy just laughed. "Never in a million years could I conceive of my dad talking to me that way. What you just described is so far removed from reality that it doesn't even register on the radar screen."

Nodding, I said, "I'm aware that many people would never consider such an approach, so we have to be honest as we admit that you didn't receive a good early send-off regarding your anger." Maintaining my belief in her innate competence, I challenged her: "Though that form of communication never happened in your childhood years, can you see how you might choose to talk to yourself in that fashion as an adult?"

She was warming up to my idea: "I suppose so, but how would it work?"

"You would need to begin with the realization that anger is not an emotion that is so thoroughly driven by impulse that it cannot be tamed. Then you could train yourself to sift through your options to determine the best path."

As I continued working with Peggy, we focused on a threefold process to help her contemplate the best way to apply choices in the midst of an angry mood. Let's examine each of those steps.

Focus on the Meaning of Your Anger at the Moment You Experience It

By now, it should be clear that anger is more than just an impulsive reaction that comes out of nowhere. When feeling angry, you are demonstrating that you have concerns regarding how you are being received by others. Your task is to determine just how necessary it is for the angry message to be communicated. Sometimes the message is quite necessary and it should be fully aired, while other times it is not.

Peggy went to her sister's home one Saturday evening to enjoy dinner with her two daughters and her nieces and nephews. While there, one of her nephews was making comments toward a sister about a failing grade she received in a college course. The nephew was not kind in his remarks, and Peggy's niece was clearly shaken. Inwardly, Peggy's anger began to build, so remembering our discussion she paused to determine why this incident was triggering an angry reaction.

Reflecting to me, she said, "When my nephew began taunting his sister about her failure, it reminded me of the way my first husband used to speak to me. He was an incredibly critical person, and he seemed to take every opportunity that he could to put me down. I realized as I observed his behavior that I was feeling empathy for my niece because I knew from my own experience how humiliating it is to have your failures held against you."

"It sounds as though your anger was tied to a legitimate cause," I commented. "Let's recall that one of the healthy functions of anger is preservation of legitimate convictions. It seems to me there was a viable message that was attached to your anger."

"That's what I thought at the time, so I felt it was something that I couldn't just let pass. I wanted to say something to my nephew."

So far, in this scene, Peggy's contemplative thinking was helping her come to terms with the anger she was experiencing. At this point, she needed to consider the second key ingredient in sifting through her choices regarding the direction she would take.

Determine How the Feeling of Anger Fits Within Your Overall Life Goals

When most people have a sudden surge of anger, they are unlikely to take time out to question: "Let's see now. How does my current feeling of agitation fit within the overall scheme of things in my life?" It may seem odd for me to suggest it, but this is precisely what is needed before the anger is communicated in words or behavior.

In my initial sessions with Peggy, she would have chafed at the idea of applying such thought to each experience of anger, but by now she was catching on to my assurance that anger can unfold in a guided process. She was willing to recognize that her thoughts could act as a governor to her previously impulsive emotional reactions.

She illustrated to me her growing confidence: "When I witnessed my nephew insulting his sister, I had two predominant thoughts about my role in the matter. First, I wanted to openly go on record that I believed in my niece, and despite the fact that she had failed she deserved to hear words of encouragement. As her aunt, I wanted to be remembered as one who would stand up for her in a trying time. Second, it hit me that I did *not* want to be known as a person whose anger is so scorching that it reduces others to rubble. I've tried that style too many times and I realized that it didn't really work."

Peggy was demonstrating a major adjustment in the management of her anger. Rather than being indiscriminate in her displays, she was appealing to a higher order of thinking. In her contemplation, she was taking into consideration how a single incident fit into the grander picture of her life's plans. She was recognizing that she could determine for herself how one communication fit with her overall approach toward life. In this incident, she reminded herself that she wanted to stand for truth, but she also wanted to model consideration in the process.

As a girl, Peggy was never trained to consider how her use of anger fit within larger plans for relationships. Nevertheless, here she was a woman in her late forties learning a new way of considering her emotional choices. This was major progress! She was recognizing how she would then apply the third step of change.

Put Your Competent Choices into Play, Even If It Does Not Feel Natural

When you have a deep habit of letting your anger run in the wrong direction, it can feel odd to attempt to channel it into more constructive behavior. The odd feeling, though, does not mean your choice is wrong. It just illustrates that sometimes the best choice is not the easiest choice.

Remember, the goal of healthy anger is to preserve worth, needs, and convictions while also upholding the dignity of the others involved. It is to be communicated respectfully; ideally, it would pave the way for cleaner communication with the one who is in conflict with you. You may find that the recipient of your assertion does not choose to respond maturely—even so, you can maintain your resolve to be dignified, even if you are alone in the effort.

Peggy chose to speak to her nephew about his belittling communication toward his sister. In the past, she would have been caustic and her goal would have been to shame him. This time, however, she consciously chose to take another path, one that was straightforward but not belittling. "Derek," she said, "I don't think it's a good idea for you to be so harsh right now toward your sister. She's struggled enough without having to be reminded of her failure. I suggest we move on to a different subject." With that, she spoke with her niece about something else, and Derek received the message and ceased berating his sister.

She later told me, "I was very deliberate in my choice to stand up for a conviction but without going into my old style of being mean. On the one hand, it felt very different because that's not at all the way I used to communicate. But on the other hand, it felt liberating because I could immediately sense that my anger didn't consume me. That's a new experience for me, and I think I could definitely get used to it!"

Peggy learned that her anger was actually a reflection of the pain perpetuated in her life, beginning with her earliest experiences. As a girl, she felt hurt and abandoned by her parents, who would not and could not take the time to use maturity in exploring why she felt as she did. Had they helped her learn to understand both the good and the bad side of anger, she likely would have had less tension as an adult. Peggy rightly concluded that she could not turn back the calendar to relive her childhood more appropriately, but she was wise enough to recognize that the competence to choose her emotional path still existed. It had simply been dormant for a long time. Focusing internally, and accepting the challenge to exercise choice, she was able to release herself from her anger trap.

No one has to be so consumed by anger that it has a permanent grip on the personality. As long as the mind is capable of sifting out choices, both positive and negative, you can free yourself from the clutches of anger gone bad.

In the next chapter, we explore how a key feature in your personality can keep you entrapped by your anger if you do not resolve it successfully. We look into how your anger is influenced by your need to be in control.

❍

For Personal Reflection

- What excuses do people often use as they try to sidestep responsibility for properly managing anger? Which excuses do you use most commonly?
- During your formative years, how were emotional matters discussed? How did this influence your adult patterns of managing anger?
- How would your patterns of anger management have been different if authority figures had taken time in your early years to listen to your emotional concerns and patiently coached you toward good alternatives?
- Adults tend to forget that they have choices in how to handle anger. In what way would your anger management improve if you became more diligent in considering choices?
- To be a contemplative thinker, you must ponder your personal goals during quiet, sober moments. As you take time to consider the person you want to be, where does anger fit within your overall plan?
- When you apply your contemplated choices regarding healthy anger, they may not always feel natural. What situations present the greatest challenge as you deliberate how best to handle your anger?
- How are your feelings of contentment affected as you succeed in laying out a well-devised plan for anger?

PART TWO

WHY PEOPLE REMAIN TRAPPED IN RAW ANGER

5

THE ILLUSION OF CONTROL

ONCE YOU LEARN to identify the purpose of your anger and recognize the options available so you can determine what to do with the emotion, you are on your way to releasing yourself from the binding nature of anger. Lurking inside your personality, though, can be tension regarding key subjects that, if left unresolved, will undermine your effort to forge a healthy path of anger management.

One primary tension that inhibits successful anger management is your struggle for control. Virtually any time you handle your anger maladaptively, you are attempting to respond to perceived control from others by grabbing control for yourself. Angry people often describe how others are bossy, invalidating, stubborn, illogical, or uncaring. Feeling offended by such behavior, you may nurse the thought: *This is unacceptable. I've got to respond in a way that clearly shows that I won't allow myself to be subjected to foul treatment.*

Although there may be a reasonable message behind the angry feeling, angry people can sabotage the legitimacy of the message as they rationalize that they can and should take the power position to get their message across. They may then resort to dogmatic statements, forceful communication, stubborn noncompliance, or closed-mindedness, just to mention a few of the many controlling behaviors that accompany anger.

Consider the three maladaptive categories of anger for the purpose of identifying how they each illustrate a desire to be in control. For instance, when people suppress their anger they are doing more than just keeping quiet. They are showing that they will expose the least amount of personal information at that time to maintain a semblance of personal control. Through quiet use of conflict avoidance, they are subtly indicating: "As I reveal very few details about myself, it allows me to feel I'm gaining the upper hand. I can't afford to be emotionally vulnerable because that would mean a loss of power." Operating on the belief that knowledge is power, they reason that the less others know about their feelings, the less control they can exert.

People who communicate anger with open aggression display their control wishes very clearly and obviously. They make little or no attempt to hide their lust for control as they speak forcefully and persuasively. It is common for them to seek an opportunity to belittle, outargue, impose an opinion, shame, or bully others into submission. Feeling strongly justified in their anger, they see their mission as force-feeding their perspective into the mind of their adversary. Their use of open aggression is their way of communicating: "I don't care if you agree with me or not, *I will be heard*."

People who use passive-aggressive forms of anger are perhaps the most controlling of all because they are adept at manipulating circumstances with the least amount of vulnerability. They make heavy use of behaviors such as noncooperation or saying one thing while doing something entirely different. They can hold stony silence, procrastinate, or give a half-hearted effort. In the midst of such behavior, they do not say the words, but they insinuate: "Try as hard as you want, but you're not going to make me do anything I don't want to do."

When I counsel angry people about how they attempt to maintain control, I first acknowledge that it is not entirely wrong to wish for some semblance of order and direction over their own lives. Anger often arises in reaction to the pushiness or insensitivity of others, and it can become a prompt that impels them to stand upon their own good convictions. There certainly is nothing wrong with that.

Most unhealthy anger, though, goes beyond the effort to preserve legitimate needs and convictions. It includes any attempt to coerce others to fit an agenda against their own choosing. The net result tends to be a painful power play between oneself and those who spark the anger.

When I first met with Jeff, I had the same reaction that most other people probably have: he seemed to be a reasonably organized man with good principles and an ambition that served him well in his professional life. In his mid-thirties, he was neatly groomed, with shortly cropped hair and the business-casual look that was so common in his world of electronic engineering. He seemed to be an engaging person, one with well-rehearsed communication skills. Everything about his outward appearance indicated that he was a man who knew who he was and where he was going.

I remembered him as a participant in one of my anger workshops, but this was the first opportunity for us to talk privately. "Basically, I'm here because my family life is falling apart," he explained, "and I can't allow that to happen. My wife has said that she's fed up with my anger and that

I get too easily upset with her and our children." I learned that he had three kids, ages six to twelve.

"Your wife says you have a problem with anger," I began, "but what do you think? In your opinion, is it truly a problem?"

"Yeah, I guess it is because we sure do argue a lot. She's got her own issues with anger, but I think it's easier for her to focus on my problems with it. I mean, I do become upset because I think she's pretty undisciplined, and I don't always agree with the way she disciplines the kids. I try to talk with her about my ideas, but it's highly predictable that she'll go into a defensive mode, and before you know it, I'm all over her case. I'm not going to say that we argue every single day, but it happens several times each week."

I went on to learn that Jeff was quite free in offering advice that was not wanted. If his wife, Katy, or one of the children expressed an opinion or preference, it was quite common for him to offer a better way or to explain how they should prioritize differently. Even though their family life had a deep history of tension because of this type of behavior from Jeff, he seemed unable to recognize the need for a new way of thinking; the result was a repetition of the same problems week after week, month after month, year after year.

In our initial discussion, we identified how he often had valid ideas that could benefit Katy and the children. He prided himself in his reading about relationships, and he had even attended special seminars on parenting and family life. Through the years, he collected quite a bit of information about how to manage a successful home, which gave him the confidence to be quite direct in telling the family what to do. We explored how he could distinguish healthy means of preserving his needs and convictions versus unhealthy means, but despite his intellectual capacity to recognize the choices in how he handled tension, he continued to have episodes of exploding at his family.

Finally I remarked, "Jeff, you seem to have a better-than-average ability to store knowledge in that brain of yours, and that's a credit to your obvious intelligence. I notice, though, that you seem unable to put your knowledge to good use if your wife and children don't join you in embracing your ideas. A high percentage of your angry outbursts seem to revolve around forcing compliance."

Jeff nodded as he absorbed my words, and then he said, "That would be fair to say. I definitely have things I want them to understand. What's so wrong with that?"

"It's not wrong to want consensus within the family," I replied. "I see, though, that you're going a step beyond wanting consensus. You're insisting that they *must* comply."

Imperative Thinking

When angry people attempt to force their way upon others, they are stuck in a pattern of thought that I call imperative thinking. Recall from your school days that an imperative statement is a direct command; it is specific, cut-and-dried. An imperative communicator says, "This is the way things are supposed to be, so let's get after it and make it happen." In our vocabulary there are numerous imperative words: *have to, must, can't, should, supposed to, ought to, need to, had better.*

I explained imperative thinking to Jeff and asked, "Does that sound familiar to you?"

He grinned as he admitted, "I only use that kind of thinking about three hundred times a day! Yeah, I'd say that pretty much summarizes my way of communicating at home."

To get an idea if your anger is fueled by imperative patterns of thinking, consider how it can be variously displayed:

- Being pushy or forceful when communicating preferences
- Using repetition when trying to make a point
- Maintaining such strong opinions that compromise is difficult
- Refusing to hear others; being so self-focused that your perception is all that matters
- Telling rather than discussing
- Feeling uncomfortable with loose ends; having a need for closure
- Maintaining a habit of annoyance or irritable reaction
- Going your own way, even when you know others are bothered by your choice
- Feeling the need to have compliance or sameness of thought
- Indulging critical thoughts
- Offering solutions when others expose their feelings or struggles
- Being impatient

In being imperative, angry people are operating as if it is their duty to make others fit an agenda. At the moment of anger, they have strong opinions about right and wrong, and they have convinced themselves that they cannot be satisfied until they force correctness. (Correctness is defined as thinking like me.) In his anger, Jeff was strongly convinced that Katy should be more organized with the kids, and he did not hesitate to let her know how she should act. Likewise, he was quite directive toward his children, correcting them in an abrupt tone of voice. No one had to guess his opinions at home.

I asked Jeff to take stock of this controlling manner of communication by considering how successfully it contributed to the emotional atmosphere at home. He paused for a moment and then replied, "Well, I guess it gets results because I can usually whip everyone into shape, but usually when I come on strong it leaves everyone unhappy. Is that what you're trying to make me see?"

"Yes. Plain and simple, people don't like feeling controlled. When you feel perturbed with your wife or children, you may truly have a worthy message, but if you speak in a controlling fashion, you dilute your good message because your method is ultimately insulting." This caused Jeff to look at me quizzically, so I explained: "Accompanying each imperative message is a hidden but powerful set of covert messages. Your overbearing style sends the impression that you don't accept the other person. It implies a low level of trust, and it indicates that you think of the other person as beneath you. Whatever right message you're trying to send is lost because the covert, or implied, messages are so distasteful."

Jeff was truly stumped because he had never really considered the covert messages attached to his controlling behavior. I explained further: "When you act imperatively, you are simultaneously using both idealistic and pessimistic thinking. You can see your idealistic thought in your insistence that others can and should apply perfect solutions to the problem at hand. There's little room given for humanness. The pessimistic thought is indicated by your feeling you have to force-feed your opinion. It shows that you have little confidence in allowing others to take the opportunity to think for themselves."

When people like Jeff consistently use imperative communication, there is a strong likelihood that this form of communication was modeled in their formative years. Most angry adults can recall many incidents of feeling controlled or forced into a mold by parents or another authority figure. This creates feelings of great dissatisfaction, so the seeds for anger are sown as the desire to preserve personal worth builds. Young people begin looking for an opportunity to illustrate that they, not their controlling counterparts, get to call the shots. Ironically, these very same people who disliked feeling controlled in their formative years become controllers themselves as they grow into adults. This perpetuates the anger cycle, and it can continue one generation after another until someone finally decides to take a much different path.

Jeff's family history was typical of angry adults who feel they must maintain control. His father was very heavy-handed in managing discipline, using lots of spanking, verbal haranguing, and insults. Jeff hated the feelings of belittlement that resulted from such treatment, as is to be expected. He certainly did not deserve such condescension. Anger would well up inside, and the emotion was handled in a variety of ways. Sometimes he would suppress it and try to "go along to get along." Other times he would feign compliance and then, behind his father's back, would do whatever he wanted. As a boy, he did not realize that such behavior was passive-aggressive anger, but that's what it was. Other times he would pitch a fit of open aggression. He could be quite argumentative, and at school he developed a reputation as an unpredictable hothead. His anger was a powerful counteraction to the feeling of being controlled.

As an adult, instead of recognizing the folly of a controlling spirit, he followed in his own father's footsteps. He did not curse or shout as often as his dad, but he was certainly heavy-handed whenever he felt inclined to preserve personal needs and convictions. Despite his powerful distaste for being controlled as a boy, he knew no other way of responding when his anger was ignited. Our task in counseling was to identify and implement a whole new approach.

Freedom Thinking

A major lapse in logic occurs every time angry people attempt to control others. They assume they have the prerogative to control others (which they do not), and they assume they actually have the ability to control others (which they also do not). In the short run, they may be fooled as they find nominal success in their effort to control, but over the course of time they inevitably find that those being controlled rebel in some form. They look for a way out. That's what Jeff did in relation to his father, and that's what was happening with his wife, who wanted to leave him.

I explained to Jeff: "Let's recognize first that control is an illusion. If you honestly think you can force your way into the minds of your wife and kids, dictating how they must think and act, you're kidding yourself. Short term, they might comply out of fear. Long term, they'll actively look for ways to express their separateness. That's a 100 percent guarantee."

Jeff looked stunned as he considered my thoughts, but immediately he recognized that we were onto something. "OK, you've got my attention. So what do I do differently?"

"First, we adjust your fundamental thinking," I explained. "Let's take all of your imperative thoughts, with all the should's and must's and had better's and duties and obligations, and throw them out the window." He visibly winced as I said this, but I continued. "In their place, let's invoke a whole new system of thinking anchored in the word *freedom.*" I paused to let him absorb what I was conveying.

Initially Jeff was taken aback by my suggestion. "Freedom? Are you trying to tell me that every person can do anything he wants, at any time or any place? If that's what you're suggesting, I'm not sure I can buy into that. That sounds like chaos to me!"

"In a sense, that's exactly what I am suggesting," I replied. "Each person does indeed have the privilege to choose how to live, at any time or place. What I am *not* suggesting is a dismissal of common sense, respectfulness, or structure. Those things are both good and necessary in any organization, whether it's a family unit, a work group, or a cluster of friends." He seemed to calm slightly as I said this.

"Free will is part of the master design that distinguishes humanity from other forms of creation," I continued. "Our Creator endowed each person with the privilege to choose how he or she will live. Of course, in our younger years, we are not yet wise enough to know what to do with unbridled freedom, so authorities need to apply guidance and consequences to help us know how to live within a group's established norms. This need for guidance continues into the adult years, since we need consequences to give people the incentive to live within agreed-upon norms in various sectors of our culture. So by saying that we need to recognize freedom, I'm not advocating irresponsibility. I am suggesting, though, that we cut as wide a swath as common sense allows so people recognize their opportunity to choose who they want to be and how they want to live."

Jeff was listening carefully, but he still had questions. I realized we needed to remove our discussion from the realm of theory and make it practical. I wanted him to discover that acceptance of the reality of freedom would represent a major step out of the trap of anger that had created so much disruption in his life.

Freedom Applied Toward Others

As you openly acknowledge the truth that others have a right to exercise free will, your methods of communication are immediately affected. For instance, if you have something to say to another person, you do so without attempting to plead or persuade. This is especially true in the midst of conflict. Likewise, keep in mind that the purpose of healthy anger is to preserve personal worth, needs, or convictions, not to rearrange another person's thoughts or priorities. When conflict and anger arise, you can still stand up for what you believe, but at the same time you leave room for others to choose for themselves how to integrate what you have communicated.

Jeff was honest in our discussion as he admitted, "When I'm angry I *am* trying to get the other person to understand my position and change. The reason I'm angry in the first place is that the other person is not cooperating. Now I'm hearing you say that my approach is wrong."

"It's not wrong," I explained, "to desire coordination or cohesion in your life with your family. It's an entirely different matter to desire coordination as opposed to forcing it. Let me give you a simple illustration. Let's suppose in talking with Katy you discover that she told one of the kids a certain activity was OK, when in fact you had told the child an hour earlier that it was not. That is a conflict that might stir up anger."

"It happens in our house all the time," he replied. He was interested to hear where I was going with this illustration.

"At that moment, there is a strong possibility that your controlling, imperative thinking will come into play." He grinned shyly as he acknowledged that I was on track. "You have options regarding what direction to take. On the one hand, you can speak coercively to your wife and explain in no uncertain terms how she should check with you first before giving permission regarding the child's activity. You can lecture about how this coordination is absolutely mandatory or the kids will grow up as manipulators." Jeff recognized that I was describing his common style of communicating frustration. I then posed the question, "Is your wife likely to receive your words with an appreciative or cooperative spirit?"

Jeff mumbled something about how this would only produce increased tension and how this problem had recurred many times. I continued, "You also have the option to acknowledge her free will. As a mother, she has the prerogative to make choices regarding the children's activities. Perhaps in this case she didn't handle the matter as you would have liked; nonetheless, she was doing what she thought was right. In your anger, you still could choose to talk with her about the need to remain coordinated, yet you could refrain from speaking in a commanding tone. With respectfulness, you could explain your preference, and then let her decide if your suggestion has merit or not. She might decide to go along with your request; she might not. Either way, you can let her know that she's free to incorporate your words any way she likes."

This prospect scared Jeff. "Well, what if she decides that my thoughts are inappropriate and that she won't give me the time of day? Am I just supposed to let her do whatever she wants?"

"There is no 'supposed to' in this formula," I reminded him. "Let me simply pose it to you this way. Which way would you like to be spoken to if the tables were reversed?"

When you recognize the freedom of others to think and feel and prioritize as they choose, a risk is inherent. They *might* decide to ignore you completely and do exactly the opposite of what you would like. In most cases, though, if you consistently approach others in a spirit of freedom, your influence *rises*. People appreciate the respect that accompanies such an attitude. Just as imperative communication conveys a covert message, freedom communication also conveys a covert message. Freedom indicates fundamental acceptance of others, as well as a sense of trust and equality. In recognizing others' freedom, you are displaying a spirit of good will, and others may be drawn toward you, wanting to blend favorably with you.

To bring balance to our discussion about freedom, I explained to Jeff, "There are times when others will use their freedom irresponsibly, and that could stoke your feelings of anger. At that point, you need not revert to controlling behavior. Instead, you can appeal to commonsense consequences. For instance, if you freely speak with your children about how to maintain harmony at home, they may predictably balk or test the limits. Consequences, in the form of lost privileges, might be applied. Likewise, if adults freely choose to disregard your legitimate needs, consequences may include your own decisive pursuit toward another course of action."

Jeff asked me, "When I implement consequences, isn't that the same as being imperative?"

"That's a good question," I replied, "and it really depends on your mindset at the moment. If you apply consequences because you're finicky, close-minded, or punitive, then that's problematic. If your consequences are an indication that you're merely attempting to maintain responsibility or respectability, you are probably on the right track. Consequences are not to be used as a means of whipping someone into submission, but to stand firmly for common sense."

As a general rule, I encourage the use of consequences that are based on broadly agreed ideals within society. Our culture has many standards about right and wrong that make up the moral fiber of life. Of course, these ideals differ according to religious beliefs, personal convictions, and the like, so there is an element of subjectivity involved. As a simple example, most would agree that lying is wrong, and therefore it can be appropriate to use consequences in the presence of such behavior. Likewise, most agree that it is reasonable to be wise in the use of money or respectful of time commitments. If these standards are breached, discerning consequences could be helpful to promote the common good in relationships. The key to using consequences is that they are truly fair and applied in a noninsulting fashion.

When you relate with people in a free manner, you are willing to cease coercive and demanding behavior. You recognize that the more you try to force correctness onto others, the more certain it is that you will be held captive by your own anger. When you acknowledge freedom, though, you are being honest about your own limitations, and you are upholding the dignity of the others involved. Your chances for relational success are enhanced.

Freedom Applied to Oneself

Even after you acknowledge that others have the privilege to be free, you can still struggle with the question of what to do with your remaining feelings of frustration. For instance, Jeff was convinced that he was wrong to deny his family the opportunity to claim ownership of their own behavior and responses. Recognizing that he did not like others telling him how to think or prioritize, it only made sense that he would give the same treatment to them as he would like in reverse. Yet even as he attempted to speak in a less controlling way, he still felt angry when he and family members were at odds.

"I realize that Katy has to feel free to make her own decisions, and it's true that my influence goes way down when I try to force-feed my ideas on her," he conceded. "But even as I give her space to think independently, I still feel upset. What am I supposed to do about that?"

"You can do anything you want with your frustration," I replied. "You're a free man, meaning anything and everything is an option."

"Huh? Are you telling me just to cut loose, and that I should just let it rip?"

"That is an option," I responded, "although keep in mind that I'm not going to pin you down to any given 'should' or 'supposed to.'" Pausing for a moment, I continued, "In my opinion, letting your anger rip is not a wise option because Katy would predictably feel insulted by such an approach. A calm explanation of your preferences seems to be more reasonable. Before you agree with my perspective, though, you need to decide if you can choose to respond in that manner."

Jeff shook his head as he stated, "Boy, this freedom thing is going to take some real getting used to. I've never really thought like this before."

It is wise to recognize others' freedom when you are angry; to tame that emotion, you would need to recognize that you too can do anything you want when you feel upset. You can yell or rant and rave. You can say ugly things about people behind their back. You can silently hold a grudge. You can state your concerns respectfully. You can forgive. Everything is an option. Your management of anger is entirely your choice.

When I encourage people like Jeff to apply full freedom at the moment they feel angry, it almost always catches them off guard. All their lives, angry people have been told that they should quit feeling so strongly, that their anger is too unruly or out of bounds. This creates conflicting feelings when they feel angry because they know that the rules say they are not supposed to get mad. Along comes Les Carter, who says that every person is free! When you feel angry, you have an array of options, and ultimately you get to decide what you'd like to do. This cuts against the grain of all that has been taught for years.

Recognizing the standards and norms that our culture generally agrees upon regarding the wisest ways of handling anger, before wildly cutting loose with unruly anger, smart people take the time to run their choices through the grid of those norms and through a well-conceived moral code. For instance, as I reminded Jeff that he was free to shout at his wife when angry, he immediately recoiled because his moral code told him doing so runs counter to human decency. When I said that holding a grudge was also an option, his mind immediately considered how that could turn disastrous.

Angry people are so commonly fixed on the illusion that they must control others to feel good that they rarely take the time to freely consider who they want to be at the moment of anger. Applying free choice to managing their own anger causes these people to ponder the question, "If I am truly free, what do I want to be?"

In the spirit of freedom, I asked Jeff, "Would you like to use the ranting-and-raving method of anger whenever your heart desires?"

Feeling somewhat exposed, he replied, "Not really. I don't like the results of that kind of communication. Nothing good comes from it."

I said, "I guess wild anger seems much less desirable once you recognize that it's a free choice. In fact, as you acknowledge the poor consequences that would accompany such a choice, the options of respectfulness and calmness and forgiveness become all the more attractive."

Handling anger with respectfulness will never become a lasting habit if it is motivated by pure duty. People who try to corral anger because they've been told they must do so don't have appropriate ownership of the right reasoning that would prompt a healthy anger response. Their efforts are similar to children who act correctly only because an adult authority figure made them do so. By factoring in freedom, angry people are more capable of weighing consequences, and they are more inclined to handle their emotions with purpose.

Jeff made an appropriate observation after we discussed the reality of his freedom to handle his anger any way he liked: "You're telling me that ultimately I'm the only person responsible for my own anger management, aren't you?" I affirmed his insight with a nod. "Looks like I've got some growing up to do," he concluded. I then asked, "Are you familiar with the phrase, 'You shall know the truth, and the truth will set you free'?" He nodded and said, "That always sounded like a wise phrase, but I never put much thought into the meaning of it." I replied, "This phrase, spoken by Jesus, prompts us to acknowledge that once we understand life's truths, we can be poised to make significant adjustments. It is a bedrock truth that we each get to choose who we will be. If you can learn to apply this truth in the midst of angry circumstances, you'll be well on the way toward significant change."

I knew right then that progress was being made.

Ultimately, controlling people unfairly attempt to shift the responsibility for their emotional stability onto others. "You've got to act right so I won't feel this way" is their message. By accepting the freedom to manage emotions in whatever way they choose, angry people can recognize that "If I'm going to have stability, it's my decision and no one else's." That is when anger has less and less of a grip on their lives.

Free Will and Assertiveness

As you understand that everyone is a free agent who gets to choose what he or she will do, coordination can still occur. Chaos is not necessarily the result. Free people who openly declare a desire to get along with one another can commit to commonsense guidelines that keep anger from getting out of hand.

Those guidelines might include a number of ideas:

- All expressions of anger are the result of choices, not just unavoidable reactions.
- You can choose to drop coercion or manipulative efforts; your aim need not be to dominate or win.
- You can choose to address needs, preferences, and perceptions with a firm yet calm disposition.
- It is not necessary to cling to a fixed agenda as to how others should respond to your message.
- If the person receiving your assertiveness disagrees, he or she is free to do so; you are not required to enter a war of point-counterpoint.
- Because you are not trying to win, you can draw conflict to a close when necessary; there is no need to engage in repetitive communication.
- You can choose to forgive or let go of your anger, not because you are supposed to do so, but because it makes sense.

Your thinking patterns directly determine how you manage your emotions. Recognizing that it is delusional to think you can control the reactions and perceptions of others, you can discover a sense of liberation never known before. You are on your way to recognizing that inner peace does not hinge on creating a predictable utopia; rather, it is the by-product of your own willingness to become anchored in qualities such as goodness, consideration, and tolerance.

In the next chapter, we explore how you can continue to find balance in your anger by maintaining a sturdy foundation of personal security. Only when you have a secure feeling of personal worth can you be expected to freely manage your anger appropriately.

For Personal Reflection

- How can your use of anger be understood as a craving to be in control? Why do you feel the need to control others?
- When has your anger been triggered by the controlling behavior of others toward you? What right message do you wish to send in those moments?
- As you engage in controlling behavior or communication, how do others respond? What effect does this have on the overall sense of harmony in your relationships?
- Why is it a virtual certainty that others will not respond well if you communicate anger in a controlling fashion?
- How was controlling anger modeled in your formative years? How did it affect you?
- What does it mean to you to be free? How would your expression of anger differ if you recognized others' privilege to be free as they determine how to respond to your feelings?
- You are free to communicate anger in any way you prefer. Knowing this, why might you choose healthy anger over unhealthy anger?
- How can you still maintain appropriate assertiveness even as you recognize that others are free to live as they choose?

6

INSECURITY'S HOLD ON ANGRY PEOPLE

IF ANGER CAN BE UNDERSTOOD as the emotion that wishes to preserve personal respect and worth, it stands to reason that chronically angry people are struggling with their sense of value. Consistently angry people are insecure people. Though they will not say so, their angry responses indicate a mind of dependency that could be summarized this way: "I'm putting you in charge of making me feel good about myself, and you can't let me down. You owe it to me to act right so I can feel worthy!" In a sense, they put others into a Godlike position, looking to the other to bestow worth upon them.

Though in many respects I am an optimistic person, my pessimism leads me to conclude that no human being is able to say or do enough of the right things to cause anyone to feel perfectly secure. Yet persistently angry people are hoping against all odds that they can somehow manipulate people and circumstances to the point of bringing them peace. Behind the persuasion and coercion that accompanies anger is a hope that others can learn to appease the angry one, causing him or her to be emotionally stable.

One such person was Gary. In his early forties, he seemed reluctant to be in my office. He explained that he had always assumed people who sought counseling were weak, so it seemed odd he was now one of those who had to get professional help. Several friends and family members had suggested in years past that he should seek help for his anger, but it was only after his supervisor at work put him on probation that he decided to meet with me. "I'm a rather intense person," this edgy and easily distracted man explained, "or at least that's what people tell me. I don't suffer fools gladly, so I've developed a reputation of getting agitated when people let me down."

I asked Gary to describe the manifestations of his anger, and his answer caused me to recognize that he was a candid person whose aggression was more open than passive. He told me that he occasionally would blurt out caustic venom, but it was usually at home with his wife and daughter. At work he was known for having exacting standards (he managed a men's clothing store). The salespeople who worked for him found him to be finicky and critical. Vendors complained that he never seemed satisfied with their efforts to serve him. He'd had several run-ins with the accountant. Even though his store showed consistent profits, the owner finally told him that he had three months to clean up his reputation or he would be fired.

Gary candidly admitted, "I know I can be hard on people, and I'm sure it has turned a lot of people off. I've always taken the attitude that if you're going to work for me, you'd better know that I'm going to have high standards. Unfortunately, it makes me seem like I'm critical, and people learn that I'm just not the kind of person who can settle for second best. I've scared off quite a few employees over the years, and my family tells me I can be hard on them, so maybe everyone else but me is onto something. I know I don't want to be fired, but at the same time I don't want to have to water down my principles."

On the surface, it seemed as though Gary's anger was tied to a system of beliefs that might be considered admirable. He believed in maintaining a solid work ethic and doing things right the first time. No one could argue against the merits of that desire. Focusing on the lofty ideals that drove him, Gary could justify most of his moments with anger. After all, who could fault him for insisting upon diligent effort? Closer examination, though, showed there was more going on that kept him trapped in patterns of perpetual anger.

Anger and Emotional Dependency

Inside every personality is the ingredient of emotional dependency. Whether we realize it consciously or not, we scan the environment every day for cues that indicate if we can feel calm or if we should be tense. "If you treat me right," so the reasoning goes, "I'll feel satisfied and stable. But if you treat me wrong, my emotions will be adversely affected." Not only is this pattern common to every person, it can be normal.

I explained to Gary, "Each time you experience anger it's because your dependency upon others has prompted you to feel that way."

Before I could say anything more, he interrupted. "Dependency? You're trying to tell me that I have a problem with dependence? I can think of a lot of ways to describe myself, but 'dependent' isn't a word I'd choose.

I'm highly independent." The agitation that accompanied his words was proof that I was right on track, so I realized I would need to be very specific in explaining what I wanted him to understand.

"Let me see if I can give you an idea of what I'm talking about," I said. "Let's suppose you're talking with one of your salespeople about the way to handle a specific procedure at the store, and it's clear that he is not catching on to what you're saying. Has that ever happened?"

With a simple chuckle Gary replied, "Only several times a week. We're constantly working to have the highest quality of service in our store. You have to if you're going to stay one step ahead of your competition."

I continued: "Let's suppose that this salesperson simply cannot or will not incorporate what you're saying. Frustration or annoyance is an inevitable response. Am I right?" He nodded and mentioned that he felt that way often. "That's your dependency at work," I said. "Let's take another example. Let's suppose you go home at the end of the day and you explain to your wife how frustrated you felt because your salesperson didn't follow your directions. Instead of giving you a supportive reply, she makes a cavalier remark and indicates disinterest. Once more your annoyance peaks. Does that sound familiar?" Again he nodded and said he became upset whenever his wife seemed indifferent to his day. "Once more," I explained, "that annoyance would be an indication of your dependence."

By this time, Gary was getting a grasp on the concept. Raising his eyebrows, he scratched his head and said, "If me reacting to others with a foul mood is dependence, I guess I'll have to plead guilty, because other people can sure put me into a bad mood. That kind of thing happens all the time." Still reluctant, though, to buy my concept completely, he added, "But I'm going to have a hard time thinking of myself as having a dependency problem."

No one is so emotionally detached from others that he or she can remain completely void of emotional reactions to the outer world. Humans simply are not wired to be robotic as they respond to the environment's many stimulations. Every day, we experience a multitude of emotional responses to an array of stimulants. For instance, our emotions can depend on the traffic, weather conditions, the way the schedule unfolds, or our financial status. Additionally, we take cues from the people we encounter each day as we react to their level of encouragement, interest, or approval. If others are rude, insensitive, or invalidating, certainly our emotions are affected. If we sense that others are defensive, bossy, incompetent, lying, or sneaky, we cannot help but have an emotional response.

Some people are more affected than others in reacting to circumstances, meaning that not all people experience the same level of dependency. No person, however, is ever so emotionally isolated from people and events that there is no response at all.

The Deepest Need

At the very moment an individual enters the world, dependency is present. A newborn infant instinctively cries, wanting some measure of assurance that the world is going to be a safe place where nurturing and sustenance are given in abundance. In the earliest days of life, children want to know if they are loved. They want to be assured that the most fundamental needs are forthcoming. If there is any hint that they are being rejected or abused, they respond with painful emotions. If they are satisfied that they are affirmed and cared for, their emotions steady. This pattern remains intact day after day and year after year. Until they take their dying breath, they desire to be affirmed as a person of value. Affirmation and love is the deepest need each person has, and there is never a day when a person can state, "OK, I've had all the affirmation I need. Don't give me any more."

As I talked with Gary about the universal experience of dependency, tying it to the most fundamental need for love, he nodded in agreement. "It's hard to argue against the fact that every person begins life with a need to be loved. I wouldn't consider myself the mushy type, but I understand what you're saying, and it makes sense to me."

Wanting to help him see the connection between the need for love and anger, I said, "Gary, when I talk with someone like yourself who has had ongoing problems with anger, I can't help but assume that there's a deep void driving the anger. At the very core of your angry reactions, you're pleading with people to show you respect. Your anger strongly speaks of feelings of hurt, and it exposes a very basic yearning to be held in higher regard. The anger tells me that you're struggling with a love deficit."

Gary sat in silence for a moment, then said quietly, "I guess I'm going to have to take some time to filter what you're saying. Until now I would never have told anyone that I have a problem with feeling unloved. Just saying it sounds like I'm speaking psychobabble." Pausing again, he then continued, "I've never really questioned if my parents loved me or not. My dad's not the most emotional guy you ever met. I mean, he sure wasn't the hugging kind of person, and we never really talked about stuff like love or hurts and pains. He was actually somewhat remote, but I knew he cared about me. And Mom, she wasn't the kind that I would gush out my feelings toward. She was nice most of the time, and even if she was in a bad mood or seemed unaccepting, it was probably because I or one of my brothers had done something to really tick her off."

When I talk with angry adults like Gary about deficient love and its accompanying dependencies, I have no desire to cast Mom or Dad in a villainous role. I merely mean to point out that in the presence of interpersonal imperfections and deficiencies, we react, and that reaction is often in the form of anger. When we persist with anger, it is a clear sign that we have not sufficiently come to terms with less-than-adequate love experiences.

Though Gary might have assumed that his anger at work (or in traffic, or in a crowded shopping mall) was not tied to the need to feel loved or affirmed, this is precisely what was driving his emotions. He was quite sensitive to any insinuation that others did not care about him. It annoyed him to no end when he felt others could not extend courtesy toward him or they did not respond to his needs appropriately.

In one session, he told me how he had gone to a nice restaurant with a friend for lunch. "The service there was lousy, and I had a hard time enjoying my meal because I couldn't get the waitress to do what she was supposed to do." He told me that she didn't refill his drink quickly enough. She failed to include a special condiment to go with his meal; she spent too much time trying to gab in friendly conversation, and she made him wait too long when taking care of his check. Though at the time he did not recognize his dependency, at the base of his building agitation was a yearning to be treated as a significant person. "Show that you value me," was the message that pushed his anger along. Even though his anger involved an unnamed waitress at a restaurant, he was so hungry to feel important that he could hardly contain his emotional responses.

In large measure, emotional dependency operates on a subconscious level. By that I mean most people do not sit on the side of the bed each morning thinking, "OK, who am I going to hand my emotional stability to today?" We do not consciously plan to become dependent upon others, but it happens whether we are aware of it or not. People who are seeking to lessen the intensity of their anger help themselves immensely if they learn to become conscious of the presence of dependency so they can then make adjustments in their thoughts and behaviors.

Primarily they need to adjust their core beliefs about personal worth.

Where Worth Comes From

Going back to the very first day of life, it is significant to note that a newborn infant has no way to merit love or affirmation, and yet they are given in large doses. Inherent in human thought is the notion of the inborn worth of the individual. This notion is certainly consistent with spiritual teachings emphasizing that human worth is a universal given, not a commodity that arbitrarily comes and goes. It's not tied to achievement or performance, nor can would-be judges decree it. It is a God-given gift that simply is. None of us acts in a manner that is perfectly consistent with innate worth, but each individual's value is nonetheless inextricably tied to the status of being human, period.

Ideally, as young children learn to interface successfully with the outer world, Mom and Dad would be quite consistent in teaching them ongoing awareness of their own value separate from external messages. In infancy and in the toddler years, this teaching would come in the form of hands-on affirmation with lots of touch, physical closeness, patience, and nurturing. As language development becomes more sophisticated during the grade school years, affirming words would be added to the nurturing as parents explain more fully to the growing child that worth is an inherent gift no one can take away. For instance, if an eight-year-old child complains to a parent that a friend has been rude, she could be told, "Sometimes people forget that you are a person of great value, so they say things that hurt. I want you to know that in our home, you will always be regarded highly, no matter what disagreements we have." Upon hearing such a message many times, the child is taught to think separately from surrounding people.

During the teen years, young people develop abstract thinking, which means they are able to claim ownership of concepts. Parents and authority figures can add to the young person's confidence by openly exploring the notion of innate worth and its application in trying circumstances. For instance, if a fifteen-year-old complains about feeling rejected by a friend, he can be reminded that the friend does not hold ultimate authority over his worth: "I understand that your friend has decided to belittle you because you haven't measured up to his standards. Remember how in our home we've discussed that worth is inherent. It's not subject to another person's moods or declarations. Let's discuss how you might handle yourself in the midst of this disappointment as you cling to the notion of your worth. How do you suppose the recognition of your own worth can guide you through such a trial?"

As I explained this idea of innate worth to Gary, I asked him, "How often did you talk with your parents about this sort of thing when you were growing up?"

He rolled his eyes in mock ridicule as he said, "You've got to be kidding. We never talked like that in my home, and I doubt we ever will. Don't get me wrong, I knew my parents loved me, but it just wasn't a topic open to deep discussion when I grew up."

Because the world can sometimes be a hostile place, developing children inevitably learn to be guarded in receiving a message of hurt or rejection from others. Experiences of conflict cause them to wonder if they have any real value at all. They need repeated reassurance from parents that their value does not have to depend upon messages from others. In the absence of such communication, children go on the hunt, wondering if someone (anyone!) will recognize their worth. This is why a capable adult like Gary can still struggle when he receives a message of devaluation. Not learning to believe fully in his inherent worth, he was still in search of a steady message to reassure him that he is deemed valuable. Whenever he perceived a rejecting response, anger was the result.

Personal Worth and Anger Management

When I counsel adults like Gary, I want them to understand that even in the absence of discussions about worth during the developmental years, it continues to exist. I told him, "Gary, things would be easier for you right now if you'd been trained to incorporate the truth about your worth into your daily reactions to the people surrounding you. There's no doubt that you would respond less severely to others' incompetence or disinterest because you wouldn't be as prone to receiving their behavior as a referendum denouncing your value."

Gary was quite pensive as he mulled over my words. Initially he did not want to believe that his security was so shaky it could hinge on the judgments others rendered toward him. Yet as he revisited in his mind the many scenes that triggered his anger, he could see how his anger was indeed a cry to be respected. His anger indicated just how hungry he was to be affirmed. Never before had he tied his eruptions to his long-standing craving to be held in high regard by others.

For instance, Gary was able to see that his anger toward a mistake-prone employee represented a yearning to be regarded more highly by the employee. Likewise, he began to recognize and admit that his anger toward his wife's occasional disinterest in him was also an indication of his hunger for affirmation. In the past, he could only see the angry expression, but now he was learning to look behind the anger to recognize the ingredients that fed the emotion.

"Okay, I admit it," he said to me. "I've been wanting people to treat me with respect, and the intensity of my anger is a clear indication of the depth of my need to feel loved. But now that I can see this problem, what am I supposed to do to make the anger disappear?"

"First," I replied, "let's recognize that it's not our goal to make your anger disappear altogether. There are times when your drive for self-preservation is appropriate, and it can lead to clean communications that could benefit your relations." Then, responding more specifically to his question, I explained, "You're going to find balance in your use of anger only as you first contemplate fully the notion of your worth. Does it hinge entirely upon the pronouncements of others, or can you find satisfaction in knowing that your worth exists even when others seem to invalidate you?"

To be released from the trap of anger, it is necessary to practice *delicate detachment*. By that I mean we can mentally separate ourselves from the judgments of others, but detachment does not have to be accompanied by a spirit of harshness. We can gently remind ourselves that the words or responses of others are not to be received as absolute truth. People can be quite fallible or nonobjective in their responses to one another, meaning it can be folly to allow our own mood or reaction to be heavily dependent on others.

Gary told me that he got upset one day with one of his salesmen because he seemed incapable of receiving instruction. Gary's anger had a legitimate base in that it prompted him to hold firmly to his belief in proper business procedures. In this incident, though, he remained in a foul mood for the entire day because of the salesman's gaffs. I told him, "That would be a time to practice delicate detachment. Without a brash spirit, you could remind yourself that the salesman's rejection of your input doesn't have to be perceived as repudiation of your value. His behavior might indicate that he has a prideful or nonteachable character, but it doesn't mean you have lesser value as a manager."

"But the guy's blunders affect the rest of the staff," he protested. "I can't help but stay ticked off when he won't do what we've outlined in our staff briefings."

"I want you to see that you're taking his negative behavior so personally that you have basically handed him the reins to your well-being, letting him determine if you're going to have a good day or not. I'm guessing that his behavior would be quite the same if he had a different boss or if he worked for another store. In other words, this salesman's behavior is not about his valuation of you. It's a commentary on his own lack of focus. Only when you remove yourself from the equation will you be able to handle your emotional response more appropriately."

In this case, Gary had good reason to feel angry, since an employee was mismanaging his responsibilities. In an assertive mode, Gary could speak respectfully to the salesman about the company's expectations, and he could openly establish consequences for failure to comply. That would be a fair exercise of appropriate anger. As he fumed for hours about the employee's poor behavior, though, he missed his opportunity to practice clean assertiveness. "How dare he not listen to me," he obsessed. "I can't stand it when someone defies my instructions."

Gary's history of less-than-adequate affirmation caused him to feel an extra measure of hurt when he received yet more evidence of a person invalidating his worth. As a child, he was not smart enough to know not to receive invalidation from others as irrefutable truth. As an adult, he now had the capacity to reason that his worth was a fixed asset, and he need not let his feelings be bruised if someone did not recognize that truth.

I explained to Gary that as he learned to trust more in the inherent nature of his own worth, he would still feel anger, but his use of anger would have a different thrust. "You can act upon your anger as a way of showing that you believe in your own worth," I remarked, "but your anger doesn't have to turn into an opportunity to establish your worth at the other person's expense."

Emotional Independence

As you learn to sidestep the invalidation of others by believing in your inherent worth, you are on your way to achieving emotional independence. That is, your emotions (specifically, your anger) do not have to depend upon others' behavior; instead you can chart your own course regarding how you respond to frustrating circumstances. Specifically, you can feel free to apply healthy traits to your undesirable circumstances rather than clamoring to make others feed your emotional neediness.

To gain mastery in emotional independence, it is helpful, then, to ponder those traits that you want to have most of the time. Do you want to be kind and patient? Do you believe in the qualities of goodness and fairness? How about rudeness and insulting communication? Do you want those traits to define you, or would you prefer to use respectfulness and encouragement instead? You might focus on other ingredients such as openness, honesty, understanding, and self-restraint. Would you choose to have qualities like these be an integral part of your relational style?

Emotionally independent people do not require that all the external factors be in place first before they can proceed with healthy plans. Armed with well-conceived priorities, they look for a way to put their best qualities into action, especially in circumstances that might otherwise evoke traits that are inconsistent with their convictions. Let's look at some simple examples of how this might work:

○ A mother is angry because her teenager is sneaky and deceptive, and he doesn't mind even after she thinks they have agreed on expected behavior. Instead of feeling lowly because the teen won't uphold her value, she can recognize that his behavior is a separate issue from her worth. Rather than talking with him in a "why are you doing this to me?" tone of voice, she can calmly and firmly discuss her convictions with him, explaining the consequences of disobedience. Her calmness is applied despite her son's attitude because this is what she believes is warranted in this situation. She has learned that her response is a function of her own sense of purpose, not his behavior.

- A man finds his brother to be cranky and annoying whenever the family gathers. He is reminded that the brother has been an antagonist dating back to their early years. Rather than fretting about why the brother chooses to be so rude to him, he decides in advance to remain respectful even as his brother operates in a predictably foul manner. He sees no reason to turn each message of condescension from his brother into a debate about why he acts so inappropriately.
- Driving in city traffic, a man knows that it would be easy to operate with tension and agitation because other motorists are so inconsiderate. He is weary of being treated like a faceless nobody who has no redeeming value, yet he does not want to sink to primitive behavior. He chooses instead to minimize the intensity of his anger by recognizing that the indifference of fellow drivers is not the ultimate factor in his beliefs about self-worth. He conducts himself in a self-respecting and patient manner because he understands that the general public does not establish his moods.

Emotional independence is possible once you recognize that you get to establish your own direction separately from the people surrounding you. Chronically angry people are so obsessed with making others respect them that they have not learned to hold confidently to their own well-chosen path.

Gary was trying to grasp the essence of my thoughts about the link between anger and worth, yet he had not fully let go of the cynicism that sometimes crept into his personality. One day he said to me, "So let me get this straight. You're telling me that if I just learn to believe in my own value I'll quit being so angry. Is that it?"

"Your use of the word *just* implies that I'm feeding you a simplistic solution that can be quickly reduced to an easy formula," I said. "The change I'm suggesting is not quite that simple, and it isn't meant to be applied in an easy 1–2–3 manner. I'm suggesting that you take time out to deeply contemplate your core beliefs about how you want to live, even while others are being antagonistic. This is something that cannot be changed in a matter of one or two days. For years, you've carried an aching spirit around, agonizing over the prospect of others rejecting you when you so desperately wanted respect. Virtually every time your anger has crossed the line into the aggressive mode, you have wished to force the person in front of you to treat you with regard."

I continued in my challenge to him. "Because people have proven to be inconsistent at best in sending you messages of worth, I'm asking you to pull back mentally for the purpose of deciding that you can be civil even when others are not. As you have more certainty about your own chosen path, you become less desperate when others choose not to be cooperative or affirming. Changing your mental approach like this is no simple process. It requires time and repetition of thoughts."

Treating Others Worthily

As you become more proficient in separating your beliefs about your inherent worth from others' pronouncements, you can learn to be so certain of the fixed reality of your own worth that you begin to see the inherent value in others too. Choosing to act like someone who can be independently secure, you develop an increasing desire to reinforce the same truth as it applies to those in your presence.

In time, Gary came to recognize that he indeed did not have to push his agenda forcefully to make others respect him. The real indicator of his changing thought process was how he chose to recognize the value of those who used to provoke his anger. He began to understand that when others acted irresponsibly, defensively, or discourteously, the behavior was a cue indicating that those people were struggling inwardly to find their own worth. Rather than reading their frustrating behavior as a repudiation of himself, he learned to empathize with their carrying a hidden hurt.

For instance, the salesman who did not always follow company procedures at Gary's store once told him, "I'm just not a red-tape kind of person. There's something in me that doesn't immediately want to embrace somebody else's way of doing things." Normally, Gary would have taken such a statement to be a rejection of his leadership, and he would have responded angrily. In this incident, though, he responded entirely differently. Recognizing that the salesman wanted to feel that his opinions mattered, he said, "It's important to feel that you have some say in the way each day unfolds. I'll tell you what, I'm still going to ask that you follow the procedures we've established here, but I also want you to feel free to talk with me about how we can help you feel that your opinions are heard. I think it's possible to create an atmosphere where each of us feels a sense of ownership regarding the policies."

Gary's approach was entirely new to him. He gave himself permission to hold firmly to his own assertions, yet he also spoke with the salesman such that he upheld his dignity. Proper anger management is most effective when accompanied by the willingness to hold onto your belief in your own value even as you let others know you value them as well.

I explained to Gary, "When you use your anger to demean others, it's a clear indication that you're not attuned to human dignity in general. At that moment, not only is your anger an attempt to bring the other person down, but you're conveying your own feelings of weakness. But if you choose to address an anger-provoking situation with a spirit of fairness, you show that you have enough awareness of your own worth that you don't need to build your worth at the other person's expense. It becomes a win-win situation."

An ancient Jewish proverb tells us that to have a friend you must be a friend. Keeping in mind that a moderate amount of dependency is normal, it is reasonable to want affirmation and to feel frustrated if it is not forthcoming. The person using anger wisely is mindful that modeling considerate behavior is far more likely to result in positive dividends than surly or insulting behavior.

Another common proverb reminds us that we reap what we sow. Angry people may be yearning for affirmation, but when they sow seeds of condescension they are likely to reap rejection. If seeds of respect are sown, they are far more likely to reap the rewards of the affirmation they so desire.

As Gary and I discussed making adjustments in his use of anger, he asked, "What if I moderate my need for acceptance and I use a more respectful approach, but I still don't get the cooperation I'm looking for?"

"You can still maintain your composure," I responded. "I'd like to be able to tell you that if you handle your anger cleanly every time you can always expect positive results. Unfortunately, that's not the case. Some people are difficult and invalidating no matter how appropriate you act. At that point, if your belief of your own worth is intact, you can choose to let go of your anger and move on with your day. Before doing so, consequences may need to be put into play, or you may decide to firmly hold your ground. Nonetheless, you can decide that the usefulness of your anger has run its course, and you can proceed with other priorities leading the way."

When people like Gary seek help for anger management, they usually have minimal awareness of its link to emotional dependency. All they know is that bad habits have become a part of their personal landscape, and something needs to change. Confronting hidden insecurity may at times be difficult or unnatural, but if we are honest with ourselves about the extensive nature of the dependency that keeps the anger alive, real change can be experienced.

Other factors also tend to lurk beneath the surface, keeping anger alive, and they too need to be exposed and understood if you are to be released from the snares of anger. In the next chapter, we explore how misguided anger can reflect pridefulness that has run afoul.

For Personal Reflection

- What is your idea of a healthy personality? List eight or nine traits that reveal your idea.
- In what circumstances are you least likely to live with those healthy traits? How do those situations pull you off track?
- How is it normal for your mood to be influenced by outer circumstances? How is it not normal for your mood to be influenced by outer circumstances?
- What love deficiencies contribute to your feelings of anger? What is the cleanest way to address those deficiencies?
- How can your behavior and communication style be positively affected if you are more mindful of your inherent worth?
- How can you use a mind-set of delicate detachment to help ease extreme feelings of anger?
- As you believe most deeply in your own worth, you are also likely to treat others worthily. How is your management of anger affected as you choose to uphold others' worth?

7

HELD CAPTIVE BY SELF-ABSORPTION

WHEN I WAS in college and graduate school, I would participate in midnight debates with fellow truth-seekers. Despite the enormous amount of brainpower exerted, we failed to solve the problems facing the Western Hemisphere. Nonetheless, we managed to grapple with questions that resulted in some productive thoughts. In those days, I was still coming to terms with my core beliefs about human nature and the origins of human struggle. One foundational question was frequently batted about: Is humanity basically good or basically evil?

My early religious training instilled in me a deep appreciation for the notion of the inherent value and dignity of each individual, as bestowed by God. The emphasis caused me to lean toward the belief that humanity is inherently good. However, I could not successfully argue against my antagonists, who would remind me that at no time in recorded history has humanity been perfectly at peace. Individuals of all eras have been prone to lie, cheat, manipulate, belittle, or deceive. Looking no further than to my own life, I could see evidence of doing wrong for little or no reason other than to simply do wrong. Certainly there is some sort of internal mechanism, I determined, that provokes people toward poor choices, even when good choices are clearly available.

In time, I came to believe in what is called the dual nature of humanity. We are a mixture of the capacity for both good and evil. No person is so thoroughly evil that he or she is incapable of good, nor is anyone so good as to be incapable of evil. We are each a mixed bag.

In the last chapter, we explored how anger is tied to the craving for love, affirmation, and significance. Spurred by lack of positive reinforcement, anger can be understood as a cry to be relieved from the pain associated with the feeling of insignificance. In that sense, we can understand anger to be linked to the side of human nature that is good, the part of the personality that finds love and acceptance to be attractive and desirable.

Sometimes, though, the impulse toward anger cannot be characterized so generously. There are times when anger is just plain mean. Some angry people seem to thrive on the possibility of lording over others or creating discomfort. Pleas to be considerate or moderate go unheeded. Anger, though perhaps linked superficially to a right reason for self-preservation, serves little real purpose beyond belittlement and humiliation.

Jeannie sought medical treatment at our clinic following years of struggling with migraine headaches and "fever blisters" that often appeared on her thighs and abdomen. To her relief, she was successfully treated by the medical doctor for these symptoms, but he wisely recognized that there was an emotional component that made her susceptible to such physical complaints. Though she did not really want "to be analyzed," Jeannie nonetheless made her way into my office to see if I could help reduce her stress.

As I first spoke with her about her lifestyle and history, nothing of significant pathology stood out. She described her childhood in generally positive terms. She was quite close to her mother and remained close to her until her death several years prior to our encounter. She admired her father, though she admitted that he was not a warm person. Quickly, she explained that he had a strong work ethic and was an excellent provider and a moral man. I got the sense that it was taboo to say anything negative about either parent. She had two younger brothers, and though I intuited that there had been tension in her relations with them, she glossed over any such details by summarizing that they all got along fine.

Now in her early forties, Jeannie was in her second marriage. The first marriage, to a high school sweetheart, did not last long, but it produced a daughter who was now in her early twenties. Giving few details about the marital break-up, she simply told me he was a bum and that he had had little to do with her or their daughter for years. Remarried for approximately ten years, she had a teenage stepson, and her husband worked hard in the insurance industry.

All the while that we talked, Jeannie maintained a guarded façade. Not wanting to appear tense or troubled, she gave the impression that not all was well, but she should be quite calculating about revealing anything that might put her in a bad light. Her words were spoken sharply and to the point; her tone of voice was stiff. Her facial features were drawn in, and the skin on her forehead had deep furrows. She did not smile easily, nor did she respond comfortably to simple chitchat.

Knowing that physical complaints such as migraine headaches can sometimes be linked to anger, I asked her to tell me what caused her to feel angry. She seemed somewhat surprised by my question and replied that although she sometimes felt frustrated, she virtually never got angry. (I interpreted this to mean she did not shout or slam doors when she felt angry.) She went on to explain, "My husband can sometimes get angry, so maybe he ought to be the one sitting in here instead of me." Knowing I would get a much fuller picture of Jeannie's emotional disposition, I suggested that it would be a good idea for him to join her in our sessions, if they both agreed that joint counseling would be helpful in confronting the stressors in her life that kept her vulnerable to physical complaints.

Sure enough, on her next visit, her husband, Darrel, accompanied her. Slightly chubby but pleasant in demeanor, he was more than willing to talk about the things in their home that created tension. He told me that he felt he had to walk on eggshells practically every day because of his wife's exacting standards. Describing Jeannie as "beyond critical," he admitted to exploding several times in their ten years together, mostly in protest against her nitpicking ways. He described himself as deeply wounded by her, and as one who was losing hope of ever achieving the love he had once thought possible in their marriage.

Jeannie refuted none of Darrel's claims, though the look on her face indicated she was clearly displeased that he would speak about their problems so candidly. When I asked if his characterization of her seemed accurate, she crisply said that she had a different perspective, but upon my further questioning she chose not to elaborate.

In time, I learned that Jeannie and Darrel had a poor pattern of managing the irritability that so easily overtook them. With low tolerance for differentness, Jeannie would scold her husband as if he were a wayward child; she often went for long periods of time without speaking to him or even looking at him. She made little effort to comprehend his feelings or perspectives, and she commonly held herself as superior to him. Life would be much finer, she reasoned, if Darrel acquiesced to her logic. Despite his reluctance to play the role of the classic hen-pecked husband, that is the way many outsiders would depict their relationship.

In response to his wife's cold and punitive demeanor, Darrel told me he would make efforts to go along to get along, but inevitably he felt weary of her bitter spirit and on occasion he would explode with a "What's wrong with you?" tirade. Rarely was the home environment joyful or peaceful.

As I talked with Jeannie about eliminating the tensions that might feed her physical problems, we eventually focused on one key ingredient in her personality. Though hesitant to explore the issue deeply, she came to recognize that her anger could be understood as an extension of the deeper issue of pridefulness.

Pridefulness Defined

There is sometimes confusion regarding the subject of pride because we use the word to denote several ideas. On the one hand, pride can be a positive trait, as we use it in relation to a feeling of inner satisfaction or pleasure; we take pride in doing a job well. We swell with pride when our children prove to be accomplished in a performance. When we hear the national anthem played, we feel patriotic pride. These emotional experiences can be quite positive, as they contribute to an overall feeling of gratification and fulfillment with life.

On the other hand, the kind of pride I detected in Jeannie's life cannot be characterized as appealing. This form of pride takes inner satisfaction and puts a wicked twist on it, prompting the individual to appear smug, self-impressed, or condescending. This egotistic pride can be defined as preoccupation with self. It is pushed along by the urge to satisfy personal cravings, preferences, or desires. It provokes the individual to become so inwardly focused that the ability to tend to the feelings and needs of others is lost.

As I observe human behavior, I have concluded that this haughty form of pride is not a learned response but innate. Its selfish spirit is a defining ingredient of humanness. To be sure, we each have received lessons regarding how to display pridefulness, but the inclination resides inside each of us regardless of the influence of the environment.

Think for a moment about the self-absorption of very young children. Most toddlers can be cute and adorable, but there is no denying that they have a tremendous capacity for tuning others out. Whether they are in the presence of other small children or accompanied by adults, toddlers can quickly change from being precious to becoming obnoxious. They need no instruction to learn how to act this way. It is natural; that is, such behavior is innate.

Recall that Jeannie had little ill will toward either parent as she drew upon memories of her childhood years. If anything, she seemed to have been trained to revere her parents. Though they certainly were not as ideal as she might depict them, neither were they demonic. A casual observer might assume, then, that the absence of overt tension in her developmental years would translate into an absence of anger in adulthood. Yet she had deep tendencies to be critical, rejecting, and condescending. She often displayed passive-aggressive behavior such as punitive withdrawal and silence. Rarely was she encouraging, but frequently she belittled. How could these forms of anger be explained if she had the positive history she claimed to have?

First, let's recognize that her idealized description of life in her family of origin may have included both denial and rationalization. Because of her overpowering need to appear together, Jeannie found honest self-examination to be unnatural. Beyond that, however, was the ongoing matter of raw, unadulterated pridefulness. As a child, she was never strongly challenged to confront the expansiveness of her own need to have self's desires satisfied. Though as a toddler it was excusable for her to display blatant selfishness, as she aged that same self-absorbed spirit went largely unchecked. In due time, she dropped the toddler tendency to fall on the floor and throw a temper tantrum, yet as she became older and more sophisticated in dealing with her public, her slyer forms of anger were accompanied by the same mentality of the toddler who just had to have her way.

The Pervasiveness of Pride

In my college and graduate school days, as I pondered the presence of good and evil within each personality, I began developing a healthy respect for the reality that each of us can slide effortlessly into patterns of relating that are not good. Even when someone seems to have had generally positive developmental experiences, the proclivity toward self-centeredness is never far away. I began seeing that this selfish dimension was inevitably at the core of *every* negative quality displayed by humans. This is quite a broad conclusion to draw, but let me challenge you to discover how selfishness is manifested in an extremely broad array of behaviors.

Think, for instance, about how self-centeredness is at the heart of openly abrasive behavior. The person who yells and curses when provoked is so consumed at that moment with the self's agenda that there is virtually no willingness or ability to factor in anyone else's feelings or needs. Likewise, when someone is recklessly rebellious, the focus is so squarely on self-gratification that little regard for others is present. The same can be said when an individual acts combatively, is openly argumentative, easily complains about foul treatment, openly expresses sarcasm, employs physical intimidation, brazenly defies the rules, or insults others for the specific purpose of injuring. Each of these openly abrasive behaviors gives evidence of pure absorption with self.

Pridefulness can also be displayed in behavior that is noncooperative yet not quite so harsh. For instance, when someone retreats into a spirit of impatience, that emotion can reveal a craving for preferential treatment. Likewise, if defensiveness is employed in communicating opposing perspectives, it can indicate unwillingness to consider thoughts beyond one's own comfort zone. Selfishness can be at the heart of interrupting communication, passing along gossip, dominating conversation with excessive chatter, or giving a lame excuse for a mistake. It can also be seen when someone treats others rudely in a public setting; tells a lie; refuses to cooperate; or whines, gripes, or frets.

The tendency toward pridefulness is seen in passive or silent behavior as well. The person who gives the silent treatment is nonverbally communicating: "I have very low regard for you, so I'm going to gloat in my own correctness even as I try to make you feel inferior to me." The same pridefulness is at the base of procrastination, which signifies an unwillingness to be moved out of one's own comfort zone. There is egotism associated with laziness, being chronically unreliable, being secretive, refusing to reveal normal humanness, indulging lustful fantasy, deliberately choosing not to be friendly, ignoring others, giving a half-hearted effort, and falsely acting as if he or she has it all together.

To say that pridefulness is an extremely broad-based trait is no exaggeration. There is virtually no end to the means that an individual goes to in illustrating that self-centeredness is a chronic feature in human personality. Certainly, inappropriate anger is a common way for that selfishness to be displayed. Those who refuse to recognize their own tendency toward this trait are destined to remain trapped in the forms of anger that prove to be most distasteful.

Jeannie was not at all inclined to admit her faults, but she also recognized that something needed to change if she could ever expect her anxiety to diminish. She proved to be less-than-open as we first began discussing how to relieve the tension that eventually left her susceptible to migraines and water blisters, but as I discussed with her the need to blame less and be more introspective, she began to recognize that personal changes were not only necessary but desirable.

Trying to ease the tension she associated with admitting a personal flaw, I said, "It seems you've learned that the presence of problems in life is bad, and therefore it should be avoided. I'm offering the idea that no human is problem-free. We each have weaknesses and negative tendencies, guaranteed. The strong person is not the one who proves to have no faults, but the one who can openly admit those faults with the intention of making improvement. As I encourage you to examine how self-centered tendencies can feed your anger, recognize that this is a trait each one of us needs to confront."

Hesitantly, yet reflectively, she said, "I know I can sometimes be hard on people, and I know I hold grudges and have difficulty forgiving. It's hard for me to admit that I've had a problem of selfishness that causes me to be angry toward people, but I guess I've got to say that it's true, I can be self-centered." With that, she grew quiet.

Such an acknowledgment was a major breakthrough for Jeannie. As I got to know her, I began to recognize that shame-based thinking was so strongly instilled in her that it was nearly impossible in her earlier years to admit fault. Her parents rarely spoke in condescending tones toward her (to the contrary, they often doted on her), but they had very strict beliefs about right and wrong. They were not bashful in pointing out their disgust for those who did not measure up to their standards, and even though Jeannie was spared from bearing the brunt of their disdain, she learned that any inclination to think or feel outside the box had to be squelched. Suppression of her anger was the result, and later this suppressed anger commonly reappeared as passive-aggressiveness.

Jeannie admitted to me, "It feels strange to say out loud that I can be prideful. I just hate to think of myself in such a negative way."

"I mean to encourage no shame by having you make such an acknowledgment," I explained. "Actually, your family would have done you a favor if they had developed a history with you where problems could be named and examined for what they were. Once you can admit a problem such as pridefulness, you've taken the first step out of the trap that is created."

Choosing Humility

If the tendency of self-centeredness can be understood as a reflection of pride, and if we can recognize that pridefulness often keeps us trapped in anger, one way to avoid angry entrapment is to set our sights on the opposite of pride: humility. Developing a deep appreciation for and commitment to this trait, we can choose to respond to adverse circumstances such that we diminish friction while increasing the possibility of harmony. Humility is not always an easy or natural choice; nonetheless, as we recognize its superiority to the selfishness that is at the center of pride, we can train our minds to give priority to responses that arise from its influence.

Humility can be defined as lack of self-preoccupation. Humble people still recognize the value of preserving worth, needs, and convictions, yet they are able to put the task of self-preservation into a larger perspective of living within a community of varying needs, preferences, and desires. Humble people are more interested in serving than in forcing servitude upon others. They embrace behavior that is openly considerate, kind, and encouraging. Humble people recognize the folly of insisting that others should cater to them, and they are wise enough to recognize personal limits.

Because of common misconceptions about humility, I have seen some interesting reactions through the years as I encourage people to choose humility as a way of life. Assuming that humble people may be pleasant yet weak, more than one or two people have challenged my emphasis. One businessman told me, "If I decided to take humility into my professional life, I'd be eaten alive. My business is very competitive, and I have to keep a sharp edge if I'm going to survive." To him, becoming humble meant becoming a marshmallow.

Not one to be so easily dissuaded, I replied, "What would you think if I told you that humility represents the ultimate strength? Humble people are not marshmallows; they are poised to be highly influential leaders. In fact, humility is the only path to true greatness."

The look on his face might have led an observer to assume that I had just zapped him! Shaking his head, he admitted, "This is going to require a major shift of my mental gears."

As I spoke with Jeannie about her various misuses of anger, I challenged her to set aside pridefulness in favor of humility. "When we feel annoyed or frustrated," I mentioned, "one of the most common problems to emerge is preoccupation with self. We each share this trait, so you're definitely not alone. To keep the anger from quickly turning sour, it will help if you set aside the focus on self and factor in the feelings and perspectives of the others involved, even if you feel they're in error."

Jeannie and I discussed several common ways for humility, instead of pride, to guide her responses of anger:

- Darrel tended to be more jovial and playful than Jeannie when they visited with family and friends. Jeannie's natural impulse was to be critical of her husband and fuss at him for being so loose. We discussed how humility could cause her to accept Darrel as he is, recognizing that an array of personality types are positive. Rather than forcing him to think like herself, she could recognize that her mannerisms did not have to be the standard by which Darrel should always be measured.
- Whenever it became clear that her teenaged stepson wasn't behaving as properly as Jeannie's older daughter would, Jeannie would give him the cold shoulder as a way of expressing disapproval. We discussed how humility could lead her to maintain a more flexible mind-set as she reminded herself that it was impossible to shape her stepson into her mold. Humility could prompt her to talk openly with him about the things that caused him to feel excited or motivated. Perhaps she could allow him to expand her interests.

○ In disagreeing with various family members, Jeannie tended to be stubborn, rarely budging from her opinions. We discussed how a mind-set of humility could prompt her to incorporate others' opinions and feelings. There would be little to gain by clinging so firmly to her own judgments that she could not or would not seek to understand their feelings. Everyone would benefit if she truly attempted to hear and digest everyone's thoughts equally.

Jeannie found that a mind-set of humility was not at all natural. For most of her life, she had given such high priority to rationalizing her own correctness that it felt to her she was compromising too much when forced to slow down long enough to consider others. I explained to her, "When you're feeling angry or tense, ultimately you wish you could have a stronger influence over the one who is in conflict with you. The self-absorbed mind-set causes you to act in a way that satisfies only your own needs, but in the end it doesn't work. Each time you give the silent treatment, or speak caustically in disagreeing, your self's needs go unmet and your influence deteriorates to almost nothing."

Continuing my thoughts, I said, "When you commit to the trait of humility, you show others that you can think beyond your own preferences. You display confidence because you're seen as someone who can handle a variety of circumstances. As you make an open attempt to be calm, reasonable, and understanding, the probability of gaining cooperation from others goes up. You can still hold onto boundaries and convictions, but it can be done without engaging in rude or condescending behavior."

Shortly after our discussion, Jeannie felt hurt because Darrel accused her of a wrong that she had not committed. The battery-charged phone he was using went dead because it had been left off the charger for several hours. When he told Jeannie that the phone had been mishandled, his tone of voice was agitated and he sounded parental. In times past, Jeannie's pride would have caused her to think, *How dare you falsely accuse* me *and speak in such a rude tone of voice.* Her response likely would have been to react haughtily, and then be silent for the rest of the evening.

Remembering our discussion about the primacy of humility, she decided not to turn Darrel's words into a referendum about herself. Calmly, she stated, "It must be frustrating to have a phone go dead in the middle of a conversation. In this case, I was not the one who mishandled the phone, but I'll certainly pay attention to the matter in the future." Her humility caused her to recognize that, right or wrong in his analysis of the problem, Darrel felt annoyed. Reminding herself that she too would have felt annoyed in a similar situation, she chose to focus on his hurt rather than her own ego.

Humility and Assertiveness

Humble people maintain an ongoing realization that they do not have to interpret all events from a "self as center of the universe" perspective. Their ego is not so fragile that emotional stability collapses every time life presents a distasteful situation. Rather than fixating on me, me, me, they can pause long enough to think, *Let me consider what you're experiencing right now. Perhaps if I demonstrate fair-mindedness, we can work this problem out together.*

As humility becomes a priority, assertive anger may still be employed amid conflict, yet it will have a decidedly broad-minded manner:

- As you consider how to react angrily, pause long enough to determine if your communication is helpful to yourself *and* the other person. True assertiveness seeks to elevate or assist others.
- Words can be spoken with an even tone of voice. Persuasion and coercion are understood to be belittling forms of communication, and therefore unnecessary.
- Make room for the possibility that others may not like what you say or do. Don't be shocked by their poor reaction, or feel the need to force immediate agreement.
- As you speak words of assertion, be open to separate or opposing feelings or viewpoints. Be willing to listen, even as you maintain firmness regarding your own beliefs.
- When you know you are right, hold firmly to your convictions, but feel no need to invalidate the other person as a way of validating yourself. In a nonargumentative way, say, "Despite your separate preference, I'll hold firmly to my conviction." If a protest is offered, you can still respectfully reply, "I realize we disagree, but that's the decision I've made."
- Be smart enough to know when not to press a point. You can let the common sense of your own words and behavior stand on their own.

Through counseling, Jeannie learned that her symptoms of headaches and blisters were closely linked to management of her emotions. She learned, too, that even though she did not display anger in wildly outrageous behavior, she was falling victim to her own anger whenever she chose to nurse bitter feelings or cling to critical thoughts. Her greatest challenge was to take the concept of humility and truly embrace it, through and through. In her childhood, she learned how to look as if she were handling problems smoothly even though she remained inwardly tense. Now as an adult, she was being challenged to give her guiding thoughts higher priority than her external behavior. This required a type of concentration that was new to her.

Stark honesty is a necessary component in making the switch from pridefulness to humility. Jeannie recognized how she could make her reasoning sound altruistic in correcting her stepson. *I'm only saying this for his own good,* she might tell herself. Eventually, she learned to ask herself, *Am I really correcting him because I love him, or is he just bugging me, and I want to make him comply for the sake of my own pleasure?* Likewise, in avoiding a family member who was acting uncooperatively, she was learning to ask herself, *Is my withdrawal intended to be seen as an act of punishment, or am I truly trying to contribute to a peaceful atmosphere?*

She once told me, "It's really easy to theorize about the differences between pride and humility, but now I recognize that sometimes I'm the only one who really knows the true motive associated with my private decisions. I've never done so much soul-searching in my life."

Wanting to help keep her on track, I reminded her of a common pitfall to avoid as she made such internal adjustments. "There will be times when you catch yourself thinking selfishly, and you'll tell yourself to broaden the scope in order to incorporate the needs and feelings of the other person. At that moment, you can feel a sense of achievement as you recognize that you're applying a good insight.

"A complication occurs, however," I continued, "if the other person chooses not to follow your example of humbleness, but instead responds to you selfishly. At that moment, you may find yourself thinking you should abandon the humble approach and respond to pride with pride. Does that seem like a distinct possibility?"

"Very much so," came her reply. "I know Darrel has told you he's frequently bothered by my selfish attitudes, but he's no angel himself. Sometimes I try to really listen to him and give him the benefit of the doubt, but instead of appreciating my efforts, he can just go on and on about how hurt he feels or about how he wishes I'd act better. Finally I can just lose heart and retreat into my world of silent withdrawal." Knowing she wanted to refrain from resorting to her self-preoccupied tendencies, she asked, "So what am I supposed to do at a time like that?"

"Well, letting your selfish side run loose is always an option," I replied. "It will get you nowhere good, but it's still a choice." Then broadening the discussion, I said, "It's also an option to recognize that Darrel's selfish response is an extension of his pain. Rather than worrying exclusively about how his behavior is creating discomfort for you, you might pause long enough to recognize that he would probably experience the same pain if he were married to someone entirely different. In other words, you could acknowledge that his disruptive behavior is not all about you. The awareness might cause you to rein in the temptation to respond punitively."

Jeannie recognized that her humility could still allow her to hold firmly to her convictions and speak openly about her needs. After all, part of the choice to serve others includes openness about matters that need interpersonal coordination. She also recognized that she could not expect others to always share the same goals that she had, no matter how right those goals might seem. In humility, she would remember that she was limited. All she could do was make right choices for herself. She was incapable of forcing others to think exactly as she did.

Setting aside preoccupation with self and choosing to consider the perspectives of others can become first nature as you repeatedly remind yourself that pridefulness ultimately does not bring good results. People are most attracted to and influenced by those whose egos can be held in check as they take the time to consider each side of an equation. Even when your efforts to invoke humility do not always result in improving someone's reaction, you still gain by choosing humility because it keeps you from wallowing in your own harmful bitterness.

For Personal Reflection

- How do you tend to openly exhibit self-absorbed thinking? How is your self-absorption displayed more subtly?
- How do others act self-absorbed toward you? What effect does this have on your anger?
- How do you define humility? How would your relational style improve if you could be consistent in your use of this trait?
- In humility, you are willing to admit that you cannot control people; nor are they obliged to live as you prefer. By accepting such ideas, how would your use of anger change?
- How is your assertiveness an act of humility? How can you tell if you are asserting with humility (not pride) leading the way?
- What would you say is the link between humility and forgiveness?
- How would your primary relationships change for the better if you consistently prioritized humility over pridefulness?

8

THE CHAINS OF FEAR

WHEN I BEGAN my practice as a psychotherapist, I often worked with young children. Though my emphasis for the past twenty-five years has been primarily with adults, I continue to draw upon my experiences with children as I determine how to respond to troubled adults. Those of us who have passed the age of twenty-one may look bigger and more sophisticated than our younger counterparts, but at the core we struggle with many of the same fundamentals.

In working with kids who had anger problems, I quickly learned that my words carried far less weight than my demeanor. If I were to have any positive impact at all on my little clients, I would need to respond to their unpredictable ways with a calm, confident mind-set. Over time, I learned not to be pulled into a response of frustration and irritability as I set aside any fear regarding a child's behavior toward me. I made it a goal not to be rattled, no matter how persistently a feisty youngster challenged or defied me.

One six-year-old tormentor, Chad, had been with me several times in my playroom, and a favorite game of his seemed to be Let's Annoy the Therapist. On this particular day, Chad found one of those dart pistols that shot darts with a little rubber suction cup on the end. Loading the dart into his pistol, he stood seven or eight feet away and aimed it directly at me. Wanting to teach him to be respectful, I explained, "Chad, I'm not for shooting. You can shoot the target over there, or you can shoot stuff on the shelves, or you can shoot into the sandbox, but I'm not for shooting."

I could almost see the wheels turning inside his head as he was trying to decide how to respond to my words ("Should I do what this guy says and aim for a different target, or should I just do what I want and shoot the sucker?"). His lips tensed and he fidgeted for a few seconds, but then with the dart gun still pointing at me, he pulled the trigger and shot me right in the chest. Bull's-eye! Standing before me with a smug look on his face, saying nary a word, Chad just stared at me to see how I would respond to his brazenness.

Picking up the dart, I handed it back to him and quietly said, "I guess you were just dying to find out what would happen if you shot me, but I'm still not for shooting." Chad was caught completely off guard. He fully expected (wanted?) me to explode, scold him, or react with at least some measure of disgust. But I didn't. He took the dart back from me, reloaded his little pistol very slowly, then reluctantly set it aside and went on to something else. (By the way, I had already determined that if he shot me a second time, the dart gun would be placed out of reach on a top shelf.)

What happened in this scenario? A six-year-old boy chose to treat me with disrespect, or at least to challenge my position of authority. Though that was not exactly how I wanted to start my afternoon, I decided that his unruly behavior did not threaten me. I was not afraid of Chad. Even though I had other ideas about how our interaction should unfold, I determined to trust in my own good sense as opposed to being drawn into an adversarial role with him. My lack of fear resulted in a greatly diminished possibility of erupting anger.

Anger Is Fear-Based

Recall some of the characters introduced in prior chapters. Steve was the fortysomething husband and stepdad who was about to lose his third marriage thanks to his angry insistence that the family must adhere to his rigid rules. Brett was the pleasant, friendly fellow who made his way to my office after pushing his wife over furniture and being arrested when the police came to settle the dispute. Peggy was the nurse whose family compelled her to seek counseling because her surly spirit kept getting her fired from good jobs. Jeannie was the tight woman whose stifled anger made her susceptible to physical complaints of migraine headaches and blisters on her legs and torso.

Though quite varied in personality and life circumstance, they shared a common denominator that kept them trapped in the torment of their own anger. They each lived in fear of the challenges that were so commonly experienced in their relationships. None of them would be inclined to admit they were acting upon fear in their incidents of anger; nonetheless, their agitated or tense response toward others communicated, "I'm threatened by the fact that you don't hold me in high regard."

I found Peggy to be a most challenging (and ultimately endearing) person because she seemed so surprised to learn how her "take no guff" exterior actually reflected more about her hidden fears than she cared to admit.

As a nurse, she was quite confident in her intelligence and abilities, and in fact many of the staff at her job sought her out for advice since they knew her to be up on the latest procedures. Her take-charge spirit did not lend itself to the immediate impression that she allowed fear to play a major role in her dealings with people. Nonetheless, I challenged her to examine how her anger masked a very real sense of dread when she felt she was at odds with others.

I gave Peggy a simple analogy. "Sometimes my little dog, Duchess, will be lounging around in our backyard. Occasionally, another person or animal may go wandering through the alley directly behind our house. Immediately Duchess will begin barking and she won't stop until the alien is a safe distance away from the house. Her bark may sound angry, but really she is displaying fear. She's thinking, *You're not going to take over my territory, are you?* People can be the same as my little Duchess. Our anger seems to be expressed for the purpose of telling others that they'd better respect our personal boundaries, when at a deeper level it reveals fear that we're being taken over by those who might run roughshod over our needs."

Peggy grinned slightly as she slowly shook her head. "Your comments catch me off guard sometimes, but I'm willing to think about what you say. Are you trying to tell me that deep inside I'm just a chicken?"

"I don't mean to overplay comparisons between you and the animal kingdom, but chicken would be an apt description." We both smiled broadly. "I want you to think about the moments you find yourself easily irritated. When people act incompetently or when they openly challenge you, your anger indicates that you can't tolerate the impropriety on display. Though you don't actually say the words, your anger reflects a thought like, *Dear me, what am I going to do? I can't handle this. This is too far outside my box*. It's almost as though your anger indicates that you've pushed an interior panic button as it holds you in a threatened state."

Recall that Peggy's father was prone to gruff put-downs, and he left no doubt he would make little room for Peggy's separate ideas or preferences. Her mother was far less condescending, but she chose disengagement as a way of responding to her unhappy feelings. Beneath young Peggy's growing penchant toward combativeness, she allowed pessimism to take hold of her guiding thoughts. "I'm afraid I don't really matter to these people," she concluded, "and there's a good chance that others will have the same lack of regard for me." Hoping to minimize her exposure to pain, she pessimistically determined to keep her guard up around others. Her approach to relationships seemed to reflect the belief that if she rejected others first, their eventual rejection of her would be less painful.

A Wall of Defense

The easiest way to determine the influence of fear upon your anger is to identify the various methods used to defend your dignity. Most fearful people do not look openly panicked, nor do they typically curl up into the fetal position when the fear comes upon them. They do, however, retreat quickly into a defensive mode, and it is often difficult to shed that defensiveness.

As an example, at her last job, Peggy had several run-ins with the same supervisor. This woman was a highly organized nurse with exacting standards for patient care. Sometimes in her zeal, she would be inclined to micromanage, giving advice that a veteran nurse like Peggy did not want or need. Instead of learning to roll with the supervisor's quirks, Peggy took issue with her so often that they finally determined Peggy had to leave. Peggy often felt she needed to justify her behavior, and she would do so with such force it generated friction that might otherwise be minimized if only she could learn to keep her cool.

Peggy explained, "Whenever this woman asked me to explain why I handled a procedure as I did, my immediate response would be to wonder who she thought she was and why she felt she could question me so readily." She went on to tell me that she had similar reactions when extended family members called her decisions into question. She summarized, "Once people get to know me, they learn not to jerk my chain. I don't like being questioned."

"What is it about being questioned that threatens you?" I asked.

"Threatens me? I'm not threatened when people second-guess me. I just don't like it. That's all."

Gently leaning on her, I pressed, "If you were so nonthreatened by others' mannerisms, you'd be far less edgy. The fact that you respond to a directive or criticism with annoyance tells me you're afraid. You can't stand the thought of being belittled. It scares you."

With that exchange, Peggy and I began exploring her history of responding to others with a strong defense leading the way. She and her sister, Rhonda, were only two years apart in age, and predictably they often argued. "Rhonda was constantly getting into my stuff, and I frequently argued with her about wearing my clothes without asking, or borrowing something like a hairbrush without returning it. We'd get into awful spats, and then one of our parents would enter the fray, and it would go from bad to worse. We didn't do a lot of listening back then because we were each too busy trying to be heard."

Tying her history of anger to her fear responses, I said, "Peggy, it would be easy to focus squarely on the anger displayed in those incidents of griping and bickering. If you look more closely into the scenario, though, you can see how fear was fueling the flames." She sat quietly as she was trying to track what I was saying. "Your anger arose from the dreaded possibility that your sister would not see you as being worthy of due consideration. You were already wondering if your parents valued you fully, and when your sister illustrated that she too would dismiss your desires as irrelevant, it was more than you could bear. Your anger showed you were threatened by the potential of chronic insignificance. The positive feature of your emotion was that you wanted to be valued. The very real threat of not being heard, though, caused you to go overboard in defending your dignity, and the pattern seems to have remained with you throughout your adult years as well."

It is not entirely wrong to experience some moments of defending yourself. Because others may genuinely misinterpret you or attack you unfairly, it is reasonable for you to stand up in preserving your needs and perspectives. But if the defensive reaction becomes too prominent or overpowering, that is the time when anger can gain a foothold and influence you to respond to your world in an unruly way. When Peggy was a girl, ideally she would have learned that her parents could be trusted to be her primary source of protection, not torment. When they repeatedly spoke ill of her, it was reasonable for her to defend. Her problems expanded, however, as she aged without letting go of the defensive approach toward the world. She never learned to incorporate a mind-set of inner trust as she faced would-be adversaries.

Here are examples of unnecessary defensiveness:

- Having a strong hesitancy to admit or reveal flaws or misjudgments
- Feeling the need to offer an airtight excuse or explanation when confronted
- Quickly throwing the focus back onto an accuser, trying to bring that person down
- Telling lies or using great spin to be perceived as acceptable
- Deliberately avoiding people who might create friction
- Refusing to receive the input or feedback offered by others; quickly invalidating their thoughts
- Being so stubborn or forceful that others learn to stay away
- Not exposing intimate feelings easily with others
- Going into a people-pleasing mode too easily
- Responding to the judgment of others with counterjudgment

With your fearful defensiveness, you reveal a fundamental lack of trust in the other person. Your quick reflex to protect shows that you assume the other person has a sinister motive that you must quickly quell. Sometimes this reflex is reasonable, but sometimes it is exaggerated. Moreover, your defensiveness shows you do not trust *yourself*. By responding self-protectively your behavior is saying, "I can't risk letting myself be exposed to your judgments or priorities. I'm too fragile to hear you out."

As Peggy and I explored how her defensiveness indicated fear, she told me about a recent run-in with one of her children. "My daughter and I were bantering about something minor," she told me, "when she just blurted out: 'Mom, you are *so* stubborn, and you always have been.' My immediate temptation was to angrily lash out at her . . . like I always have done in the past. But then I thought about our discussion about defensiveness being tied to our fear, and I had to ask myself if I was afraid to look at her assessment of me."

Peggy was right on track. Had she defended herself angrily against the accusation that she was stubborn, she would have shown herself to be so weak as to be incapable of considering an unflattering perception. As an alternative, she decided that despite her daughter's less-than-wonderful impression of her, she was strong enough to consider the feedback being offered. The net result was that her diminished need to defend canceled her impulse to respond angrily.

Three Types of Defensiveness

To diminish the influence of fear on your anger level, it is first necessary to identify how you tend to act defensively. Though defensiveness can be displayed through many behaviors, there are three general patterns to watch for: denial, evasiveness, and reversal. Let's look briefly at each.

The Defense of Denial

Without exception, everyone has character defects or lapses in judgment. None of us is so close to perfection that we succeed day after day in responding to people and events ideally. This means anyone who has ongoing exposure to another person eventually witnesses their flaws, and oftentimes comments are made regarding those imperfections. Sometimes the comments are offered positively, while at other times they are spoken with a measure of condescension or judgment.

Self-trusting, secure people accept the reality that their flaws (or sometimes just their differences) are on display and may generate friction. They listen to the input being offered and respond appropriately. They do not necessarily enjoy being told what is wrong, but they are wise enough to consider all perspectives, even the ones that may be erroneous or hurtful.

Fearful people, however, tremble at the possibility of having their flaws brought out into the open. Invariably, their personal history included incidents when negative things were said about them for destructive purposes. For instance, Peggy vividly recalled how her father would "camp out" on mistakes that she made, pouring shame upon her for being a mere human. So distasteful was he in his way of discussing her flaws with her that she dreaded interacting with him, knowing he would draw attention to her imperfections.

If people learn to fear the motives of those who speak disparagingly about their flaws, they easily gravitate toward the use of denial. So painful are the accuser's sentiments that they subconsciously reason that if the accusations can be deemed null and void, they can be freed from the pain accompanying the accusation. In her childhood years, Peggy learned to respond to her father's harshness by saying things such as, "That's not so," or "You don't know what you're talking about," or "I didn't do that." She knew she would probably never convince her dad she was a decent person, but if she could at least convince herself that the case brought against her was untrue, she could proceed with some dignity intact.

These are some common uses of denial:

- *The "know-it-all" defense.* People of this persuasion have convinced themselves they are so enlightened that no one else has quite the same handle on truth. This allows them to readily dismiss any and all perceptions of others that are not in agreement.
- *Rationalization.* This defense is typified by an airtight explanation for the concerns levied by others. Using self-serving rationale, they can explain why they are innocent of any negative implications. There is rarely a time when they can consider a conflicting view as viable.
- *Magical thinking.* Some people are so afraid to grapple with the pain and complexity of life that they train their mind to be overly optimistic. They quickly dismiss problems by saying, "It's not all that bad," or "Hey, we'll just work it out," or "Yeah, but let's focus on all the things that are good." They have made a commitment to ignore the troublesome elements of life.
- *Playing incompetent.* Some people remove themselves from the responsibility of grappling with conflict by assuming that the effort to manage conflict is too difficult. "Someone else besides me is going to have to make the effort to get things right," the reasoning goes. "I'm not even sure I know what you're talking about."

The Defense of Evasiveness

One hallmark of a healthy personality is the willingness to sit face to face with those who create conflict for the purpose of openly exchanging feelings and needs. Given the breadth of personality types, it should come as no surprise that individuals think separately from each other. Some people's experience with the open approach, however, has been so distasteful that they make it their goal to avoid personal sharing, particularly if the subject is potentially controversial. Here are examples of evasive defensiveness:

- *"I don't care" mentality.* Rather than denying a problem, evasive defenders show their fear of conflict by feigning indifference. Portrayal of indifference is often a cover for such thoughts as "I'd hate to let you know how important this subject is to me because we might never see eye to eye on it."
- *Hiding out.* In Chapter Three, passive-aggressiveness was described as a way of communicating anger with the least vulnerability. Being physically unavailable can indicate annoyance or agitation, but on a deeper level it illustrates that an open exchange of feelings and ideas is frightful. Evasiveness shows a person to be threatened by the possibility of having to be vulnerable or accountable.
- *Changing the subject.* If a topic of discussion becomes too personal, some maneuver as quickly as possible to another topic. This is a controlling tactic, but on a deeper level it exposes insecurity about facing unpleasant issues. Sometimes these people work extra hard not to let a particular subject come up in conversation in the first place.

The Defense of Reversal

In any conflict, to successfully navigate through the tension attention may be given evenly to both sides of the disagreement. Fear is displayed when an individual attempts to keep any uncomfortable attention away by slinging the focus back toward the one initiating the uncomfortable confrontation. This form of communication is sure to keep anger alive, even as it demonstrates the fear that renders the person incapable of considering other perspectives or feelings. Here are examples of reversal:

- *"What about you?"* Inevitably in any ongoing relationship, the other person feels the need to point out a problem area. Confident individuals listen carefully to what is said, either in the hope of learning or for the purpose of respecting the other's thoughts. Fearful people, however, quickly refocus attention onto the sender of the message. In so doing, they insinuate, "I'm threatened by the discussion of my humanness."

○ *Blaming.* Some angry people are not as interested in finding resolution to conflict as they are in affixing blame. Seeing conflict as a sure path toward judgment, they quickly determine that they can soften their own hurt by putting the responsibility for wrong onto the other person. Anyone who thinks differently is immediately deemed an adversary, not a fellow seeker of harmony or growth.

○ *"If only."* Sometimes people defend themselves by faulting circumstances for the problems they experience. They do not deny the existence of their difficulties, but they refuse to embrace any responsibility as they suggest that things would be fine if only the external world offered up the preferred ingredient. This approach illustrates that the erring person is threatened by the prospect of being proven fallible.

Breaking the Grip of Fear

As I spoke with Peggy about how pervasive defensiveness was in her life, she began to gain a clear picture of the influence of fear in her anger. She told me, "Now that I'm beginning to identify how many ways I attempt to defend myself, I'm amazed at the extent of this trend in my relationships. I never realized before now that so much of my emotional energy was being spent trying to protect myself from the onslaughts of others."

Reflecting on her early history, she said, "In my childhood years, it seems that every one of us in the family was in a strong defensive mode. If I ever hinted to my dad that I disagreed with him or that I felt displeased, he would be highly offended and launch into an attack." Shaking her head, she concluded, "That was his defensiveness playing out, wasn't it? Imagine that. He was so afraid of me as a little girl that he couldn't set aside his own ego long enough to just listen. Even if I was completely off base in my thoughts, there was little to lose by just hearing me out—but he couldn't do it!"

To keep fear from playing too prominent a role in our emotional management, trust is vital. As family members, spouses, friends, and coworkers show themselves to be trustworthy, defense becomes unnecessary and openness is given priority. Self-revelation can be practiced with ease, and anger is not employed since the need for self-preservation is minimal.

I explained to Peggy the importance of developing trust as a safeguard against fear, and she quickly took issue with me: "How am I supposed to start trusting people when I have a lifetime of experiences that tell me others can't be trusted? I can honestly say that I have had very few close relationships with anyone who proved to be fully safe or trustworthy. Does this mean that I'm going to be bound by fear and defensiveness for the rest of my life?"

"If your emotional stability hinged completely on the attitude and behavior of others," I replied, "I guess we'd have to conclude that you are sunk. I know you're not making things up when you say people can let you down or fall short of trustworthiness. Fortunately, though, you can still find emotional stability even when others remain antagonistic, indifferent, or critical. You need not buckle under the weight of fear and its resulting anger."

Though Peggy indeed could not trust the motives of many individuals, I challenged her to look inward for her solution. "Would you be able to trust in your own good judgment even when others do not share a flattering opinion about you?" By putting the focus back into her own personality, I was letting her know that inner peace was the key to breaking free from the chains of fear.

Tying my suggestion to a practical application, I posed a potential scenario. "Let's suppose one of your adult daughters is speaking with you about coordinating plans with the extended family, and she suddenly disagrees with the way you have prioritized your schedule. In other words, a conflict becomes apparent."

"You've been looking in my windows, haven't you!?" Peggy was tuned in as I continued.

"That would present an easy opportunity," I said, "to allow your defensiveness to take over, and it could quickly prompt you to respond irritably. Let's add to this potential dilemma by supposing that you explain your decision to your daughter, but instead of giving you the respect you desire, she continues pressing her point. Your conversation with her could easily turn into an offensive and defensive exchange, and your resulting anger would show that you feel threatened by her attack."

I could almost see the wheels turning in Peggy's mind as she tried to apply our discussion to this imaginary scenario. "So you're suggesting to me that I should be less worried about her motives and more focused instead on my own good qualities that my daughter might be overlooking at the moment? And that if I could truly trust that my reasoning was sound, I'd be less fearful and defensive even if she kept pressing the issue?"

"That's exactly what I'm suggesting," I said. We went on to discuss how her trust in herself might prompt her to say something like, "I'll certainly consider what you're saying." Or it might cause her to calmly say, "I'm comfortable with the way I make my decisions, and I don't feel I need to change that." If her daughter kept pressing the issue, she could reply, confidently yet gently, "Well, that's the decision I've made." No further defense is necessary.

Calm firmness is a better alternative to defensive anger when you are in conflict with others. To succeed in maintaining such a trait, you would need to incorporate two key ingredients into your style of managing offensive exchange: objectivity and listening.

Objectivity

People who quickly respond to conflict with defensiveness and its resulting anger are primarily *subjective* in their approach. That is, their response is so readily driven by emotional impulse that little reasoning is immediately applied to the troublesome situation. This subjective habit is at the base of a parent's defensive response to a child's challenge, and it is also the force behind an agitated reply when a family member questions a decision. Subjectively motivated people typically display erratic emotions because they allow their feelings to run loose without making a deliberate effort to consult the facts. The results can be disastrous.

Objectivity is the better alternative in trying to decide how to respond to conflict, especially if the conflict might tempt you to be condescending, judgmental, or rejecting. It is defined by the ability to weigh facts with logic and reason, resulting in a measured response to the situation at hand. Objectivity requires self-restraint as it governs responses that might otherwise be solely impulsive in nature. Being objective does not mean feelings are ignored; rather, feelings are not allowed to be overwhelming or irrational. Applying objectivity can only happen if you pause at the moment anger is experienced for the purpose of thinking clearly about what you will do next.

I wanted Peggy to put some perspective on her pattern of responding to anger-provoking circumstances. "When you feel ticked off or frustrated," I asked, "how often do you slow down to consider what's happening and why?"

A blank look crossed her face as she answered, "I'm not sure that I really take any time to analyze problems, particularly when I'm right in the middle of tension. Are you trying to tell me that I'm supposed to analyze every single situation before I react?"

"I'm not telling you that you have to do anything," I replied, "since you can choose for yourself how you'd like to manage your life. I do want you to recognize that your angry expression can become more than a habitual knee-jerk response." She nodded as she recognized this to be true. "I'm also suggesting you will discover that when you pull back for a moment to consider what's provoking your anger, a strong defensive or self-protective response isn't really necessary."

Objective people can usually recognize that conflict has a multilayered impetus and is often driven by issues that go far beyond the immediate circumstances. For instance, a wife may feel offended because her husband cannot or will not take time to factor in her feelings as he makes a decision. In pure subjectivity, she might feel provoked to think, *Why does he always do this to me? I hate it when he's this rude.* Her emotions could take over as she responds to him with an argumentative or worrisome reaction. With objectivity, this same wife might be able to respond with a different mind-set to her husband's insensitivity. She might remind herself: "This behavior is nothing new. His family of origin did little to teach him how to respond kindly to a woman, and all through his adult years he's shown little interest in personal soul searching." Grasping these facts, she could conclude that griping or pleading did little to advance her cause, yet she could still choose to stand firmly in her own beliefs as she moves forward with him in the matter at hand.

Common sense and hard-earned experience clearly indicate that defensiveness, fearfulness, worry, and agitation don't work. Subjective people ignore this truth as they repeatedly respond to conflicts in the same, tired, maladaptive way. Objective people can accept truth for what it is, with no illusion that they can somehow force anyone to act according to their better notions. They are still committed to appropriate self-preservation, but it is accomplished without flailing, fretting, and coercion.

Listening

Once you objectively choose to trust in your own good judgment to keep from being sucked into an unnecessary defensive mode, you can expend greater emotional energy listening to the other person. Rather than angrily defending your own decency, you can make an effort to comprehend what really motivates your antagonist. Listeners recognize that there is merit in learning what the other person thinks and feels. They respond to conflict with the realization that teamwork produces better results than an adversarial spirit.

Peggy came to recognize that despite her crusty exterior, her defensiveness was evidence of a scared little girl who remained in charge of her emotional expressions. Applying objectivity, she was able to conclude that although her defenses were a reasonable response for a developing girl who did not yet know how to handle invalidating messages from her parents, those defenses were no longer necessary now that she had established herself as a responsible, reasonable adult. If others chose to be as insensitive as her parents once were, she could now recognize that their behavior did not have to be received as a referendum regarding her personal worth. Clinging to her own belief in her inherent decency, she was able to recognize that their contentious behavior spoke more about their own inner tension than about her personal issues.

In one of our discussions, she excitedly told me how she let go of her defensiveness and was able to turn a potentially damaging exchange into a positive interaction. "A couple of days ago, my sister chided me because she disagreed with a financial decision that I made involving one of my daughter's needs. In the past, I would have blasted her for sticking her nose where it doesn't belong, and predictably it would have produced a minifeud. Instead, I asked myself why I should feel threatened if my sister disagrees with my choices regarding finances. I turned the confrontation around by asking her to explain why she felt as she did. As she talked, it became evident that she was in the middle of her own budget crunch, and I realized she was projecting her anxiety onto me. We spent several minutes talking about her worries, and I didn't even feel the need to address her criticism toward me."

In many instances of conflict, a good listener can discern that the other person's tension is being pushed along by issues not fully related to the current focus. Fearful people, by contrast, put so much energy into unnecessarily defending themselves that they may never see behind the scenes for the purpose of understanding their detractor more fully. As listening produces increased insight and understanding, anger is often seen as an unnecessary response. Even if anger is warranted, a good listener usually concludes that the anger does not need to be accompanied by forcefulness or manipulation. Increased comprehension of the other person's humanness has a way of stilling the impulses that might otherwise produce fruitless aggression.

For Personal Reflection

- In what way does your anger indicate fear? What threatens you most as you interact with others?
- When are you most prone to defending yourself? What is it during those moments that causes you to feel you must protect yourself?
- When do you use denial as you are in conflict with others? Why is it so difficult to receive others' perceptions that seem misinformed?
- How do you protect yourself by being evasive? What are you hoping to accomplish with such a tactic?
- When do you defend yourself by reversing the focus, putting the spotlight back on the one accusing you? How does this affect your overall success at communication?

- What is it about your character that is trustworthy? How would your use of anger improve if you could more consistently abide in your own trustworthiness?
- If you could apply objectivity more consistently in conflict, how would your fear diminish? What positive effect would this have upon your anger?
- If you defended less and listened more, how would your anger management change?

9

MYTHS THAT PERPETUATE ANGER

IT'S FUN TO DREAM, isn't it? Admit it; when you hear of someone winning $10 million in the lottery, don't you entertain thoughts about what you would do if you ever won? I suppose it can be harmless to dream about utopian circumstances from time to time, yet people trying to maintain healthy emotional balance recognize that it is not wise to camp out very long in dreamland, lest it create a sour response to common reality.

Whether they recognize it or not, people who repeatedly respond to life with unseemly anger are clinging to dreamlike wishes. They often find their real world experiences to be negative or hurtful, so they nurse a fantasy about life under much more pleasing circumstances. In fact, they can invest their emotional stability so heavily in fantasy that they convince themselves their lives would be bankrupt in the absence of ideal conditions. The anger can represent a yearning to force life into an ideal paradigm.

As Roger sat in my office, tension was written all over his face, and his tone of voice hinted at thoughts of incredulity as he tried to make sense of his world. Speaking in a higher pitch than normal, he complained, "What is it with people these days? I mean, everywhere I go I try to be decent and considerate. I'm not one of those selfish types who barrels over anyone in the way; instead, I make it my business to factor in the feelings or preferences of the other person, then I act with that person's needs in mind. I get *very* frustrated, though, whenever I realize that others can't or won't make similar efforts in reverse. People can be so blind and insensitive!" He was shaking his head in disgust.

"Let me give you an idea of what I'm talking about," he said. "It's my responsibility at work to follow up on the deals that our salespeople make with our customers. We provide Internet services to a wide variety of businesses, and as you might guess our industry is very competitive, so we've got to be a little better than the other guys to keep our advantage. I'm constantly encountering problems, though, when I learn that our salespeople promise more than our company can deliver. I've talked with them over and over about this, but they just don't hear me. Once I begin working with the customers, they have expectations, and if I don't meet them, they're ready to walk.

"And that brings up another problem." He was on a roll now. "Because our customers know how competitive our industry is, they seem to operate with the assumption that they can treat me any old way they like, knowing that I've got to put up with their bull for fear that they might take their business elsewhere. I *hate* condescending people, but these folks feel they're in the position to look down on a peon like me."

Adding insult to injury, he said, "Then I go home and try to let my wife know that I've had a grinding day, and her only response is 'That's why they call it work.' She doesn't seem to appreciate the sacrifices I make so she and our daughter can have a good life. I've never been able to open up to her because she doesn't really care about my feelings. To her I'm just a paycheck!" Summarizing his outlook, Roger said dejectedly, "I'm the only person I know who really tries to be sensitive and tuned in. Why can't anyone else make the effort to have appropriate people skills?"

Roger came to my office because he was experiencing anger outbursts with increasing frequency. Listening to some of his concerns, I could understand why he would feel angry. Anyone struggling with a lack of support and understanding on the work front and at home is sure to feel agitated. Roger was not wrong to feel what he felt. He was compounding his problem with anger, though, as he entertained a dreamlike fantasy about how life should unfold in more ideal circumstances.

Repeatedly, Roger obsessed upon thoughts about receiving greater respect from his coworkers. "Why can't they take the time to appreciate how hard I work to make their jobs go more smoothly?" he would ask himself. Likewise, he would frequently pause to ponder more ideal responses from his customers with thoughts like: "Wouldn't it be nice if they could recognize that we are all regular people with regular feelings and needs? It seems like they could remind themselves that they need to factor in the human dimension." In addition, he would dream about better conditions at home as he wondered: "I wish I could figure out what it would take to get Leah to appreciate what I do for her. I can't believe that she shows such low regard for my efforts."

Mythical Thinking

Without recognizing it, Roger's anger was being fed by *mythical thinking*—indulgence of fantasy regarding how life might be under ideal circumstances. Although it is good, and even necessary, to maintain ideals that can generate a positive pull on personal goals and ambitions, it is possible to have too much of a good thing. This is what happens when people employ mythical thinking. Not only do they aspire to lofty standards but these people convince themselves they cannot find peace in the absence of those standards. People trapped by mythical thoughts are sure to use phrases like these:

- "I can't believe . . ."
- "Why can't you just . . ."
- "If only you would . . ."
- "It seems to me that . . ."
- "I just wish . . ."
- "I don't understand why . . ."
- "Won't you at least consider . . ."

So focused are they on the notion that life can and should run smoothly that they make little room for the possibility that others do not adhere to the fantasy. When it becomes obvious that the fantasy is not coming true, anger spills over.

Roger had a tendency to brood and fume when he felt angry, which was a fairly frequent occurrence. In his angry moments, this fuming would be expressed with agitation as he might say to a coworker or to his wife: "What's the deal around here? What's it going to take to get you to see that we can't go on doing things in the same old tired ways?" Whenever he inevitably received a less-than-satisfactory response, that is when his anger might get nasty. "I am sick and tired of having to put up with your incompetence," he might shout. "It's ridiculous that I've got to accept senseless behavior from senseless people!" Of course, each time he exploded like this, his cause would be set back several steps as the recipient thought something like: "Get me away from this jerk. I don't know who put a burr in his britches, but I don't have to put up with this junk!"

Ugly Truth

When people like Roger cling to mythical thinking, they fail to make room for ugly truth. It is a fact that people and events will disappoint. It is not a pleasant fact, but the unpleasantness does not make it any less true. No matter how powerfully we wish things to be different, we each encounter circumstances that create frustration. Stable people can adjust to the thought; perpetually angry people refuse to accommodate such a reality.

As I explained mythical thinking to Roger and encouraged him to incorporate ugly truths, he shook his head in great frustration. "I don't mind saying that I've put up with lousy treatment from others my entire life, and frankly I'm not interested in hearing you or anyone else telling me that I've just got to accept things as they are. I *don't* have to accept incompetence and insensitivity. I grew up with a mother who was the ultimate grouch. She was always in a bad mood, and she was a pro at making life miserable for anyone in her presence. Dad was a decent enough fellow, but he was gone a lot, and frankly I think he was actively trying to avoid my mother."

He went on to tell me that in his early family life arguing and friction typified relations among the three siblings. Mealtimes were especially unpleasant, and any attempt to coordinate family schedules predictably ended with someone angry at someone else. "I used to dream of the day," Roger told me, "that I could be rid of all that tension. I was so tired of the bickering and complaining in my household that I determined I would *not* live that way as an adult."

As Roger elaborated about the pain he experienced in his developmental years, I began getting a clearer picture of his adulthood anger. I learned that young Roger soothed his pain by wishing for a life that was friction free. In his college and early adult years, he became a student of human relations, devouring books that spelled out a better way to live. He prided himself on how he would act and communicate differently from his family of origin. "I am committed to the right way of living," he would say, "and surely I can find a few good people who will share the same positive goals."

I explained to Roger that I applauded his desire to build a better life than what he knew with his family of origin. Then I said, "It's almost as though you've oversold yourself on the notion that you can reinvent your world. It's good to have a forward-leaning approach toward life, but you still can't get around the fact that humans are prone to mistakes and blunders. Some are more aggravating than others, but nonetheless, ineptitude is always a part of the human equation."

As a simple way of making my point, I asked Roger to keep a writing pad handy for the next several days so he could jot down some of the ugly truths he encountered that were not likely to change soon. Here is a sample of what he wrote down over a week's time:

- My daughter does not put the same premium on punctuality as I do.
- When I'm dealing with clerks at the grocery store, or in any store, a high percentage act as if they don't care about me, the customer.
- Idiots drive on the same roads that I drive on every day.
- My wife misunderstands my motives frequently. She can be unnecessarily defensive.
- My supervisor at work tends to be so busy that she often brushes me off in conversation.
- When I get my supervisor's attention, she may not have a clue about the issue at hand.
- I'm good about staying in touch with my friends, but they don't really go out of their way to stay in touch with me. My friendships often feel like a one-way street.
- My mother is a rotten listener. She constantly interrupts or changes the subject.
- My wife is not much better at communication than my mother, and neither is my sister. My brother doesn't know how to have a deep conversation.
- My main customer is very slippery in the way he discusses things. I have a hard time determining if he's lying or telling the truth.
- Even though I make a decent income, we never seem to have enough money. When I try to talk to my wife and daughter about it, they say what I want to hear, then they go right back to wasting money.
- Just when I feel I'm doing OK financially, the car will break down or the water heater will go out.

As I read this list during our next visit, I looked over my glasses at Roger and said, "Wow! You've got plenty of imperfections in your daily routine. It looks like there's no shortage of anger-producing circumstances!" It made sense to me that Roger would feel angry in the face of these unwanted realities. For each example on his list, we could develop a rationale for using assertive communication or behavior. So I explained: "I'm not suggesting that we eliminate your emotional responses to each of these scenarios. That would be impossible, or unwise. What I am suggesting is that you become aware of the tendency to indulge in mythical thinking every time you feel stymied by these situations. You'll need to develop a strategy for emotional stability other than just wishing that things would be better. The minute you refuse to accept that life is not running parallel to your dreams, that's when you become susceptible to the unhealthy forms of anger."

Pain Exists

When you allow mythical thinking to infiltrate your response to conflict or unwanted circumstances, you attempt to remove the presence of pain in your life. You also accept a low view of yourself, as you convince yourself that you are too weak or frail to handle the distasteful elements in life. In a sense, the angry people who cling to mythical thinking are expressing a form of shock. Their anger reveals a thought that might go like this: "Oh no! I'm doomed! I'm certain I can't handle the problem before me. I must have more favorable conditions or I'll fall apart."

Roger snickered as I pointed out to him this notion of shock and pain avoidance. "I never have thought of myself as one who pushes the panic button when things don't go my way, but maybe you're onto something." Speaking slowly he added, "I'll give this a lot of thought."

As Roger and I began to look specifically at how his anger revealed mythical thoughts, I challenged him to identify how it revealed pain-avoidant wishes:

- After conferring with a salesperson at his company regarding the best way to handle a new account, the salesperson reneged on their agreed approach and made an agreement with the customer that Roger could not endorse. Roger was very edgy and agitated for two days afterward. He was able to recognize that even though his anger had legitimate roots, its excess revealed his thinking: "This is more agonizing than I can manage. I can't believe a coworker would do something like this. I'm now going to fall apart."
- He had an explosive episode with his grade-school-age daughter because she forgot a major homework assignment and was frantically scrambling at the last minute to get it done. Roger had a legitimate lesson to communicate to her, yet he handled it so sloppily that his daughter was reduced to tearful arguing. Roger was able to admit that his anger revealed the thought: "I'm deeply wounded when my daughter lives contrary to my preferences. The discomfort is more than I can bear; therefore I have to force compliance."
- Roger learned that his sister-in-law had broken an expensive kitchen appliance that she borrowed from Leah, and he became angry because she

did not immediately volunteer to replace it with a new one. He fumed and griped about it to his wife, to the point that she would no longer discuss the matter with him. He later recognized that his thinking could be summarized this way: "I find it so painful that a family member would disappoint me that I can't contain my emotions. Woe is me! This is too much to handle!"

As Roger and I broke down these experiences of anger to discover how his emotion was fueled by the fantasy that his life should proceed pain-free, he was able to acknowledge that he secretly wished he could somehow become the first person in history to eliminate all discomfort. "I think I'm catching on to the fact that I'm setting myself up for my own problems by my refusal to admit to myself that life basically cannot be counted on to be a bed of roses," he admitted.

I explained to Roger that I usually find that people who convince themselves they have to have ideal circumstances to fend off life's pain tend to draw upon one of two family backdrops. The first possibility is one similar to Roger's history. Many angry adults, like Roger, can recall far too many experiences in their past that were filled with insensitively managed conflict. Perhaps a parent was persistently harsh, invalidating, or picky. Perhaps the family digressed too easily into bickering and arguing. In some cases, the child suffered from abusive treatment.

When young people feel trapped by chronic mistreatment or ongoing and unresolved friction, they eventually look to the future with the hope of being able to escape such frustration. "One of these days . . ." becomes the phrase that gives them hope. They nurse the thought that one of these days their life will be free from the condescension they currently must abide. One of these days, they'll be separated from a tormenting sibling. One of these days, people will actually listen and give credibility to their feelings.

The desire to separate from pain-producing circumstances is entirely normal, yet without a guide to keep their hopes anchored in reality these young people can become adults whose expectations are unattainable. They so crave a better life that they feel cheated when they learn that even in adulthood they continue to be exposed to pain. The disillusionment caused by this recognition becomes the seed for anger. "I thought I could get to a place of avoiding the junk that reminds me of all the problems I had to endure from my past," they reason.

The other historical backdrop that feeds mythical thinking is much more idyllic. Some adults look back to their early years and conclude that it was an almost perfect time. One woman looked dreamy-eyed at me and said, "I don't think I could have had two finer parents. We never argued in our home. My dad was the perfect gentleman and my mother became one of my best friends. All my friends loved coming to our house, and there was always something going on there." This woman struggled with anxiety and irritability as an adult because she was unable to reproduce such perfection in her own home. Her husband was a good man, but not as good as she remembered Daddy being. She complained because he could sometimes be impatient, and he struggled in a career that did not reward him financially, as she thought it should. In addition, this woman found that she was unable to re-create the best-friend relationship with her children that she once had with her mother. Her daughter was more of a tomboy than she would have liked, and her son used far too many grunts and shoulder shrugs when she tried to communicate with him.

This woman's anxiety was fed by a steady diet of frustration, hurt feelings, and critical thoughts. Because she did not often shout or scream, she would not identify herself as angry. Nonetheless, that was a major problem she needed to address if she wanted to reduce her anxiety.

Incorporating Truth

Whether the tendency toward mythical thinking has its roots in a history of torment or one of presumed idealism, angry adults find balance only after they learn to exchange their myths for truth. Once they do so, they can make plans to address the legitimate aspects of their anger constructively and assertively.

I explained to Roger: "I like the fact that you've made yourself a student of healthy relationship skills. I'm like you in the sense that I too wish more people would make greater efforts to treat people with thoughtfulness. Yet, as long as we live on this side of Heaven, we're not going to have the luxury of being with people who do everything right. That being the case, I suggest we set aside your myths and figure out how to let truth guide your emotional responses."

Roger and I were able to zero in on several myths that perpetuated his anger, and as we did, we identified the corresponding truth he could incorporate:

MYTH: I NEED PEOPLE TO BE FAIR-MINDED
SO I WON'T HAVE PROBLEMS WITH ANGER

TRUTH: I CAN MANAGE MY ANGER
WELL DESPITE OTHERS' FLAWS

Roger made a conscious effort to be fair in the way he responded to others, and that was a noble goal. In his zeal to do things right, however, he convinced himself that he could not have peace if others chose not to reciprocate. Stung by memories of early family life that was often unfair and unloving, he concluded that he absolutely needed others to give an equal effort. I pointed out to him: "Not only have you not succeeded in positioning yourself among highly sensitive people, each time you allow yourself to dream of total fairness you're that much farther from being personally stable. I'm willing to proceed with the belief that you can figure out a way to manage your anger even when it seems you're in the Lone Ranger role."

"But I just can't stand it when I feel I'm being appropriate, only to have others take advantage of my good nature," he protested.

"Is perfect interaction your goal," I asked, "or is your goal to be emotionally healthy? I'm encouraging you to consider how to manage your anger best, knowing that you can't expect life to play out in a completely wonderful fashion."

Roger was mistakenly fusing his choices regarding anger with the issue of fairness, which is a separate matter altogether. I reminded him that all sorts of unfair things happen to everybody, and though he need not pretend those things never bothered him, neither did he have to consider them ruinous to his emotional well-being. Little children in a temper tantrum can be excused for crying over the seeming lack of fairness in their lives because they know no better. Adults, like Roger, need to drop the myth that life is fair and remember that they can choose appropriate assertiveness or release of anger because that is what they deem to be wisest.

MYTH: BEING FORCEFUL IS A SIGN OF STRENGTH

TRUTH: GENTLENESS IS A SIGN OF STRENGTH

Roger recalled many moments as a boy when his mother would communicate in an overbearing and demanding tone. He distinctly remembered how weary he felt as he seemed to be the one in their home who was chronically holding the short straw. "Power was the name of the game for my mother," he told me. "I decided very early in life that I would do all I could to become the one with the upper hand because I was so tired of being verbally beat up by her."

We discussed how indeed Roger had learned various ways to position himself in strength. For instance, he had a witty sense of humor and often used sarcastically funny comments to put people in their place. Also, friends and family members knew not to try to win an argument with him because Roger was quite a capable debater and could readily find the loopholes in another's position. Likewise, he was known as stubborn, and he had infinite willingness to hold onto his biases, even when they were shown to be erroneous.

As we talked, I remembered that he seemed stuck in the role of the hurt little boy who was fighting to prove to his mother that he was somebody to be reckoned with. "Her winning technique was the overpowering approach too," I mentioned. "Before you commit any more of your life to perfecting the same technique, I think it would be interesting for you to consider what she won with her so-called strength."

That comment caught Roger off guard. He quietly nodded as he picked up on my line of reasoning. "I guess she gained nothing but trouble by using the overpowering approach, and I suppose you're trying to tell me that I can expect the same."

Wanting to put his mythical thinking into a logical perspective, I asked, "Does the overpowering approach work in your closest relations today? Do people seem more inclined to cooperate once they've felt demeaned?"

Assertive anger is the preferred alternative to aggressive forms of anger, and you need not be overpowering to be successfully assertive. Firmness can still be accompanied by calmness and gentleness. It allows you to display your respect for the other person even as you maintain a commitment to what you know is right. For instance, Roger had an episode at work where he felt a customer was being far too pushy regarding the time frame for finishing a project. In the past he would have suppressed his anger when interfacing with the customer, and then he would have displaced it later toward an office clerk, or perhaps gone home in a foul mood and unloaded his irritability onto family members.

In this case, though, he decided he needed to display strength toward the customer, but he would illustrate his strength delicately. "I know you want the project finished ASAP," he said in an even tone of voice, "and I can certainly appreciate the need to wrap things up in a timely fashion. I think you can see that I'm giving the project my best effort, so I'm asking you to respect that fact." The customer couldn't quite let go of his complaint and retorted with a less-than-supportive reply. Roger stayed with the same calm voice and answered, "Nonetheless, I'm giving you my best effort. I'll handle this in the most efficient way that I can."

Later, as we discussed this incident, he beamed and told me how clean he felt because he had remained true to his boundaries, yet he also kept his dignity intact. It was then that he realized that the gentle-but-firm approach was clearly a display of true confidence. He also recognized that a whining or complaining wish for power would have shown how defeated he allowed himself to feel.

MYTH: OTHERS OWE IT TO ME TO ACT RIGHT

TRUTH: A MIND OF ENTITLEMENT DOES NOT PREVAIL

When anger is mismanaged, it is almost always accompanied by an attitude of deservedness. A "you owe me" mentality is evidenced by the presence of a coercive or demanding method of communication. Somehow, angry people have convinced themselves that it is their right to expect others to cater to them, either because of their position of authority or because they have bought the right to good treatment by their own correct behavior.

For instance, Roger told me about an angry episode involving his wife. It was Saturday, and he had asked Leah for some help with a chore in the garage. She told Roger she would be there to help in about five minutes, but she became preoccupied on a telephone call and then forgot to go to the garage to help him. Thirty minutes later, Roger found her in the house and exploded. In his anger, he listed half a dozen helpful things he had done for her in the last few days, and then he shouted, "And the only thing I can count on from you is your forgetfulness. I'm there for you, but you sure aren't there for me!"

Was Roger's anger mistaken? Not entirely. It would have been appropriate for him to assertively remind Leah that he still needed her help, and that her consideration would be appreciated. The anger became aggressive, however, as it was fed by the mythical idea that his good deeds somehow demanded that she must repay him. She was now in his debt.

I told Roger, "When you begin to list your good deeds and demand that she repay you, it spoils the goodness that accompanied your original acts. You're going to be much steadier in your emotions as you choose to be kind with no expectations and no scorekeeping. Relationships sour quickly when you operate with a mind of deservedness."

Love, goodness, and kindness are qualities that by definition exist even when the recipient cannot or will not give the same in return. Roger's anger would have been far more effective if before his outburst he had reminded himself, *My good behaviors toward Leah are a separate issue. They are not part of this equation.* He could have focused calmly and exclusively on the issue of her forgetfulness, and his words likely would have had a much greater impact because her mind would not have been cluttered with having to sift through the issue of his earlier deeds.

MYTH: ACCEPTING IMPERFECTION MEANS ACCEPTING DEFEAT

TRUTH: ACCEPTING IMPERFECTION IS A SIGN OF MATURITY, AND NOT ALL PEOPLE SHARE THAT QUALITY

People who have balance in their anger management know the value of releasing anger. They are direct enough to speak specifically and constructively about the things that bother them, but they also are wise enough to know when to cease from self-preservation efforts. They value qualities such as forgiveness, acceptance, and tolerance, and they are willing to let go of their anger when they recognize that it suffocates positive priorities.

When people hold onto their anger and stubbornly insist upon forcing their agenda, they typically do so because they fear that acceptance of others is tantamount to giving up on all that is right or good. Their minds are so strongly influenced by a win-or-lose style of thought that they mistakenly assume an accommodating spirit is the same as conceding defeat.

I recall one man who told me about bitter feelings he held toward a former business partner who colluded with a major customer and broke their business arrangement to begin a new company. This maneuver caused the original company to collapse, and my client had to file bankruptcy and then struggled to find new employment. Truly it was an unethical move by the partner, and the man had reasons to feel angry. When I asked how recently this had happened, his reply was, "Twelve years ago."

Twelve years had passed, and he still held onto the anger! His wife told me that the anger was so deeply entrenched that he had lost several friendships and developed a reputation as a grouch who could only see the negative elements in life. When I asked if anyone had spoken with him about accepting the loss or forgiving so he could move forward with his life, he nodded and told me that the subject was broached many times. When I asked why he chose not to accept or forgive, he looked incredulous and said, "Are you kidding? That would mean I let him win!" Apparently he believed that holding on to bitter anger meant he was the winner, but he could not recognize that his winning prize was an emotional prison.

Someone who incorporates truth, even when it is ugly, is willing to admit that painful events happen, yet they do not have to ultimately define a person. By accepting the negative circumstances in their lives, such people are not necessarily letting go of their legitimate convictions; they are acknowledging there are other priorities in life that they want to accentuate. For instance, this man whose business collapsed could have decided that he did not want to give his angry feelings highest attention. He could have chosen to establish a new life that incorporated the hard lessons learned in his ordeal, meaning he would be careful to establish clear boundaries with business associates. Then he could have determined that goodness and an encouraging spirit would hold greater appeal than grouchiness.

Taking the better path of emotional maturity may at times feel uncomfortable when it becomes apparent that others will not join that effort, yet group commitment to emotional well-being is deemed less reliable than individual choice. Mythical thinkers can make the mistake of dreaming of better conditions "out there," and in the meantime they miss the reality that "in here" is their best chance for contentment.

MYTH: GOOD RELATIONSHIPS SHOULDN'T REQUIRE MUCH WORK

TRUTH: EVEN THE BEST RELATIONSHIPS REQUIRE ONGOING PLANNING

Once Roger looked straight at me and in all seriousness said, "Relationships shouldn't have to be so much work." I thought about the conflicts he had discussed with me: coworkers who did a poor job of coordinating, customers who were unrealistic in demands, a spouse who did not know how to voice support. In my reflections, I realized that Roger truly experienced aggravation that *could* be averted if only the participants chose to use healthy relational skills. I could only nod my head in agreement and say, "Wouldn't it be nice if we could snap our fingers and make each key person in your life considerate and understanding?"

Roger grinned as he said emphatically, "*But.* I know exactly where you're going with your thoughts, and there is a huge *but* waiting, isn't there?"

Returning the grin, I said, "Well, as a matter of fact, yes there is a *but.* Personalities and the perspectives we each have about life can be so varied that there is only one certainty: we all differ greatly from one another. Relationships require ongoing adjustment and lots of willingness to bend and flex. Sometimes the need to calculate moves can feel tedious. Nonetheless, there will never be a relationship so ideal that it just naturally falls into place."

Individuals who learn to tame their anger are realistic in their expectations, and they make lots of room for the fact that people and events can and will disappoint. When possible, they make the effort to adjust circumstances to their needs, yet they are under no illusion that they have everything as they wish.

"You're trying to make me think first before I engage my anger," Roger reflected. Indeed, that statement summarized my hopes for our therapeutic process.

"Most of us have a certain amount of psychological laziness," I explained, "that causes us to seek the shortest path to emotional well-being. Deep down, we know that life doesn't just fall into a neatly designed pattern, yet our mythical thinking can delude us into thinking it can be that simple. For you to contain your moods of anger, you'll need to acclimate your mind to realize that just when you think you've got your life perfectly wired, there is always going to be an unexpected or undesirable twist that challenges you. It's very easy to be calm and pleasant in your mood when everything fits according to your ideal fantasies. The mark of a truly healthy person, though, is to maintain calmness even when you encounter ugliness."

Summarizing my thoughts about how mythical thinking influenced his anger, I challenged Roger to focus on three key adjustments:

1. Become very honest about how you set yourself up for disappointment by clinging to your many fantasies, which are just that—fantasies.
2. Accept the reality that circumstances can be ugly, even when they involve people who seemingly should know better than to live with distasteful behaviors.
3. Recognize that your anger is fed by a shock reaction ("I can't believe this is happening to me"), and drop the shock. Removing histrionics allows you to choose more wisely if you proceed with clean assertiveness, or choose to release your anger altogether.

He could always go back to the option of trying to rewrite truth, and in doing so angrily attempt to force others to accept his version of how things ought to be. But we readily concluded that doing so would bring the same results as banging his head against a brick wall. He was ready, instead, to recognize that such an effort at pain avoidance only created greater pain.

For Personal Reflection

- What are some ideal circumstances you wish to experience? In what way is it good to have these ideals? In what way is it harmful to have them?
- What are some painful realities in your life that cannot be completely eliminated? How is your anger affected when you try to force those painful circumstances to go away?
- How did your early family life equip you to handle unwanted frustration? What thought adjustments do you have to make in overcoming the lack of full training from your early years?
- How could you be assertive as you address circumstances that generate pain? How would your emotional balance improve if you made more allowance for pain?

- How have you deluded yourself into thinking that forcefulness proves you are strong? How would calmness or gentleness be a better display of strength?
- How would your anger management be positively affected if you dropped the assumption that others owe it to you to treat you right?
- In what ways does your anger indicate emotional laziness?

PART THREE

CHOOSING THE BETTER PATH

10

AGONY'S UPSIDE

WHEN I FIRST met Thomas, I knew there was something very special about him. Balding, with premature white hair, he looked older than most men in their late forties, yet his trim, athletic build indicated it was not for a lack of effort. Thomas made his way to counseling only after much personal strain, and his story was not pretty, yet I knew almost instantly that we were going to see great results once we got to the bottom of his issues. Sometimes I get the sense that a client's case will become something special, and I knew his was going to be one of those.

Thomas had just lost his job because he embezzled funds and was caught red-handed. At the time he began counseling with me, he was uncertain if he would spend time in prison. Later, complications arose in the prosecutor's case, and what seemed like a sure ticket to prison became a probated sentence, for which Thomas felt greatly relieved.

"Something catastrophic like this needed to happen to get me to seek professional help," Thomas told me, "but now that I'm here I'm very glad to be doing this. I've known for a long time that I needed to talk with someone." The choices that resulted in his legal woes took up a good portion of our early sessions, but in time we began exploring the deeper roots of his problems; to no surprise, I learned that he had been sitting on years of stifled anger.

Born into a home dominated by a crass, demanding father, Thomas struggled mightily as a boy to feel secure. A former athletic wannabe, his father pushed his only son (of five children) to be a star athlete. Actually, Thomas enjoyed sports, and he especially looked forward to attending games featuring local college and professional teams. Yet in time, Thomas despised his own participation in team sports because his father was always so mean as he insisted that he be the best.

"My dad thought nothing about cursing at me in front of other kids or my sisters or my mother," Thomas recalled. "I actually felt relieved when he called me names like *wimp* or *sissy* because they were much milder than some of the other more horrible names he often used. He was really rough on me because he felt that as the only boy in the family, I should be the one to make the rest proud. And it wasn't just sports that caused him to lay into me. It was everything! I was held to a high standard in all my subjects at school, and I had to be exemplary in my manners both at home and in public."

"Sounds like dad had one speed when he became angry," I reflected to him, "and that was full throttle."

"That's totally correct," Thomas shot back, "and I'm sorry to say that I grew to hate him for it. When I was younger, in grade school, I was a pretty subservient kid because I was afraid of what he might do if I caused him to lose his temper. In my teens, though, I was so worn out by his domineering ways that I started pushing back. We had some pretty strong shouting matches, and I think it really caught the old man off guard when I chose to speak to him with the same filthy words he used on me. I quit all my sports involvement in the tenth grade, and it was at that point that he went into a deep freeze toward me. Don't get me wrong, he'd still spout off criticisms and insults freely, but aside from that he might go days at a time without even looking at me."

Thomas could not get out the door quickly enough when he finished high school, and after a stint in the military he buckled down and finished college in three years and settled into a career as a CPA. He married and had two girls of his own. By observing him, few people would suspect he might have a major anger problem.

Though he became known as a clean, churchgoing family man, there was a dark side to Thomas that few outside his family would see. Working as an in-house accountant for a small manufacturing company, he hated being told what to do, and he would fume quietly whenever the company's owner seemed to micromanage him. As the years passed, the owner's son took the reins, which annoyed Thomas no end because he thought of him as a buffoon. Repeatedly he considered leaving for another line of work, but he convinced himself that he was too specialized in his niche, presumably stuck with nowhere else to go. In time, it was all he could do to keep a lid on his seething contempt for his employer.

While Thomas became a master at disguising his anger in public, his home life was another story. His wife, Charlotte, told me that she and the two girls kept a tight line of communication among themselves to determine if he was in one of his foul moods or not. On his worst days, he would snap at one or all of them with scathing criticism, while at other times he was just silently unapproachable. On a few occasions, he could relax and act friendly, but this mostly perpetuated confusion; his family feared responding too happily because they knew the friendliness would soon fade.

Charlotte brought her own insecurities into the marriage, and her mood vacillated easily among fretfulness, irritability, appeasement, and defensiveness. Their college-aged daughter, Jessica, told me that there always seemed to be a cloud of tension hanging over their home, causing everyone to live a guarded life for fear that any false move would generate an eruption. "It was definitely not a happy home," she sighed.

After Thomas was caught mismanaging company funds, for the first time ever he wept bitterly over the way his life had turned out. He felt "beyond humiliated" as the news swept quickly through his community. He explained, "There I was, this supposedly respected businessman and pillar of the church, with egg all over my face. What's worse, my family wasn't very sympathetic and I had no one else to blame but myself. I had dug myself into this hole because I trained my mind to rationalize that since I had not gotten from life what I deserved, I could take matters into my own hands, even if it meant acting like I was above the law." Shaking his head in disgust, he openly chided himself. "Who did I think I was? I knew that what I had planned was wrong, but I did it anyway." Then burying his head in his hands, he said, barely audibly, "I'm a worthless fool."

There have been many moments when I hear people make self-deprecating comments that prompt me to speak in a lovingly corrective way about such self-talk. This incident with Thomas was not such a moment. Throughout his adult life, he had built his self-esteem upon a foundation of deluded thoughts about his own deservedness, and now that foundation was crumbling. Though painful to watch, I knew he had to go through this agony before he could build upon an entirely new manner of thought.

The Grace of Agony

Grace is often defined as the offering of forgiveness or kindness when it is not earned. For instance, if Thomas's employer had set aside any prosecution of his wrongdoing and pardoned him unconditionally from his crime, that would have been a merciful act of grace. Likewise, if Charlotte had responded to his cold moods with sheer goodness, that too would have exemplified grace.

Grace indeed is illustrated by the gift of unmerited favor, but it is actually broader than that. God recognizes that no human has the natural capacity to live a perfectly healthy life, so he is willing to provide guidance even amid failure. When someone like Thomas fails yet somehow discovers a God-given strength to grow and learn, he or she experiences *sustaining grace*. This can be most profoundly experienced when agony is at its peak.

During the time Thomas began working with me, if his boss or his wife had pronounced total forgiveness immediately, it probably would not have been a good thing. Without having to grapple with the seriousness of his ill-chosen ways, he might have fallen back quickly into the patterns that were part of his demise. Frankly, Thomas needed to hurt, not because hurt is a good way to make a scoundrel feel debased but because hurt would cause him to search for priorities in life that were more dignified. Hurt can sometimes be a teacher, prompting someone to grow in a way that might not otherwise occur.

No Meaningless Pain

Angry people are in pain. They inflict pain upon others, but that is because they have not come to terms with their own deep wounds, and a primary way they have learned to relieve themselves of their own aching is to give it away. As a result, it may feel odd for someone like Thomas to appreciate the value that can be derived by allowing one's own hurt to run its full course. To people like him, it might seem more appropriate to suggest that all pain should be eliminated in order for personal growth to occur, yet such reasoning is not necessarily true.

An analogy helps explain my appreciation for the graceful role that pain can play. A friend once told me about a bum knee that had plagued him off and on for months. "I didn't want to deal with the aggravation of surgery," he explained, "so my doctor gave me a shot of cortisone. Wow! That stuff really worked, in the sense that it relieved my pain greatly. It did nothing to heal my damaged ligaments and cartilage, mind you, but I sure *felt* better." In the absence of pain, however, my friend encountered a whole new problem. The lack of pain emboldened him to be more physically aggressive, and soon he was pivoting on the knee and pushing it beyond its capacity. Over the course of weeks, the damage to his knee worsened, making surgery all the more necessary. The cortisone had inhibited his body's pain sensors from doing their full work, which was to alert my friend regarding the adjustments he could make to prevent a worsening of his situation. The lack of pain weakened him.

Pain can be a gift, albeit one that is not welcomed by many. When I work with angry people like Thomas, I often emphasize the need to listen carefully to the message being sent by emotional pain. Just as physical pain prompts someone to make healing adjustments within the body, emotional pain can prompt change within the personality. Ignoring its signals can prove disastrous in the sense of a needed lesson being lost.

On the day that Thomas sat before me calling himself a worthless fool, my response was to ask him to elaborate on what that meant. Tears came as he spoke, and he bore the look of the broken man he had become. "All my life I've tried to prove my dad wrong," he said dejectedly. "As a kid he almost had me convinced that I was a nobody if I didn't do exactly as he wanted, but when I reached my late teens, I decided that no one ever again would get away with telling me what to do. I was the master of my own ship, and I'd live with no barriers holding me back."

Heaving a great sigh, he continued, "Through the years I've tried to build a protective armor of toughness around me. I'd remind myself of my vow that no one would ever again dictate my life. But in my efforts to be a stronger person, I've basically perpetuated my father's angry personality. I'm not as openly mean as he was, and that is by design. Yet I've got to be honest and admit that I'm just mean in a different way. I can be cold and vindictive. I've become secretive. I'm a liar. I definitely hold grudges. I *hate* what I have allowed myself to become."

Over the course of several counseling sessions, Thomas and I examined several examples from his adult life that depicted how insensitively his anger was manifested. Given the breadth of his callous disregard for others' dignity, I did not rush him through this exercise, and I often asked questions that would prompt him to identify the rationalizations that allowed him to continue in these behaviors. Our discussions covered a range of misdeeds. He confessed how he was consistently grouchy as he coordinated efforts with coworkers. He rued the many times he used foul language to intimidate his wife into submission. He admitted making few efforts to factor in his family's needs as he scheduled outings involving golf or a hunting trip. He recognized openly that he seemed to take a perverse delight in being known as surly, critical, and insulting. As he detailed these matters, I would prod him to explore why he made such choices, and we both agreed that "I don't know" was not a sufficient answer. Confronting himself, no matter how uncomfortable the process, had to be thorough and incisive.

"This hurts," Thomas said. "For so long I just allowed myself to run roughshod over people and act like a privileged character, but now it's humbling to look directly into my mannerisms to recognize the damage that I have done."

On several occasions, Charlotte joined in our sessions. After hearing him admit the many ways he had harmed others, she remarked that this openness was entirely out of character for him. "I've never known him to be this honest before," she said. "Usually if he admitted a flaw it was immediately followed by blame or by excuses." Then she added, "Something very different is going on here, and I like it."

Disgust Is Motivating

A woman in her midthirties once explained to me why she chose not to drink alcoholic beverages. "About fifteen years ago I attended a fraternity party at my college. The music was loud, and the atmosphere was uninhibited as the alcohol flowed. I have no idea how many drinks I took in that night, but I was just trying to keep up with my friends. Eventually some of the behavior between the young men and women became lewd and bawdy, and I joined right in. I did things sexually that night that I am not proud of, and the next day I had the most miserable hangover that a person could have. The nausea was so severe that I can still remember it. I honestly wanted to die that day. Since then I recognized that while alcohol does not always lead to such extremes, it was no friend of mine. If I was so susceptible to the poor decisions that can accompany its intake, then I had no business putting it into my body ever again. I've not touched a drop since then." Her disgust with her poor choices, though uncomfortable, created a response that served her well years after the fact.

Angry people often have a good reason for feeling angry. Thomas did, at least in the beginning. His anger started as a protest against the condescension his father so easily displayed. Even some of his adult episodes of anger could be linked to a reasonable desire to stand up for his own dignity. Most people like Thomas, however, recognize that there have been too many incidents where the anger became an impetus to treat people foully. If they have no disgust for such a turn of the emotion, they are likely to repeatedly misuse the anger. If they can recall the painful truth that the anger had a ruinous effect on their behavior, they can develop a resolve never to repeat the misuse of anger again.

In my years of counseling, I have encountered many people who hold so tightly to guilt that they remain stuck in patterns of insecurity and shame. It is my delight to teach them that they can let go of their guilt and shame, to pursue more wholesome thoughts. I often explain that there is a difference between true guilt and false guilt. The false guilt that holds so many people captive can be understood as a spirit of judgment that is misapplied or completely unnecessary. I teach that they need not commit themselves to an emotion resulting in perpetual self-condemnation.

There are times, though, when the emphasis on removing guilt from the personality proves to be harmful to personal growth. If people develop a pattern of ongoing irresponsibility, they *need* to feel badly about their choices, not permanently but long enough for the seriousness of those wrong choices to register. True guilt is defined as a sense of regret or remorse that prompts corrective adjustment. Without feelings of true guilt, angry people might never choose to explore the possibilities for personal improvement:

- If a father treats his children with contempt during an angry episode of discipline, the parent needs to feel badly about such poor communication because it can cause him to consider more appropriate ways to speak words of discipline.
- If a driver joins with other motorists in being rude, the guilt can cause him to regret the pervasiveness of disrespect on the road. A commitment to kindness could result.
- If a friend brazenly disregards the needs of another, guilt could motivate her to seek forgiveness and make restitution.
- If a husband has a habit of barking orders angrily at his wife, the ensuing guilt could prompt him to choose a more respectful way to express his needs.
- If a wife allows edginess or coldness to infiltrate her communication with her husband, the guilt could cue her to consider more pleasant alternatives.

Guilt can be good. There are times when self-directed disgust is necessary. I explained to Thomas, "When you were a boy, your dad seemed to have no qualms about motivating you through guilt or intimidation. His message was wrong, and you were right to decide that you would not live in the perpetual shame that he so easily dished out. He was applying false guilt, and your anger was a valid refutation of that false guilt.

"Unfortunately, as you became an adult, your anger took a wrong turn. Instead of building upon your resolve to uphold dignity in your closest relationships, you chose to erase your own feelings of shame by becoming the one who held contemptuous feelings toward others. Your commitment to being dominant or agitated evolved so effortlessly over time that you might not have been fully conscious of it; nonetheless, it happened. Your adult thinking was intact as you chose harshness over kindness."

Again, that broken look came over Thomas's face. "It's all so clear. I guess I never would have been so open in years past to say that I had made my own commitment to anger or rebellion, but the evidence is so compelling that I have to acknowledge the truthfulness of what you're saying. Point blank: I allowed myself to become a jerk."

As the full weight of his recognition sank in, I wanted him to feel the disgust that would become the springboard for change, but I also wanted him to recognize that positive alternatives awaited him. "You know I'm pulling for you, and I want things to be very different from this point forward," I said gently. Thomas nodded; he knew that I meant what I said. I continued. "Thomas, there is a great upside to your personality. Beginning in your boyhood years you knew that there had to be a better way of life than the one portrayed by your dad. He must have been a very hurt man himself, and you were right to recognize that you did not need to be pulled along by his mistaken ways. I want us to reconnect with the appropriate self-preservation you desired as the receiver of his mistreatment, so you can more clearly focus on healthier ways of addressing people when you must draw attention to your needs."

As you allow your self-directed feelings of disgust or guilt to run their course, consider three key awarenesses that can lead you toward personal healing.

Awareness Number One: Recognize That Harmful Anger Never Succeeds

People like Thomas have numerous ways to let their anger show, and usually they do not produce good results. In Thomas's case, his anger was usually displayed through his "don't tell me what to do" attitude, his easy griping, and his caustic condescension. Presumably, he handled his anger in these forms because he allowed himself to believe that they would be the most effective way to gain influence.

"I never really consciously thought that my harmful use of anger would give me greater influence," Thomas said as I mentioned this thought to him. "That's just the way my anger happened to come out."

"Whoa. Hold off on that thought," I replied. "Angry expressions don't just fall out of your brain. They are chosen. Though your patterns of anger may have become habituated, at some level in your mind you knew you had other options, but rebellion or agitation were the options you selected. You'll need to take responsibility for the fact that you chose to be the way you were."

"OK. I see your point. But where do I go from here?"

"Acknowledge that those choices are always available to you, but that they don't work. I'm hoping that the painful consequences that have followed your angry choices will be an ever-present reminder that you do not want to return to those options."

Openly aggressive and passive-aggressive expressions of anger never get good results, no matter how legitimate the original reason for anger may be. Thomas, for instance, began to take inventory regarding how he would stand up for his needs and convictions with his coworkers, his wife, and his daughters. He would gripe, pout, criticize, intimidate, or yell. And what did he receive for his efforts? Temporarily, he felt a surge of power. But over time, his influence in the lives of these people eroded to the point that they respected him less and less.

So I told him: "Thomas, right now you're feeling like your world has bottomed out, and most of your problems can be traced to unrestrained anger. As you resolve to make personal improvements, I'm hoping that you won't soon forget how painful the repercussions of your anger can be. Your father's anger got him nothing good in life, and neither has your anger. Each time you're faced with the opportunity to make an unhealthy choice with your anger, perhaps your painful memories will remind you that those choices won't work."

A home builder who was in business for himself for several years once talked with me about his motivation to build a house using the highest standards of quality workmanship. "In my early years in the business," he said, "I worked for a builder who wanted to get houses up as quickly as possible, and it meant nothing to him to cut corners or use slipshod practices along the way. He succeeded in getting people into houses in a short time, but I was bowled over by the number of complaints we would get from our customers. What he intended as a means for personal gain became a source of great stress for all of us. I determined then that when I was the one running my own business, I would never cut corners or try to get away with cheap products. In the long run, it was never worth the hassle."

What was it that caused this businessman to commit to high standards? Painful memories. It is not pleasurable (which is what our twenty-first-century mentality demands) to remember the pain, but it is ultimately profitable. Likewise, people who look back upon the disasters associated with their anger episodes may not find the exercise enjoyable, but it can be useful if they feel prompted to choose behaviors that serve the best interests of all without generating further misery.

Awareness Number Two: See Yourself as the One Who Can Break the Generational Cycle

In an extremely high percentage of cases involving people who create pain by misuse of anger, the generations preceding them mishandled anger too. Since learning is accomplished through modeling, the lessons a developing child receives can become the foundation for later adult behavior, and unless a determination is made to take a healthier approach, troublesome patterns remain.

This is what befell Thomas. Though he intensely disliked his father's mismanagement of anger, and though he had said to himself on many occasions that he did not want to be like him, Thomas never really put full effort into analyzing his anger for the purpose of putting much better options into play. To his credit, he chose to refrain from some of the grossly inappropriate behavior displayed by his father, yet he only succeeded in choosing other maladaptive forms of anger. Now he was in a time of serious soul searching, and I wanted to capitalize on the opportunity it gave us.

"Just out of curiosity," I asked Thomas, "what do you know about your father's developmental years, and specifically his exposure to anger in his family of origin?"

"My dad had an awful childhood," he reflected. "I heard stories about how his father worked two jobs while he was growing up in the Depression years, and how they struggled because every extra dollar he made went to his drinking habits. Apparently, his father was a pretty mean drunk, and the rule at home was to never do anything to make their dad angry. A couple of times my dad remarked how he would be spanked severely with a razor strap, but he didn't really like to talk much about his childhood. I think it was pretty chaotic, though, and my dad never recovered from the emotional scars."

"It's sad," I mentioned, "that even though he was on the receiving end of inappropriate anger, when it came his turn to be the guy in charge of the family, your father picked right up where his dad left off."

Quickly picking up on my line of thinking, Thomas chimed in, "Yeah, and then I've carried on in the same angry tradition. I'd rationalize to myself that I was never as bad as my father or grandfather, but truthfully I didn't go far enough in my resolve to clean up our family's act." Shaking his head, he stated, "This insanity has got to stop."

There is no need to assume that an extended family's pattern of handling anger is so fixed it can never be altered. As you observe the painful results of poorly chosen anger in family members, you can choose to remain in your own dysfunctional habits, or you can choose to pursue a better route.

Decades ago, a reporter interviewed Richard Nixon while he was in the Oval Office, but before his Watergate scandal. She asked him to identify the most important quality that would prepare a person to become president. Thoughtfully, Nixon replied, "Above all else, you have to have a keen understanding of our country's history. You cannot make good plans for the present and future if you are unaware of the right and wrong decisions that brought us to our current place in time." Whatever inconsistencies he displayed in not adhering to this response, it can be said that this answer warrants attention in the sense that it could be applied to personal matters.

The same can be said for families. Individuals who reflect minimally upon their own family's pluses and minuses are bound to make few, if any, inroads into improving a long-standing pattern. Those who can learn from historical mistakes, however, and build upon the success can expect positive dividends.

Awareness Number Three: See Traits Such as Respectfulness and Goodness as Desirable, Not Dutiful

You have known people (perhaps you are one of them) who implemented a diet and lost weight, only to gain the pounds back in the ensuing months. In many of these cases, the dieter saw the loss of weight as desirable, but the process involved was treated as a duty or obligation. Only when the process (not just the end result) becomes desirable can the weight loss be permanently maintained. Those seeking to change need to worry less about the final outcome and focus more on the change of mentality that will get them what they want.

As you seek to make changes in managing your anger, the same principle applies. Most angry people would like to have a life defined by calmness or pleasantness, but they may feel reluctant to embrace the traits that are required for the process of change: self-restraint, humility, discipline, and the like. Rather than wishing to have the final outcome in place, they would increase their chances for personal success if they appreciated the journey that leads to change.

In one of our early sessions, Thomas remarked that he was tired of being an angry middle-aged man, and that he wanted to be a more even-tempered person instead. I replied, "I suppose you realize that to get what you want, you need to be much more committed to being a good listener, choosing patience, and accepting people where they are."

Almost dejectedly he said, "I knew you'd say something like that."

Thomas was thinking like an athlete who wants to be fit and trim but doesn't want to exercise to reach the goal. I spoke words of encouragement at that point. "Thomas, you insinuate that the ingredients required to help bring balance to your anger are distasteful. I'm hoping that you will *enjoy* learning to be a better listener, just as you will enjoy practicing patience and acceptance. Don't look at those qualities as a means to an end. See them for the positive traits they are, and eagerly look for the opportunity to put them into practice. As you appreciate the fact that a whole new way of living is available to you, you'll see change as a privilege, not a duty."

Once people become deeply cognizant of the misery that is produced by anger, they can become eager to seek better alternatives. Think of this analogy. Perhaps you have traveled to a destination that was impoverished and dilapidated. You have witnessed the squalor that others live in, and you are saddened by the poor diet and poor clothing that is available. Once you return to your own home and all its nice amenities, what thoughts flood your mind? If you are like most, you think: "Wow! Am I glad to be home." You have a renewed appreciation for the simple things that you could so easily take for granted.

When I counsel people who have experienced great agony and misery thanks to their own anger, my desire is to help them move to a new "home." It is a place of contentment, respectfulness, and kindness. Along the way, they are required to use traits such as empathy, encouragement, and tolerance. My hope is that if they are tempted to think of the new effort as drudgery, they will quickly call up the memories of the pain associated with misapplied anger, and upon doing so see the new effort as a privilege, not a duty.

A full year passed after Thomas originally stepped into my office, and he was in an especially pensive mind-set as he spoke with me one day. "I can easily say that I have never had a more difficult and a more wonderful year than this past one." I smiled as he spoke in these contradictory terms because I knew exactly what he meant. "I can be a proud person," he continued, "and because of that I never was very inclined to be forthcoming about my flaws, but once I was arrested it was pretty hard to hide the truth about what I had become. The humiliation was awful, but it set into motion a process of introspection like I've never experienced before. Until now, I could cite why it was better to be kind or encouraging or honest, but I never was really committed to those traits as a way of life. Now, I *want* to have goodness and purity and kindness because I have seen what the alternative looks like, and I never want to return there."

I cannot say that I was glad Thomas had experienced so much pain because I do not want to seem inhumane. Yet once the agony of his life choices brought to light the repercussions of his previous priorities, his personal growth was a pleasure to behold. His pain became the greatest teacher he could have, and fortunately he was willing to listen to its message.

For Personal Reflection

- In what circumstances have you felt humiliated by your own poor choices? Why is it good that you felt such a difficult emotion?
- In what circumstances have you made poor choices, yet you did not feel humiliated by them? What is it about such an occurrence that is not good?

- In what way might your emotional pain be understood as a gift?
- In incidents involving your wrong treatment of others, what was it in your feelings of anger that was valid? How was the validity of that anger buried by your poor expression of it?
- When is it right to feel guilty? What good can you expect from your struggles with guilt?
- Harmful anger never succeeds. Why is it so necessary to acknowledge such a truth? How will your use of anger be altered as you incorporate this belief?
- What is it about your use of anger that can be traced to past generations of mismanaged anger? What can you do to break this generational cycle?

11

FORGIVENESS AND ACCEPTANCE

WHEN CONFLICT AND AGGRAVATION ARISE, anger is expressed because of a desire for closure. The anger-producing circumstances represent an unwanted intrusion, and the angry person immediately wishes to put an end to the disruption. It is this desire, for instance, that prompts an employee to speak too forcefully with a coworker, or a parent to snap at a complaining child, or a husband to gripe at his disagreeing wife. Most people do not like loose ends, so they convince themselves that they must eliminate the elements in their lives that are outside the realm of what ought to be.

The desire for closure is certainly not strange, nor is it wrong. In its most appropriate form, the effort to tie up loose ends results in assertive communication that brings order and respect into a relationship. Problems arise, however, when the need for closure is so strong that individuals convince themselves they cannot find peace until they succeed in ordering their world to be precisely as they wish. Common sense tells us that a perfect structure does not exist, at least not on this side of Heaven, but if a person becomes consumed with anger and frustration, common sense goes flying out the window. Angry people have difficulty admitting that assertiveness is limited and that it will never eliminate all intrusions.

When I counsel people individually, and when I speak at workshops and conferences, I teach that assertiveness is a better way to gain influence as conflicts are addressed and healing is sought. People can train their minds to set aside maladaptive forms of anger in order to give priority to anger that is constructive and respectful. I also emphasize that assertiveness does not always generate the desired results. Sometimes you can be textbook-perfect in addressing conflicts with an appropriate tone of voice and a cooperative spirit, yet the person on the receiving end may continue in a combative, disinterested, or uncooperative mode. The option exists to attempt to force your good assertion, but usually such a choice leads to aggression or bitterness. Wisdom requires that a separate effort be made in those moments, the effort to accept or forgive.

When I speak with people about reducing their anger by way of acceptance and forgiveness, I often hear words of protest. "So I'm just supposed to let people get away with gross insensitivities, is that what you're telling me?" Such a protest indicates that the person is still clinging to the illusion that closure can always be accomplished, and to suggest otherwise is a form of quitting, or perhaps a display of weakness. I reply that when we each survey our common, everyday experience we are forced to admit that some conflicts simply cannot be satisfactorily resolved. Some people truly do not care how you feel, or at least they are not willing to expend the energy to make a simple change. In those circumstances, if you continue to insist upon closure you are bound to remain entrapped by your own foul mood—guaranteed.

Carol, who was in her early thirties, elected to take a break from her career in pharmaceutical sales to stay home with her young son. Full of energy and ambition, she never thought of herself as a stay-at-home wife. Nonetheless, this is what she had become, and she found that she enjoyed the role more than she once thought she would. Her toddler, Ryan, was a true delight, and she loved tending to his needs. Along the way, she made friends with other young mothers, which she found to be rewarding.

A major problem, however, kept Carol stuck in a pattern of ongoing anger and resentment. She considered her husband, Grant, to be highly insensitive and controlling, and she rarely felt that her efforts to talk with him about their differences proved productive. "He's *very* defensive," she told me, "and he can dissect my arguments so quickly that I often feel bewildered and empty. He never was a great communicator before we became parents, but his behavior didn't affect me as much then because I at least felt like I had some semblance of control over my life. He's very stingy with money, but when we had my extra income, it wasn't as big an issue. Now that he's the sole breadwinner, he seems to think that he's even more in the position of telling me what to do. We've had some pretty ugly knockdown fights over it, and I'm afraid there's no end in sight."

In our counseling, Carol and I explored ways to assert her needs cleanly, and we acknowledged that sometimes she would need to do what she knew to be appropriate even if it meant not having Grant's approval. As a simple illustration, she once bought extra baby supplies because they were on sale. Grant scolded her for spending extra money, and even after she explained that her choice would actually save them money he still fumed and griped. In the past, she would have used such an incident to launch into warfare tactics, but as a result of our counseling, she learned to calmly hold her ground, saying something like "That's the choice I made, and it needs no further explanation." She was learning that she could choose to calmly remain true to her convictions so she would not store a grudge for days on end. Despite Grant's inability to see the good in her assertions, she knew she had to exercise the freedom to make her own choices and judgments. Not to do so would cause her to lose her own self-respect.

Repeatedly, however, Carol would speak to me with great sighs. "How long am I going to have to put up with my husband's bossiness? I despise the fact that he thinks it's OK to lord himself over me. I've tried and I've tried to make him understand that he is not the final authority on every issue in our home, but I haven't gotten very far with that message."

Complicating Carol's emotion was the fact that she had felt unnecessarily confined as a youth by her parents. "My mother and I were at odds frequently," she would recall. "She had a short fuse, so when a problem arose she was virtually incapable of talking things over in a sane fashion. She had lots of eruptions and she was very moody. Dad wasn't much help back then, either. He'd be Mr. Mellow for a while, then suddenly he would erupt! Sometimes I felt like I could count on him to be fair, but he was so inconsistent, I never really felt his good moods could be trusted. Both of my parents were way too restrictive, and I vowed I would never live that way again once I became an adult." Then heaving one of her great sighs, she said, "Grant makes my mother and father's problems seem mild in comparison. When I married him I went from a somewhat controlled life to a *really* controlled life."

I did not disagree with Carol's desire to be released from the debilitating effects of a controlling home environment, but I emphasized that there was only one person in the world she could change, and it wasn't Grant or either of her parents. "Despite your exposure to others who may never think as deeply as you do about emotional maturity, you can still make great steps toward being the kind of person you want to be. Straightforward confrontation can have its place, but even if it's not received you can still choose healthiness. There are many moments when your best option is to accept things as they are, and often you may need to forgive others for their insensitivity."

The first time we discussed the subject, Carol nodded in agreement, and she admitted she could sometimes be so self-righteous that she found forgiveness and acceptance difficult. She vowed to give highest priority to the matter. Afterward, she had several episodes with Grant where she decided that her assertiveness was applied as fully as possible, so it would be advisable to accept him as he was. Likewise, she began making good strides in her relationship with her mother, choosing to show a higher degree of acceptance than in the past.

One day, however, Carol expressed exasperation as she admitted, "Acceptance is such a tedious task. I keep wishing Grant, in particular, would appreciate my efforts and learn to love me more fully. He doesn't seem to recognize that we could have a much fuller life if he would quit being so anal and just trust me more." Then, being very honest, she admitted, "It's going to take a monumental effort for me to keep from becoming filled with resentment."

"Carol," I replied, "most of the examples you cite as reasons for ongoing anger make me recognize that you truly are trying to apply common sense in your relationships with Grant and with your mother. This makes the task of forgiveness all the more frustrating since it's so tempting to question why they can't accept your reasonable ideas. That said, I want to remind you of an analogy you may have heard elsewhere. Holding onto anger and bitterness makes as much sense as you drinking poison, hoping it will kill the other person."

We both chuckled at the absurdity of this analogy, and then I said, "We'll need to stay focused on your efforts to keep your anger from dominating. Rather than counting on these other people to always adjust with you, you can still make headway despite their intransigence."

Acceptance and Forgiveness—An Alternative to Anger

When I talk with people like Carol about choosing acceptance and forgiveness as the better alternative to anger, there are several ideas that we discuss. Let's examine some here.

Bitterness Is Always a Choice

As odd as it may seem, it is good to begin with the reminder that bitterness is always an option as you decide what to do with your anger. In particular, people who have had strong religious teachings feel so compelled to do the right thing that it feels strange to think of bitterness and forgiveness in terms of choice. Many immediately protest: "I'd never *choose* to be bitter; that's a preposterous thought!" Such a protest suggests that once an emotion like bitterness creeps into the personality, it just stays there until some mysterious something makes it go away. Choice is removed from the equation.

Too often, it is tempting to think of forgiveness as an obligation, not one choice among many. Keeping the opposite of forgiveness in the equation can force the angry person to question why forgiveness would be a preferable option. Do you really believe it can be wise to accept others as they are? Do you see yourself as capable of giving priority to personality traits other than anger? Can you really draw upon inner resolve to overcome external frustration? Questions like these can force you to grapple with your true guiding thoughts.

I spoke with Carol about this: "By acknowledging that you could choose to give full energy to your bitterness, I'm asking you to look deeply into your personal priorities. You need to compare what you could gain by clinging to bitterness with what you would gain by forgiving or acceptance."

This approach was new for Carol because she had not been trained to think of emotional responses as a matter of choice. She was accustomed to being told what to do, first by her parents and then by her husband. Now, here was this therapist telling her that she could choose to keep her bitterness, just as she could choose to accept and forgive! The concept made sense to her, yet she was not yet convinced that she liked the full weight of the responsibility that this placed squarely upon her shoulders.

As the days passed, Carol thought frequently about the challenge to weigh the benefits of forgiveness over bitterness. To crystallize her thoughts, she kept a journal and recorded various reflections about her options. Here are a few examples of what she wrote:

- If I choose bitterness, I could make myself feel morally superior to Grant. He'd never change, but I could quietly gloat about my higher reasoning.
- Accepting Grant for what he is would allow me to mentally move on to other more pleasant thoughts, like how blessed I am to be a mother and to have the friends I have.
- Forgiving would mean that I could stop keeping score of right and wrong. Maybe I wouldn't be as petty in my obsession over all the little things I don't like.
- Bitterness would drain me of my ability to be friendly, whereas acceptance would free me to be friendly.
- Thinking about becoming a forgiving person would mean that I have to put more energy into developing my spiritual life, and I like that thought.
- Bitterness means they win; they have charge over my personality. Acceptance means that I would be choosing to stay out of the battle altogether.
- Forgiveness and acceptance cause my influence to rise. No one pays much attention to the right things that a bitter person has to say.

I smiled as Carol read these comments to me, and I remarked, "If you let it happen, lousy circumstances can bring out the best in you. They can force you to question who you really are and whether you can be a decent person even in the midst of undesirable circumstances."

Speaking reflectively, Carol admitted, "When my anger is at its peak, I am mentally at my laziest. I want Grant or whoever is in front of me to do the changing so I won't have to work so hard at it myself. When you told me that bitterness is a choice, it made me realize that forgiving and acceptance are harder, but they're choices too."

I often ponder what perverse pleasure people find when they allow a bitter spirit to take up residence in their hearts. Usually the choice of bitterness allows them to feel temporarily powerful, but it also blinds them from seeing how their good qualities erode, and they eventually become a shell of their optimal selves. As an example, I got Carol to recognize that on the occasions when bitterness gained a foothold, she was less inclined to show her son positive attention. She would withdraw from friends. She was prone to depression.

The cost of choosing bitterness is high, meaning its alternative could prove rewarding.

Understand What Forgiveness Is and What Forgiveness Is Not

Carol made a great effort to be firm in maintaining appropriate boundaries with Grant and to act and speak assertively when necessary. Certainly she had no lack of opportunities to do so because her husband was so consistently out of touch with her needs and feelings. She told me, "I become most disheartened when I realize the permanence of our differences. It doesn't matter how clearly I speak with him about a subject, I can never trust that he's going to be able to digest my thoughts fully and learn to bend a little toward the middle."

Grant continued to criticize often, giving advice when it was not needed. He repeatedly failed to follow through on requests Carol made. Money was an ever-present issue, and despite Carol's genuine efforts to stay within the budget he would fret about finances. In public, Grant would appear friendly and considerate, but away from outsiders he would repeatedly tell his wife what she should have done differently. An exasperated Carol told me, "I know that I'm limited in my ability to change him, but Grant creates more problems than I think I can handle. Some days he's impossible! Accepting him as he is will be a major effort, just as it is to forgive him for his wrongs. He's such a jerk sometimes!"

Carol once mentioned that it seemed that forgiveness would require her to give up on some of her deepest convictions, so I wanted to assure her she could still be true to her beliefs even as she tried to find a way to keep her emotional composure with Grant. In our discussions, we delineated what forgiveness is and what it is not. Here are some ideas we came up with. Forgiveness is not:

- Letting go of healthy communication of anger
- Allowing others to continue disrespectful behavior
- Pretending that everything is normal, as if nothing has happened
- Communicating that past wrongs are insignificant and that everything is fine now
- Acting as though you are best buddies with the one who has done wrong
- Denying the real pain that misdeeds create

Choosing to forgive does not mean going into a pattern of enabling the wrongdoer, or ceasing from being firm in your beliefs. There can be moments when the forgiving person must give a reminder that he or she still wants respect and cooperative behavior. Forgiveness is:

- Dropping the demand for repayment, particularly when efforts have been made to seek restitution and conciliatory response
- Refraining from insulting the wrongdoer, even if the negative sentiment feels justified
- Letting go of the illusion that you can control the wrongdoer's choices
- Choosing to give higher priority to traits like kindness and calmness
- Ceasing obsession about why the wrongdoer acts as he or she does
- Letting God be the final judge regarding another person's misdeeds

I remind people like Carol that forgiveness is usually chosen not because the other person has earned it but because it represents a commitment to internal wholeness. She was quite realistic as she recognized that Grant's problems could go on for years to come. She was not at a point of divorcing him because she realized that the price for such a decision would be too steep, especially now that they had Ryan. Her decision to forgive Grant therefore had to be motivated by her own commitment to self-respect, driven by the fact that she wanted to be the healthiest person possible, even if her husband did not join in the effort.

Love Is More Desirable than Anger

Once you choose to refrain from clinging to bitterness, and you recognize that forgiveness is a reasonable option, you then need to focus on a higher calling. You must determine if love can become more prominent than anger. Most people recognize that it is easy to love when all the right ingredients are in place, but the true test of love comes when conditions do not meet the ideal standards.

Many angry people balk at the idea of trading in their angry responses for more loving alternatives, as if they are being required to act like a Milquetoast weakling. Such a response indicates a grand misunderstanding of the nature of love. Primary among the qualities of love are such traits as patience, kindness, and lack of arrogance. To love means that goodness is prioritized, as is self-restraint. None of these traits is indicative of weakness. They all show inner resolve.

We often confuse the notion of love by thinking that we must be "in love" with the person in question. Imagine a crusty truck driver thinking he must be in love with other crass or crude men before he can get a handle on his anger. Let's just say that such a notion would not carry much weight with someone of that persuasion.

Love is much more than just a sweet, airy feeling. It is commitment to decency, and willingness to release others from conditions that earn acceptance. Love prioritizes a spirit of encouragement over criticism, and it seeks to find what is good, even when the task seems unnatural. Love refuses to remain fixed on the things that have produced pain; instead, it looks toward the possibility of healing.

As I spoke with Carol about giving love priority over anger, she admitted, "I've heard for a long time that love is more than a feeling; it's a choice. Until the last couple of years, I had no idea that it would be so hard. I keep looking for signs from Grant that lead me to believe that he's on the right track with me, but mostly I'm disappointed. This is all coming down to a real test of my willpower."

"If you're like the rest of us humans," I commented, "it's quite easy to let your critical thoughts run away with you. We all want to be right, so it can be incredibly annoying to accept the notion that some relationships may never be fully right."

Carol found that she had to make a choice to love, scene-by-scene. For instance, one Sunday Grant seemed to be in a particularly finicky mood as he complained about several decisions Carol had made. Wisely she told him that her patience was waning, and that they needed to spend a couple of hours apart. She used the time to refocus her emotional direction, and she determined that she would not participate in any further discussion that day regarding her husband's complaints. As she summarized it to me: "I reminded myself that I was going to prioritize patience and tolerance because I believe that such loving efforts are in everyone's best interests. I can still give myself permission to speak firmly if necessary, but I don't want to get drawn into a hateful spirit. Grant is what he is." Specifically, she did not tell herself that she had to act loving for the rest of her life. She only knew that it was Sunday afternoon, and she could choose to apply love's qualities for the next couple of hours.

Loving others often means that you bypass the opportunity to hold another person in contempt as you remind yourself you can ill afford to give priority to your worst traits.

Recognize That High Awareness Comes with a Price

People seeking to curb their anger by way of forgiveness and acceptance recognize that they can succeed only as the mind takes precedence over raw emotional expression. Awareness and insight are valued more than impulsive outburst. Those who succeed in getting out of the anger trap do so as they contemplate who they want to be and how they want to conduct themselves. Thoughtfulness, not blind reaction, is the factor that drives change.

People like Carol who try to apply awareness to their struggle with anger experience both a blessing and a curse. The blessing comes in the form of self-respect as they realize they are taking appropriate responsibility for their own emotional direction. The curse comes as they recognize that significant people in their lives do not have the same desire to be aware and responsible. This leaves them feeling as if their lives are a solo act and that others cannot be counted upon to pull their fair share of the relationship load. They struggle to accept the truth that many people float from one poorly handled circumstance to another without deeply thinking about how to handle problems. They often wonder if they can somehow compel unaware people to become more reflective, thoughtful, and inquisitive about making changes.

Carol once told me, "In our first few years together, I tried to talk with Grant about ways that we could improve our relationship, and specifically how we could handle conflict without it turning into catastrophe. I'd drag him with me to counselors and I'd sign us up for marriage conferences and I'd read books that explained how we could make changes for the better. Finally, I stopped pushing him, and I just lowered my expectations greatly. Now that we have a child, though, I can easily work myself into anger again because I know that eventually his rudeness is going to rub off on our son, and I can hardly bear the thought."

I felt bad for Carol as I listened to her concerns; I knew she was feeling isolated because of Grant's unwillingness to join her in the effort to assimilate a relationship game plan. She knew that our emphasis upon acceptance and forgiveness was the best path to take if she was going to succeed in calming her angry impulses; she just wished that Grant could help at least *some*.

"You're struggling with an issue that's common in many relationships," I reflected. "Whether it's a marriage we're examining, relationships within an extended family, a working partnership, or a friendship, a common problem often emerges. That is, one person shows himself or herself to be willing to apply insights while the other keeps blundering along making no internal adjustments and showing no particular interest in learning anything new or helpful."

"That describes exactly what I'm up against," she said. "Getting Grant to be introspective is about as easy as pushing a rope uphill! It won't happen."

Those like Carol who operate with higher awareness than their counterparts have a choice to make. They can keep attempting to force change in the other person. (This probably will not work, but it is an option.) They can cease efforts to handle their own anger correctly and revert to a poorer form of anger. (This too does not work since it only puts them deeper into a pit of turmoil.) Or they can proceed with a balance between assertion and forgiveness.

I talked with Carol about these options. "Most of us like to see measurable results, so it is tempting to revert back to the anger that seems so justifiable. If you choose to forgive Grant, your reward is internal, not external, and you move forward in your relationship with him knowing you're making the greater effort. Are you up to it?"

She thought carefully about the subject that we were discussing, which made me appreciate her commitment to reply meaningfully to my questions. "I have to admit," she stated pensively, "that I'd like to be rewarded for my good choices by having my husband show appreciation for my efforts, and by having him become a partner with me in being emotionally balanced." Then she added, "I know that's not going to happen anytime soon, but I *can* say that I like *me* better when I let go of my anger and choose to accept him for what he is. If that's the intrinsic reward you're referring to, I can draw some satisfaction from it."

Carol was glad she had a productive mind that could grasp concepts that helped her control her anger. Though she did not receive fully what she wanted in her relationship with Grant, she reminded herself that choosing to forgive was better than remaining committed to destructive anger.

Resist the Urge for Vengeance

One day Carol came for a counseling session, and it was clear that she was very unhappy. Even as we walked in the hallway toward my office, she began telling me about a recent incident in which her mother acted like her old pushy self. Positioning herself on the front of the chair, angry words came spewing forth as Carol told me what happened. "Mother visited me at my house yesterday, and I was having an unusually difficult time with Ryan. He's been in one of those defiant spells, saying no to just about everything, so I was really struggling just to keep my composure. She hadn't done it lately, but this time Mother seized the opportunity to comment on everything I was doing wrong, which meant she was verbally whaling away at me. It reminded me of all the times she criticized me as a child, and how she acted like she was the only person on the planet who knew what was right. I *hate* it when she goes into her condescending mode, and I was ready to scream at her."

"Well, did you?"

"Not quite, but I *did* tell her that I was having a bad day and that I needed some space. She took the hint and left earlier than she had planned. Dr. Carter, I want to go to her and tell her in no uncertain terms how she has loused up my life over and over. I want so badly to remind her that I have a few bad days here and there, but when I was a girl, every day for her was a bad day. She was a bully toward me as a child, and I want her to know she has absolutely no right to come into *my* home talking to me as if I'm obliged to live according to her stupid principles that never worked for her when she was in my position."

Did Carol have a reason to feel angry toward her mother? From what she told me, it seemed she felt violated by her mother's criticisms and her poor timing in speaking words of instruction. I did not fault Carol for wanting to preserve her dignity, and she probably did the right thing when she told her mother that she needed space. This was a good example of assertive anger that needed to be communicated.

What concerned me about Carol's anger was the desire for vengeance that it revealed. I believe good can come when people like her speak openly with others about the hurts that have come over the course of a relationship. I have witnessed firsthand how healing can result when hurt individuals are willing to expose wounds from the past for the purpose of drawing past abuse and conflict to a close. I did not sense, however, that it was for healing reasons that Carol wanted to speak to her mother about their history of frustrating exchanges. Carol was hurt, which prompted her to want to hurt her mother. Virtually never does such an impetus for communication produce anything good.

Vengeance represents a form of anger that is both punitive and humiliating in nature. Some acts (crime, abuse, gross manipulation, and irresponsibility) warrant a form of punishment, but anger in general is not resolved if accompanied by a desire to humiliate. If justice requires punishment, so be it, but the angry person is not helped if a spirit of vengeance persists.

Carol's frustration with her mother is a good illustration that shows the need for ongoing assertiveness, and perhaps even an attempt to discuss past problems for the purpose of their creating a new view of one another. If, however, Carol pressed forward in an attempt to humiliate her mother, she would succeed only in perpetuating the very behavior she chided her mother for having.

I wanted Carol to aim for something higher than what she received as a hurt girl. Part of her pain reduction could come as she identified the wrongs perpetuated by her mother so that she could then identify the better alternatives and commit to them. For instance, she and I talked about the qualities she wished her mother had shown during Carol's own childhood. Carol identified traits such as understanding, patience, and flexibility that would have made a positive difference in her childhood home. I then challenged her: "When you see your mother acting contrary to these good qualities, it's reasonable to set boundaries and refuse to become drawn into a pattern that generates further pain. Once that happens, you can then determine that your life will become a living illustration of the better way. Personal composure, not vengeance, is your greatest pronouncement that you believe in your own ethic. By rising above the temptation to squash an antagonist, you have a better chance for personal peace and your influence over the antagonist can potentially increase."

Pursuing vengeance inevitably requires a deeper commitment to anger. Forgiving the wrongdoer does not have to preclude appropriate retribution or addressing of the problem, but it does imply that there is a commitment to move forward in life without repeatedly drawing upon past wrongs. One man who chose forgiveness over vengeance described his decision this way: "I have learned that when I focus so heavily in extracting payback for someone's wrong deeds, my personality is so flooded with spite that I have become the very kind of person that creates anger in me. I don't want to be hypocritical, so that means I need to model the behavior that I'm asking from the other person."

Acknowledge That You Too Need Forgiveness

The only person who truly has the prerogative not to forgive is the one who has never done wrong. Humanity's innate inclination to err is the great equalizer that prohibits one person from holding too strongly to an attitude of superiority over another. My wrongdoing may not seem as awful as your wrongdoing, but the fact that I do wrong means that I am never capable of being so objective that I can accurately pronounce judgment upon another. It is this awareness that is behind the Christian instruction, "Judge not, lest you be judged."

Admitting your own need for forgiveness can be difficult because you don't want to think you are on the same low level as the one who needs your forgiveness. I tell people who struggle with this issue that it is wisest not to keep score regarding who is a better or worse human. We each are influenced by such diverse environmental, historical, and biological factors that it is virtually impossible to correctly determine who is healthy and who is not. I teach instead that the choice to refrain from lording over wrongdoers is essential, if for no other reason than that it keeps the forgiving person free from being emotionally chained to the one who has brought hurt.

Carol and I spoke about the truth that forgiveness could be a major factor in keeping her anger balanced: "You genuinely have good reasons to feel annoyed as you contend with the ongoing problem of your husband's and mother's insensitivities. Yet I'm going to guess that if I spoke with each of them about their interactions with you, they would be able to cite incidents when they felt they received less-than-honorable treatment in reverse."

"You'd be guessing correctly," she said. "It's no secret that in my frustrated moments I'm capable of saying and doing things that don't help matters at all. I can be bombastic and harsh sometimes."

I asked how she would prefer to be treated when she erred, and she quickly replied, "I'd like to be forgiven." Then she grinned and asked, "Are you about to give me a 'Do unto others as you would have them do unto you' speech?"

"Hmm. I don't think I need to because you already know that speech by heart."

You know how uncomfortable you feel when others refuse to release you from wrong deeds, indicating an unwillingness to accept you as you are. You also know that when you experience forgiveness and acceptance, you are more inclined to show a cooperative spirit toward the one offering it. Your own appreciation for the act of forgiveness can become the motivating factor for you to give it freely to those who have wronged you.

Forgiveness is a gift that is offered, freely chosen, with no strings attached. Although pure forgiveness is accomplished with no expectation of a reward from the recipient, the prospects for a cooperative atmosphere increase once it is offered. Angry people look for relief from painful experiences, and just as they sometimes find that proper assertiveness can generate the desired response, so too might they learn that forgiveness creates improved relations.

Even if you do not receive in full measure what you have given, you still prosper because the resulting calmness is far more rewarding than remaining inside your anger trap.

For Personal Reflection

- In what circumstances have you considered being assertive, only to determine that it would not achieve the desired results? Who in your world do you need to forgive?
- In what circumstances might you be tempted to justify clinging to bitterness? Why would forgiveness or acceptance be a better alternative?
- What misconception have you had about the nature of forgiveness? How can you know that forgiveness is a demonstration of strength, not defeat?
- What do you believe about the idea that love is more desirable than anger? How would such a belief guide you as you consider forgiving others?
- To forgive, you may have to accept that others will not appreciate or even recognize the goodness of your effort. What is the best way to handle such a possibility?
- Why is vengeance ultimately harmful to your quality of life?
- In what circumstances do you need to be forgiven? How can awareness of this need assist you as you determine how to handle your anger?

12

A MIND OF EQUALITY

ONE OF THE GREATEST hindrances to anger being appropriately communicated is the tendency of angry people to speak or act condescendingly. Even when the message of anger is reasonable, the receiver of the message is likely to reject it if it is accompanied by a manner that attempts to belittle. In common terminology, we refer to this as "talking down" to the other person. Anyone who has misused anger (and that includes all of us) has done this many times, whether with open aggression or passive-aggressiveness.

Each time anger is expressed, the receiver has to sift through two messages, the overt and the covert. The overt message is the spoken word, while the covert is the insinuated, implied meaning. Practically always, the covert message is the more dominant, so even if the overt message is reasonable, when it is accompanied by a condescending covert message it is lost.

For instance, suppose you are working on a project and you get the distinct impression that your partner thinks poorly of your methods. He is stubborn and unhelpful, and he openly second-guesses your decisions. Receiving this less-than-cooperative treatment, you are likely to feel as if you are in the "down" position. How would you respond? Many people in such a predicament look for a way to gain the upper position. You might convince yourself that he is so inept that his thoughts carry no weight at all. You might respond to his suggestions with a quick rebuttal detailing the error of the suggestion. Perhaps you would look for an opportunity to speak to a third party, cataloguing all the ways that he displays ineptness. It could be that you respond with quiet noncooperation, driven by an "I'll show you" attitude.

Whenever you feel that another person thinks of you in a lowly manner, you are highly likely to be tempted to reverse the situation by somehow putting yourself above your antagonist. It is this dynamic that commonly keeps individuals stuck in nonproductive forms of anger. Rather than speaking respectfully about needs and convictions, they turn their communications into a battle for superiority.

Let's revisit Jeff, the electronic engineer introduced in Chapter Five who regular erupted with his wife, Katy, and their three children. As I tried to get him to acknowledge the futility of control, I wanted him to recognize that he would unwittingly play a one-up, one-down game with others when he got angry. This approach almost never produced good results.

With memories of a heavy-handed father lodged in his mind, he was determined never to feel belittled again as he had been in his youth. Because of his history of feeling abased, Jeff tended to interpret others' noncooperation as a personal affront, as if he were considered lowly and of no consequence. One evening he and Katy were trying to juggle their schedules, and they were having a hard time agreeing how to proceed. When Katy made known a preference, he responded forcefully with, "That's ridiculous." When she asked him to clarify his own preferences, he snapped: "I know what I'm talking about, so I don't need you trying to pick my words apart."

As we sat in my office discussing how his anger was mishandled in this simple incident, I asked, "Do you recognize how powerfully you attempt to speak from a position of superiority when you and Katy are at odds?"

A puzzled look crossed his face as he replied, in all innocence, "You're going to have to explain that one to me, Doc, because I don't see it."

"Take your comment, 'That's ridiculous.' I don't fault you for having a separate opinion from Katy's, but it seems that you took her expression as an invitation to go to battle. Through that simple comment, you were attempting to establish that your order of reasoning is higher, and that you could not stoop to her lower, inadequate reasoning. At that moment, the discussion turned from an effort to weigh the options to a battle for supremacy."

Jeff was able to recognize that indeed his words represented an attempt to put Katy into a lower position, and as we continued to discuss the matter he cited many other incidents of a similar pattern. For instance, he often assumed a judgmental attitude toward family members who thought differently from him. In a disagreement, he would interrupt frequently because he was convinced his opinions were more valid. He struggled to be patient with his children because he hated their not maintaining his high standards. I explained to him, "Each time you belittle, invalidate, or criticize, you are assuming a position of superiority, as if you have the higher order of thought."

Being candid, Jeff admitted, "Quite honestly, there are times when I feel that my opinions *are* superior. My wife can come up with some really dopey ways of doing things, and my kids' reasoning is usually childish. I think it would be wrong to just let my family run loose with inadequate rationale."

"I'm glad you have confidence in your perceptions," I mentioned. "I'm not hinting that you should abandon good principles. I *am* assuming, however, that your wife and kids believe their perceptions make sense, or at least to them. That being the case, it would serve everyone's best interest to allow each person involved in a conflict to have the same right to an opinion as anyone else."

Performance Standards

A common mistake made by angry people is to overlook the human dimension, relating instead as if others were mere performers. Rather than recognizing that every individual is bound to bring his or her emotions and perceptions to the relationship, they focus too heavily on measurable results, or they attempt to reduce people to a logical machine. If the performance or logic does not measure up to the angry person's criteria, the other person is dismissed as inadequate.

Jeff had already talked with me about his memories of his own father being bombastic and free with criticism. He elaborated: "My dad put a very high premium on doing things right. He could not tolerate illogic, nor would he stand by idly when a person showed weakness. He just *had* to correct you, and when he did it was never pleasant."

"How would that leave you feeling?"

"Angry and sad. I'd be angry because he never would make the effort to really know me from the inside out. I felt sad because it hurt that he couldn't accept anything short of his standards." Jeff went on to explain that he felt his father wanted to remove the emotional side of his personality, turning him into something like a trained seal. He explained, "If I could just learn to jump through his hoops, he'd have been totally satisfied."

Evaluation Emphasis

Many angry people, like Jeff, grew up with an emphasis on making the grade, or doing things right. Whenever they exposed a need, a hurt, or a unique perspective, they were quickly confronted with the requirement to conform to a fixed standard. If Jeff told his dad he was frustrated because a friend had disappointed him, he was abruptly told that it was not good to let someone have that kind of hold on him; he should learn to proceed without worrying about what the friend did. No discussion was pursued regarding the emotional dimension of his dilemma. Likewise, if he struggled with a homework assignment, he was told he'd better figure it out so he would not receive a bad grade. Again, no attention was paid to his emotions.

Jeff summarized, "I felt like I was always being compared to some perfect standard and always falling short." Indeed, his father apparently was unable to understand that people exist for reasons other than making the grade. So uncomfortable was he with the nonperformance aspects of life that he was unable to know his son as a person. Ironically, although Jeff complained easily about his father's stiffness, once he became a husband and a dad he unwittingly incorporated the relational patterns he had disliked in his father.

Performance is a part of every life. From the earliest years, children are taught to clean their room, finish schoolwork, get ready for bed in a timely fashion, or help with domestic chores. It is reasonable to emphasize excellence in the many performances of life, and it is irresponsible not to attempt to perform well. Simply put, productivity and reliability are core ingredients of a healthy personality.

Some people, however, put so much emphasis on correct performance that it seems as if little else matters. A telltale sign of this imbalance is heavy use of evaluative words: *excellent, good, poor, terrific, so-so, outstanding, awful.* As they observe life, performance-based people can hardly refrain from giving a grade to the things they witness. As an example, if Katy had difficulty getting their child to obey, he would comment, "That's not good." If a fellow employee finished a project early, he might comment, "This is excellent." If the same employee struggled to get a project completed, Jeff would mutter under his breath, "This is ridiculous." He seemed to perpetually measure people by their achievement and habitually pass judgment on the result of their effort.

As I discussed this matter with him, Jeff asked, "What's so bad about that?"

"It's not inherently wrong to have standards and evaluations for performance. In fact, at times it can be good when we exhort each other to do our best. I'm concerned about the possibility of emphasizing evaluation to the extent that you hold yourself as one who has the right to judge, and you forget that this is a human being you're referring to, someone with real feelings and needs that can be addressed."

As an example, when Jeff witnessed Katy struggling to discipline their child, rather than evaluating her ("This is not good") he could take the time to explore the frustration she felt at that moment. If an employee finished a task ahead of schedule, he could comment on the gratification he felt, and if the employee struggled to complete a task he could talk about the difficulties experienced. Rather than merely assessing the person's skills or logic, he could address the inside of the person.

To get an idea of whether you relate with a strong evaluative emphasis, look over these indicators. Do any seem familiar?

- ❍ Strong emphasis on achievement and doing things right
- ❍ Discomfort when others' feelings are different or outside the box
- ❍ Upon hearing others' problems, telling them how to handle the problem
- ❍ Being known for having unbending standards
- ❍ An easy inclination to think critically
- ❍ Difficulty revealing personal weakness or need
- ❍ Tendency to carry too much guilt, or to motivate others through guilt
- ❍ Being careful to maintain a proper image with friends and acquaintances
- ❍ Assuming that people who have failed should be given less credibility
- ❍ Expressing opinions far more easily than expressing feelings

As you overemphasize the performance aspects of life, you are unwittingly caught in a mind-set that assumes some people are higher in value and some are lower. When frustration and irritability come upon you, the one-up, one-down mentality can play out fully. Sometimes you express anger because you feel that others think of you as inferior, and your anger compels you to show that you indeed are not inferior, but superior. At other times, you experience anger because you cannot tolerate presumably inferior behavior from others, and you feel it is your job to uphold the standard. Either way, the anger you express leads to increased tension.

Finding Perspective

As Jeff and I discussed his inclination toward anger, it became clear to him how quickly he turned a common exchange into a referendum about the superiority of his thinking. We agreed that as long as he continued to do so, he could expect trouble since it was highly predictable that no one in his world would gladly receive the label of inferior. I explained to him, "As you make the necessary adjustments in your anger, it would be helpful to gain a full perspective regarding the origins of this pattern."

Focusing on his early years, I suggested: "When you were a boy, you learned very early that there was a definite pecking order in relationships. Numerous times each day, you were reminded that the adults got to call the shots, and whether you liked it or not, you had to comply. They were in the high position; you were in the low position." He mentioned learning at an early age that he'd better respect adult authority, so yes, he could relate to what I was saying.

"Adding to this way of thinking," I said, "as you aged you also became aware that your peer group would be divided into the have's and have not's. Some gained significance because they made higher grades. Others were known as having the best social skills. Some gained prominence because they looked good or had athletic skills, or they had more money, or they knew the right people. No doubt, you learned early in life that some people seemed capable of shedding any label of inferiority by gaining status through these various means. In fact, many of the relational efforts made by young people are for the purpose of establishing themselves as having higher qualities while distancing themselves from lower qualities. If you ever found yourself being tagged as a person on the lower end of any of these scales, you learned to compensate for the feeling of inadequacy by discounting those who thought of themselves as higher than you."

"That is so true," Jeff reflected. "I never really thought of it very deeply before now, but it's clear that childhood consists of great efforts to posture for positioning. I can see that it occurred within my family, and it certainly occurred among my friends, especially when I was in my teens. In fact, I can see this very pattern every day in my own kids' lives. It's a big deal to each of them to be thought of as having some superior qualities."

"Of course, this trend doesn't cease once people enter adulthood," I mentioned. "We adults like to think of ourselves as more polished than our youthful counterparts, but in many respects we're the same. We grade each other on the kind of car we drive, or the size of our home, or the type of work we do. In social settings, we are careful to conceal personal failures, but we don't mind people learning about our successes. We want to look right and be associated with the best people. It's all part of the lifelong process of wanting to be deemed as a little better than the next person."

Jeff queried, "Do you really think this posturing for superiority is *that* prominent?"

"Sure it is," I said. "Think of the simplest ways that we adults try to one-up each other. For example, if you tell someone about a good restaurant that you went to, she'll tell you about a favorite restaurant that's just a little better. If you talk about a home run that your son hit in a ball game, someone is likely to chime in and tell about the time his son hit two home runs! We do this sort of thing with each other all the time." We both chuckled as we recognized just how common this habit is.

It was then that I asked Jeff, "Can you see how this vying for the upper position takes its toll on emotional healthiness? I'd guess you're like me in the sense that you feel weary from the effort to stay one up. Anger can be aroused when you feel wrongly judged by others, and you provoke anger in others when you act as if they're beneath you. We all play the game at one time or another, yet we each feel annoyed as it happens."

A Mind of Equality

When I counsel angry people for the purpose of bringing balance to their emotions, I try to shift their emphasis away from the effort to be superior by emphasizing that we can relate with an understanding that humans are equal to one another. This concept is certainly not new to the people I talk with, and most agree theoretically with my words. Yet I find that much mental adjustment is required as we grapple with the implications of equality.

I spoke about it with Jeff: "When you were young you recognized that different people possessed different amounts of authority or privilege. For example, adults got to drive a car while the grade school kids could not. Likewise, the adults were able to establish the rules of the house and the children had to obey, and if they did not they experienced consequences. In addition, you became aware that your peers possessed separate talents and skills, and as a result some seemed to enjoy more rewards while others enjoyed fewer."

Then shifting gears, I posed this thought: "Did anyone take the time to discuss with you that these differences could be understood as just that? They were simply differences. Having dissimilar skills or positions or experiences meant nothing more than that we're not the same. Differentness is not an indication of being superior or inferior. Instead, our differentness highlights the reality that we are each a unique individual living a unique life and experiencing unique outcomes. Nothing more, nothing less."

Shaking his head, Jeff said, "No one ever talked with me about those kinds of things. If anything, we had more of an emphasis on the opposite way of thinking. If I had total recall, I could recount hundreds of things that were said to compartmentalize people. I can remember, as an example, how my father would refer to unskilled laborers as losers. Also, he was not kind toward people of other ethnic groups. And if he ever learned about someone failing or experiencing difficulties, he could be brutal in his cutting remarks. I guess you could say that the concept of equality was nonexistent in my home."

"Staying with my line of reasoning," I responded, "would you be willing to amend your thoughts about unskilled laborers as losers?" Jeff nodded, and I realized that it frustrated him that such foul thinking had ever been planted in his mind. I continued, "It would be appropriate to recognize them as people of equal value who happen to perform functions that differ from other workers. Likewise, there's no need to think of people of other ethnic groups as being higher or lower. They simply have a separate heritage to draw from. The same could be said of people who have failed or experienced problems. Their struggles do not have to detract from their standing among others, given the fact that we each can struggle in some way with life's imperfections."

Descriptive Thinking

To develop a mind of equality, it is helpful to set aside the chronic tendency to grade one another, and to think descriptively instead. This requires great discipline, since most people have lived most of their lives giving and receiving evaluations. The difference comes in the refusal to place a judgment upon someone's feelings or experience. Instead, we can focus on the internal elements experienced in a given event.

Suppose a family member promised to do you a favor but failed to follow through. You could evaluate the behavior by stating that it is lousy and stupid. You could chastise the person by calling him an idiot. You could defame his character by telling others that he is no good. In the end, what have you gained? Perhaps you feel a temporary surge of superiority, and you would be the holder of anger and cynicism. You would certainly not be a better person for dwelling on such thoughts.

On the other hand, you could respond to the one who has failed to deliver as promised by using descriptive thoughts. First, you could admit that you feel disappointed. You could recognize that the other person has had a tendency to manage time in a less-than-efficient manner. You could even choose not to include that person in vital plans in the future. All the while, you could refrain from judging or grading the person.

I explained to Jeff, "When you choose not to grade another person, you are not requiring yourself to deny your feelings or to cease having standards. You *are,* however, recognizing that you do not need to think of yourself as better than anyone. Honestly describe what you are feeling and thinking while accepting the truth that you serve no good purpose when you hold a person in contempt, as if he is beneath you."

Shortly after this discussion, Jeff had several opportunities to be descriptive while refraining from taking a superior position. Here are a couple of the things that happened:

- Two of his children were arguing vigorously over something trivial. In the past, he would have verbally blasted the youngsters and reprimanded them for being so impossible to live with. This time, however, Jeff said: "Looks like you two have some strong concerns that need to be addressed. Let's take a thirty-minute time-out to let cooler heads prevail, then I'd like to hear from each of you separately. I'm sure you'll both have something valid you want the other to understand."
- One Saturday, his wife spent more money than he would have liked for some household supplies. In the past, he would have labeled her irresponsible, and it would have set off a major argument. This time Jeff said: "I guess there were more items on your wish list than we had anticipated. Let's talk about how we can keep this from becoming too much of a burden on the budget."

When I asked Jeff what made a difference in his approach, he showed great insight. He told me, "For years my anger has been conveyed as if I were the only perfect person on the planet, and I had the misfortune of having to bide my time with people who were beneath me. I can't keep doing that, so I put myself in their position as I tried to think of how I'd like to be addressed if the roles were reversed. I've got to admit that this way of thinking isn't 100 percent natural yet, but it sure does decrease the amount of anger and tension. I can definitely get used to that!"

Thinking descriptively requires you to enter into the humanity of the other person. What is he or she feeling? What is the rationale behind his or her choices? Why would this person respond in that manner? What does he or she want you to understand? As you think in this manner, you are less likely to judge and more likely to think of others as equal partners.

The Personal Touch

Prior to counseling, Jeff frequently rationalized his condescending treatment toward his wife. "Maybe I can be impatient," he might have said, "but it's because she's such a poor time manager." Or "I know I shouldn't speak so forcefully, but how else am I supposed to get her to listen? She just tunes people out!" His own problematic behavior was dismissed as he put a greater focus on the other person's lower status.

As I got to know Jeff, I would regularly call his hand when he verbally put Katy in the down position for her humanness. For instance, when he blamed his impatience on her time management skills, I would respond: "Even if you don't like the way she prioritizes, she's still a real person with real value. You could choose to factor that in as you discuss how to coordinate time with her." Likewise, when he blamed his being forceful on her lack of attentiveness, I would say, "You could address your needs openly even as you show a willingness to comprehend what she has on her mind. If you treat her as an equal, you will gain a greater level of cooperation."

In time, Jeff was able to admit that his problematic anger was experienced in direct proportion to his willingness to act as if he were higher than others. His wife, children, and coworkers were not always ideal in their behavior, but neither was he the easiest person to live with. Acting superior meant he was conveniently forgetting his own humanness.

As you embrace the mind of equality and choose to speak as one equal to another, specific changes can be observed in addressing anger-provoking circumstances. Here are some of the most common.

The Goal Is Not to Win

When in a dispute, you can proceed with the realization that it is not your ultimate goal to win.

Many angry exchanges are accompanied by a convincing effort, an attempt to prove that your way of thinking is the winning way, while the other person's is the losing way. To succeed in convincing, you have to reduce the other person to underling status. (Our English word *convince* is derived from a Latin root word meaning "to conquer.")

A healthy person wants nothing to do with the desire to verbally conquer others. In winning, you only build your feeling of security by causing someone else to feel lowly. It is a hollow victory indeed. Instead of setting out to win, you can make it your goal to clearly explain your feelings or thoughts—nothing more, nothing less. It is not your job to force-feed your thoughts, only to be true to what you believe.

Give the Other Person Time

Once you have expressed yourself, allow the other person the opportunity to digest your thoughts at his or her own pace.

Remaining in a mind-set of equality, you can recognize that there is no fixed way for people to absorb one another's thoughts. Some process confrontation from another person quickly, while others need time to mull it over. An argumentative spirit represents an attempt to think on behalf of the other person. Allowing the other person the chance to receive information in his or her own time is a show of respect. This means being succinct in your expression, rather than repeating yourself or being unnecessarily wordy.

You Have Options in Responding

If others are not cooperative or understanding, you need not respond in kind.

Even as you make the effort to manage your anger clearly, there is no certainty that others will join in the same good efforts. When you attempt to address conflict, for example, as one equal speaking with another, a response could take the form of an invitation to join in competing for the superior position. At such a time, you can choose not to join in such unnecessary posturing.

For instance, Jeff was convinced he should be far less authoritarian in speaking with his children during conflict. Though he still wanted to maintain a leadership role with them, he recognized that his children could be treated as individuals of equal value to himself. In one situation, he reprimanded his son for not following through on a task. In the process, he was determined to speak in a respectful, even tone of voice. The son's response was a clear attempt to establish superiority: "You're not perfect, so why should I be expected to be perfect?" His voice was animated and challenging. In the past, Jeff would have taken such a response as an opportunity to prove who *really* had the superiority. This time, however, he chose to continue with his spirit of equality. Knowing that in his past he too had spoken defiantly to authority figures, he kept calm and said, "I know that you and I are not seeing eye to eye right now, but I'm still holding to my request. It needs to be done." Jeff wisely recognized that his willingness to speak respectfully did not need to be derailed because of another person's errant agenda.

Stick to the Point

As you express assertiveness, stick to the subject.

A common tactic used by angry people is piling on subjects to be corrected by the other person. In this scenario, a need to confront a specific problem is accompanied by the worry that the subject will be summarily dismissed. To add strength to the confrontation, then, angry people may recall other problematic behaviors that are not really germane to the original topic. This represents a blatant attempt to establish superiority in the sense that it is done deliberately to weaken any retort that might be given by the other person. If enough evidence is offered, the reasoning goes, to prove that the other person's overall behavior is indeed inferior, the angry confronter can gain the superior position and thereby win.

People operating from equality have nothing to do with such tactics. Not wanting to demean, they speak about the subject at hand with the assumption that it is fair to let the confrontation stand on its own merit with no attempt to posture for a higher position over the other.

No Exaggeration

Avoid terms of exaggeration.

You have probably noticed that angry individuals often resort to exaggeration as they attempt to share feelings of hurt or disappointment. They may say something like "You're so impossible that I don't know what to do," or "I cannot imagine why anyone would possibly choose to treat someone the way you treat me." They may have a valid point, but exaggerating has one primary goal: to shame the other person into submission. It represents an attempt to generate feelings of inferiority in the other person for the purpose of being above. People committed to equality stick to the subject, and they feel no need to create a lowly feeling by making problems out to appear larger than they really are.

Refrain from Character Assassination or Other Forms of Condescension

In anger, the temptation exists to make the other person seem inadequate by means of speaking poorly about his or her character. For instance, more than once, Jeff said to Katy something like "Why should I trust you when you have such a long history of not honoring your word?" or "I wouldn't be nearly so frustrated if I were sure you were someone who truly knew how to love, but you're nothing more than a taker." Whatever idea he wanted her to consider would be completely lost, as she would feel deeply hurt and insulted by such jabs.

In time, Jeff recognized that character assassination had no place in a thriving relationship. Even when he detected flaws in his wife's character, he would remind himself that he too had personal defects. Rather than engaging in slanderous communication, he determined to let his feelings be addressed directly, with no judgment given regarding her integrity. This adjustment caused Katy to feel he was confronting her for the purpose of finding harmony as opposed to finding dominance.

Give Away Respect

See respectfulness as a gift to give away, especially in moments of conflict.

I make the assumption that anyone can act respectfully if others are behaving exactly as one would want. When others think, feel, or respond less than ideally, it can be tempting to seek the superior position. "Permission" is taken to treat others as inferior because, well, they are acting lowly.

When others behave in a less-than-respectful or dignified manner, it is a signal that they are struggling to find their own significance. They are hurting and are confused. Those operating with an attitude of equality can recall that they too have had episodes of feeling insignificant or hurt. Rather than using the other person's poor behavior as an opportunity to pounce, they maintain dignity. They refuse to seize upon another person's pain as a chance to establish superiority. They recognize instead that respect is maintained even when others are struggling to keep their own self-respect intact.

As Jeff contemplated how he could adjust his anger communication to incorporate an attitude of equality, he illustrated that a positive, fundamental shift in his thinking was occurring: "For years, I would take my cues from others as I would choose how to manage my anger, and that was dangerous. I'm realizing that I can't let my emotions be so haphazard. Even if others are way off base in their treatment of me, I can operate with my own game plan. I have to stop to think how I'd want to be treated, and then proceed accordingly. I'm tired of turning conflict into a win-lose situation because every time I do so, we all lose."

Jeff was catching on to the notion that the secret to clean anger management lies in rearranging inner attitude, not external circumstance.

o

For Personal Reflection

- In what way is anger an attempt to one-up another person? What methods do you commonly use to accomplish this?
- Why do you allow yourself to be drawn into competition to outargue another person? What are you hoping to accomplish?
- In your early years, how important was it for you to receive good evaluation? What effect did your drive to achieve have on your emotions?

- Why do some people struggle to treat others as equals? In what circumstances do you struggle to treat someone as an equal?
- If you were to give higher priority to the equal value of every person, how would your methods of managing anger improve?
- How would your communication of anger change if you chose to judge less, opting instead to describe your feelings and perceptions?
- Even as you attempt to relate as an equal to another, others still might act as if they are superior to you. How can you keep from becoming drawn into a futile war of one-up, one-down communication?

13

THE WAY OF THE OVERCOMER

ONE MONDAY in the lunchroom at our clinic, a staff doctor was clearly in a foul mood. Rather than joining in the friendly chitchat of the rest of the employees, he was sullen and quiet. A frown seemed permanently etched on his face, and he was curt in his remarks. An avid football fan, he had attended a college football game two days prior, and his team unexpectedly lost. He spoke dejectedly about the lousy game plan put together by the coaches and the poor performance by the players. Clearly, in his estimation, the day had been a disaster and given him nothing to feel good about. "Leave me alone" was written all over him.

At the same time, another doctor was acting quite friendly and upbeat. He had positive things to say to the other staff members, and he was unable to remove the smile on his face. He too had gone to a football game the prior Saturday. In fact, it was the same game attended by the other doctor. He spoke of the excellent play, praised the coaches, and was clearly buoyed by the fact that the best team won.

Two men had participated in the same experience, and yet their emotional responses differed greatly. How did that happen? Of course, they each cheered for their own team, and their reactions reflected the final score of the game. More tellingly, their separate emotions illustrated that they each had a mental filtering system that prompted them to interpret the event in their own way.

Whether you are aware of it or not, in every circumstance your mind filters the events in front of you and tells you how to react. That filter consists of attitudes, priorities, biases, prior experiences, needs, desires, and expectations. Sometimes your filter tells you to respond with enthusiasm, other times with boredom. Your filter may tell you that you should feel sad, or to be wary, or it may prompt feelings of contentment.

Because of the subjective nature of the key ingredients in this mental filter, there is no certainty that it will cause an emotional response to be sound, mature, or stable. In fact, the problem of disruptive anger illustrates that some people are predisposed to a foul mood because their filtering system causes them to assume that the world is a difficult place and that the only way to respond to its stimulation is with force, stubbornness, punitive measures, or withdrawal. There may be poor logic involved in the response, yet the filter system can be so powerful that it causes an individual to shun reason and respond in a way that ultimately creates more problems than solutions.

A Mind of Distress

When people are trapped by their own ongoing anger, inevitably they develop a distressed approach toward other people and circumstances. A mind of distress can be defined as a tendency to interpret events with pessimism and futility, leading to a reaction of tension or emotional collapse. People in ongoing distress have a mental filter that tells them the world is bad and not to be trusted. They cite anecdotal evidence of situations that turned sour, to justify to themselves why they are right in responding to their environment harshly or defensively.

Recall Carol, the young mother who was taking time out from her career to stay home with her young son. Most people meeting her would assume she was optimistic and upbeat, given her friendly and extroverted temperament. She always enjoyed being with friends, and her life as a mom certainly gave her many opportunities to get to know other women with similar lifestyles.

Despite her sanguine demeanor, she tended to live with an edge of irritability and aggravation while interacting with her mother and her husband, Grant. Earlier in her life, she indeed had reason to feel angry with her mother because of their history of broken communication and poorly managed conflict. Likewise, she also could justify her anger toward Grant, given his critical demeanor and difficulty in processing emotions with her. As she and I discussed handling her anger with clean assertions and establishment of relationship boundaries, I noted that Carol had a habit of clinging to her anger even after it had seemingly played out its usefulness.

As an example, one weekend she sensed that Grant seemed out of it as he went about the routine matters that consumed their time together. He spoke in one-word responses and seemed quite disinterested in the things Carol had to say. Appropriately, she talked with him about his behavior, and she expressed the hope that he would snap out of his funk and join her in making their weekend a pleasant and relaxing experience. To his credit, Grant received her words well and made specific attempts to adjust.

A few days later, as Carol spoke with me about their time together, she commented, "Even though Grant's mood changed for the better, I found myself struggling with irritability for the rest of the weekend. It bothered me that I had to ask him to be nice. It seems that the only way I can get him to become a decent person is to spell it out very clearly to him. He's a grown man! Why can't he be a good person without having to be prodded first?"

Carol responded to a negative situation with assertiveness, and it paid positive dividends. Yet she continued to struggle with simmering anger. What was going on? Her mental filter system told her that she could not be satisfied with Grant's response because she knew that it did not represent a full and permanent adjustment. Given his track record, she knew his adjustment was temporary, and she was already borrowing frustration from future circumstances that would be similar to the current one. More important, her mind was telling her: "He's done this to me too many times. I can't go on like this. It's too difficult."

Feelings of Victimization

Subtly, Carol's mind of distress allowed her to take on the role of the victim. Although she was understandably upset at having spent years trying to figure out how to respond to others' moods, she obsessed about the unfairness of life's predicament to the extent that she could not shake her feeling of aggravation.

Victimization is a common experience among angry people. "Look what you've done to make my life difficult" is the common complaint they levy against others. In many cases, hurt and annoyance are valid, so it would be wrong to state that people who feel angry because of others' mistreatment are imbalanced for feeling as they do. A victim is defined as one who has received undue subjection to suffering, injury, or loss. Certainly, in many anger-provoking circumstances the one experiencing the anger is right to want to stand up against foul treatment.

Carol could recall many episodes when Grant was harshly critical, neglectful, or unreliable. Sometimes, he was just mean in how he treated her. Likewise, Carol could tell of numerous times, past and present, when her parents were anything but supportive of her. Her mother, in particular, could be argumentative, and she often left Carol feeling baffled by her unwillingness to show flexibility or extend kindness.

Was Carol a victim? According to the definition, yes. She certainly was unduly subjected to suffering, injury, and loss. As such, she had good reason to be assertive, explaining her needs clearly and setting stipulations where necessary. In our counseling, though, we discussed how she would need to take care not to allow her victimization to become so central to her emotions that she lost her initiative to get beyond her anger once it ran its course.

Some people turn their victim status into a centerpiece, placing a disproportionate amount of emphasis upon their suffering. They can exaggerate their anger until it becomes inappropriate rage or chronic agitation, and their personality can be consumed by the need to have others prove that they will never again subject them to injurious feelings. They either express anger too strongly or frequently toward the one who has mistreated, or displace their anger onto those who are not directly involved in victimizing.

During one holiday celebration, Carol was at the home of a relative when her mother made a critical comment about something relatively minor. To be sure, the comment was unnecessary, but it was also innocuous enough that it could have been ignored. For several minutes, Carol silently stewed about her mother's insensitivity; then, without warning, she motioned for her husband and son to step to the front porch of the relative's home. Informing them that it was time to leave, the family drove off without saying a word to the rest.

Carol had convinced herself that her mother would make the rest of the visit miserable, so her anger prompted her to make a preemptive strike. In that instant, she was not just acting as a victim but as *the* victim. So focused was she on the potential for suffering at the hand of her mother that she could not contain her anger. Her mother had actually made improvement in the months prior to the incident and shown some receptiveness to Carol's assertions. Nonetheless, it was difficult for her to shed her victim status because it had defined her for so many years.

The Defeatist Attitude

Alongside the problem of victimization is an attitude of defeat within an angry person stuck in a mind of distress. Defeatism can be defined as succumbing to a position of hopelessness resulting in chronic cynicism, bitterness, or depression. Effort might be made to overcome problems, only to fail again. "Who cares?" and "What's the use?" are commonly heard from people who suffer from defeatism.

I recall talking with a single man in his forties who had been disappointed in key relationships in his past. His father abandoned the family in his childhood and never played a significant role in his life as an adult. During his college years, his mother remarried and moved to another state, becoming less available to him. He married, only to have his wife commit adultery with not one man but two. Several friends deserted him along the way, and he was employed in a career that paid the bills but did not offer great stimulation or challenge.

As this man talked to me, he told me he had been dating a woman for two years and could find no serious flaws in her. She was kind, loyal, and responsible. Yet despite her positive qualities, he allowed a sour spirit to become prominent, and she was complaining about his being increasingly moody and erratic. He explained to me, "Quite candidly, I'm afraid to love her. She's shown no inclination to treat me in any way other than good. I guess I'm so used to having relationships fall apart that I'm just expecting it to happen even when the evidence tells me otherwise."

Cynicism is a prominent feature in defeatists. Their circumstances have taught them it is wise to be skeptical of people and events, but they have taken the need for vigilance a step too far by assuming the worst, even when it is not warranted. As this occurs, innocent people are drawn into the circle of anger. Little effort is put into healthy expression of boundaries and assertiveness since there is an exaggeratedly low expectation that it will do any good. Forgiveness and releasing anger are not done because it seems too lenient to let people off the hook like that.

As I spoke with Carol specifically about releasing her anger toward her mother, her mind of defeat clearly showed. She said it wouldn't do any good to change her response toward her mother now because their dysfunctional communication was so deeply entrenched. Even when her mother showed signs of willingness to change, Carol would shrug and say she had heard that line before. She couldn't afford to hope again.

Carol was dangerously close to letting her mind become accustomed to defeat; she had nearly conceded that she could expect nothing good to come from her primary relationships. It seemed she was resigned to a life of tension and anger. She would not necessarily admit she had chosen to dwell upon such pessimistic beliefs, yet the persistence of tense moods indicated that she had let go of the possibility of being anything other than irritable.

People like Carol can remain in a mind-set of distress because they place too much emphasis on others to make their anger and pessimism go away. Given the fact that it is certain that others can and will disappoint, they remain in their anger until they realize they can in fact choose a better way. They can choose to overcome.

The Overcomer's Mind-Set

There is a special group of people who learn to respond to adversity with an attitude of optimism. They are the overcomers, those who refuse to sink in ultimate defeat when faced with adverse circumstances. When they encounter difficulties, their mental filter tells them they have an opportunity to respond in a manner that promotes relationship growth and harmony. Rather than being threatened by conflict, they recognize that it represents an opportunity to display goodness, integrity, or fairness. They realize that essentially anyone can maintain emotional composure when things are going right, but they have recognized that the real opportunity to forge solid relationships is in proper management of tension, and they do not want to waste the opportunity once it comes along.

One such overcomer was Jim, a middle-aged man who admittedly had been through the experience of defeat in his family and professional life. Now single, he divorced several years prior to our meeting. He had a college-aged son, Patrick, who lived with him during his last two years of high school. Patrick experimented rather heavily in alcohol abuse, and Jim recognized that the only way to help his son was to develop better parenting skills, as opposed to verbal harassment or any other means of being disrespectful.

"I always prided myself," he told me, "in being a hands-on father who could talk straight with my son. You can imagine the shock and anger I felt once I learned that he had turned into a devious kid who hung out with the wrong crowd. Once he turned sixteen, it was like a switch was thrown in his mind and all his common sense was erased. He began cutting classes and not turning in homework and making bad grades. He frequently was not where he told me he would be. His friends were losers who had no accountability with their parents. Almost every weekend, he would make his way to a keg party somewhere and consume beer foolishly with these new friends. He dropped out of sports and quit going to the youth organizations that promoted good values. It was like I hardly knew him anymore."

My curiosity was piqued. "So how did you deal with all the ramifications this created? It must have been a tough haul for you."

"It *was* tough," Jim admitted. "My first reaction was to question how I had failed. I also became angry and wanted to make him know in no uncertain terms that I was not about to subsidize a life of stupidity and irresponsibility." Then shifting gears, Jim said, "I realized that my son's behaviors indicated that he was hurting, so I decided that my best chance to help him was to get to know him more fully."

Jim could have used his anger to verbally pound Patrick into submission. Such an approach would not have produced good results; nonetheless, he would have been able to rationalize it, given his son's irresponsibility. Instead, he sought counseling for the purpose of learning how to communicate boundaries without eroding his relationship with Patrick any further. His opening statement in his first session was, "I need to learn how to handle my anger because I need to help my son learn how to handle his anger." Right then, I knew we would make progress because he lacked a blaming or defeatist spirit.

In our sessions, we discussed many of the concepts that are so commonly associated with the issue of anger. We outlined the options, both positive and negative, for his management of the emotion, and we determined why assertiveness and releasing anger were the preferred choices. We discussed freedom, balanced by an understanding of the role of consequences. We talked about the role of insecurity in his own emotional expressions, and how he could ill afford to allow his son's erratic choices to dictate his moods. Jim was eager to learn, and he was especially skilled at applying the ideas we discussed in changed behavior. He was determined to give his best effort.

Jim's mental filtering system primed him to believe that his anger problems could be resolved in some manner. He predetermined that even if Patrick did not react to his positive initiatives as he would like, Jim would still become a better parent and a more balanced person. His attitude could be summarized this way: "Though I have no control over the outside influences that challenge me each day, no one but me possesses my insides." Jim acknowledged in the very beginning of our work that only he was in charge of the direction of his anger.

As overcomers determine how to respond to anger-provoking circumstances, several key attitudes begin to surface. Let's examine them.

You Can Always Grow

Your experience of negative circumstances is the beginning of your resolve to be a healthier person.

People caught in the web of their own anger take their emotional cues from others. "If you act the way I want," the reasoning goes, "then I can be emotionally stable. But if you treat me badly, I guess I'm obliged to let my anger run its course." Gone is any evidence of inner strength, as the mind of distress kicks into full gear. In essence, this approach guarantees ongoing mismanagement of anger since it is reactionary, void of well-conceived initiatives.

Overcomers realize that the presence of conflict is not a time for quick reflexive reaction, but for thinking, planning, and separating from the emotions of others that are destructive. Repeatedly, I hear angry people claim that their own harsh emotions just happen. The surge of anger comes on so rapidly and powerfully, they claim, that there is no time to plan a reasonable response. When I suggest that their emotional response is the result of choice, they often protest, claiming that it is all so lightning quick that they have no control over their impulse. If that is true, I retort, then they are truly doomed to a life of irrationality.

Overcomers recognize that although emotional surges often happen quickly, they still can choose a response. Self-restraint is always an option. They also know that the ability to plan how to respond to conflict is enhanced as they rehearse in advance how they would like to respond to adversity. They do not leave emotional expression to last-minute impulsiveness. As a result, they have predetermined not to get pulled into others' dysfunction, as they think instead about how to use a moment of conflict as an opportunity to expand their leadership and positive influence.

I had a conversation with Carol about how she could adjust her mental filtering system as it related to responding to both her husband and her mother. "You've told me about numerous run-ins that you've had with your mother," I reflected, "and how she has exhibited the same insensitive attitude in most of those instances. And I detect that you tend to respond to her initiatives in a similar, predictable way. It seems like you've lost any hope that things could be any different." Then challenging her, I asked, "Would you be willing to view the next conflict you have with her as an opportunity to demonstrate growth and maturity?"

Physically, Carol pulled back as she sat in her chair. She stammered slightly as she gave the response that she supposed I wanted to hear: "Well, uh, yeah, I guess. I mean, I suppose I don't have to go on giving her the same responses as I always have, if that's what you're getting at."

"That's exactly what I'm getting at," I said. "For years, you've been allowing your mother to set the pace for your emotional well-being, and the strategy hasn't exactly been a smashing success. I'd say it's time to change course, with determination from within yourself that is focused on being the healthiest person possible, regardless of her response."

Carol had never thought of her emotions as being part of an overall strategy. She just assumed they were what they were, and she had to go with the flow. By contrast, Jim recognized that his anger was more than just an inevitable reaction. He could handle his anger with rudeness and insecurity, or he could handle it with reason and calmness. He would choose the positive route because he determined it was more consistent with his life goals.

Most growth in relationship is not found at a time of peace, but in the midst of conflict. It is in a moment of tension or crisis that we reveal our true strength and character to one another. Overcomers do not necessarily look forward to conflict, but neither do they dread it. They have the wisdom to recognize it is through conflict that they truly learn what resides inside themselves, and in the meantime they also know it is a time when they can exert substantial influence by maintaining a commitment to fairness and reasonableness.

You Are Separate from the Other

You are able to see yourself as separate from the persons creating grief.

A primary reason overcomers can positively respond to conflict is their ability to think autonomously. For instance, many people who operate with the mind of distress think, "We are having tension in our relations; therefore I'm in a troubled state." Their anger is held captive by the matter of collective emotional energy. Overcomers, however, recognize, "This is my life, so I'll need to make the most of my choices even if others around me do not."

Carol showed solid insight in one of our sessions as she recalled recent tension involving Grant. "It was a Friday evening, and we were having a quiet evening at home," she recounted. "It seemed like out of the blue Grant just had a moody reaction to something minor I told him regarding our son. He became accusing and belittling, and it really hurt my feelings. Normally, I would have seen this as a marital problem, and I would have jumped right in with my attitude of distress leading the way. This time, however, I realized we were not having a marital problem. Grant was having an emotional meltdown, but I was not going to join him. It was the end of his week, and he was physically and emotionally depleted. I, however, was glad that the weekend was upon us, and I was in a good mood. I decided right then that I'd take a break from him for a little while, but that I would also stay my course separate from him."

I recall a conversation from years ago with a woman who told me why she had a consistently optimistic and infectious spirit, even amid strain and turmoil. She was born out of wedlock to a disadvantaged teenager and adopted by a couple in their late thirties who were unable to have children. Before her sixth birthday, her adoptive mother died of cancer. The father was not a sensitive person, alternating between sullenness and irritability. He eventually remarried, and her stepmother clearly did not want to take the nurturing role upon herself. Her teen years were lonely; she struggled to have any social life. Not surprisingly, she married the first person available shortly after high school, and it ended in divorce by the time she was in her early twenties.

This woman explained to me, "It was at that point that I realized I was my own separate person. Literally from day one in my life, I had been exposed to people who did not know how to manage my needs, so I had to pay the price. I recognized, though, that my life did not have to be determined by the things that happened to me. I realized that I am my own separate person with my own unique skills and with options every step along the way. I had always admired people who were upbeat and seemed to know where they were going, and I decided there was no reason for me not to be one of those types of people."

Anger management and the security that underlies it don't have to be driven by group processes. Cooperation in all relationships is desirable, but it is not essential to making wise choices. Overcomers see their mind as a separate tool that doesn't have to be subjected to the prevailing experience of surrounding influences.

Optimism About the Future Is Possible

Optimism is possible as you recognize that you can change only what lies in the future, not the past.

Most of the pessimism that drives the anger of people in distress is from reminders of painful experiences in the past (whether immediate or distant). Their mental filter reminds them that conflict perpetuated a distasteful feeling of inadequacy or insignificance; therefore, they think, all current and future conflict will also produce the same. Held down by historical pain, they respond as if they have no other option than to repeat what has gone before.

Overcomers, however, hold no such assumption. Seeing past failure as a learning experience, they respond to present and future problems with the anticipation that something totally different can happen. They take time to reflect upon their own historical missteps, and they specifically mull over how they would like to turn future episodes into a chance to illustrate to themselves that they can make healthy adjustment.

Jim once told me, "When I was married to Patrick's mother, I did not think of myself as capable of contributing good qualities during bad times. My ex-wife and I argued strongly, and sometimes it bordered on violence. Of course, Patrick would sometimes bear the brunt of our problems because it was so easy for my own bad mood to spill over on him. After years of being caught in this crazy cycle, I decided I couldn't keep going down the same path. Whether my ex would change or not, I wanted to be more civil, kind, friendly, and calm. I couldn't undo the past problems we had been entangled in, but I could decide that I would be a better man because of what I had experienced."

In dealing with Patrick's teenage rebellion, Jim recognized he could return to his old antics of ranting and raving. That would always be an option. It would produce no better results than the past, but it was an option. He decided instead that even though Patrick indeed needed instruction and accountability, he could certainly manage to communicate with a tone of respect, even as he maintained his resolve. Drawing upon failed experience from the past, Jim knew that the skills of well-timed assertiveness would serve his purpose of standing up for his belief in responsibility and wise social habits. He knew Patrick would not necessarily be receptive to his assertions immediately, so even as he let consequences run their course he decided that patience was an ally as he held his ground.

Jim looked content as he talked about his experiences with Patrick. "It hasn't been an easy time for the two of us, yet it has been gratifying in its own odd way. I never liked it when I would learn that Patrick had done something wrong again, but I did like the fact that I could see myself becoming a different person. I simply could not go back to the old days of yelling whenever I felt angry. I honestly believe that the best way for me to make inroads with my son is to be firm and dignified at the same time. My past shapes me, but it doesn't define me. It shapes me in the sense that it reminds me of what doesn't work. Today is a new day, and I've decided that as I make choices that reflect greater care and wisdom, I don't have to cling to painful regret. I'm learning, and that's what matters."

Continue a Commitment to Goodness

You can be motivated to accept and forgive because of your commitment to be healthy.

A major mistake that accompanies the effort to be assertive is to expect that results can and will meet expectations. Sometimes the effort to be direct is met with cooperation on the part of those in conflict. When that happens, the effort to maintain composure is simple. At other times, assertion can be managed with great care and maturity, yet the results are disappointing and the conflict remains.

When receiving poor results, people in a mind-set of distress allow defeat to engulf them, which only ensures that anger remains in an unpleasant form. So convinced are they that they must have the cooperation of others before finding personal peace, they forget other choices are available.

Overcomers are committed to being direct and respectful in addressing anger, but they are wise enough to recognize that circumstances do not always unfold as desired. Rather than letting such disappointment derail their personal stability, they can also opt for releasing anger. They are committed to acts and communication of self-preservation, yet they are even more committed to decency, goodness, and self-restraint.

Jim told me about a shift in thinking that, frankly, is needed by many people. He said, "When I was an adolescent and young adult, I thought it was fruity for a man to say he prioritized peace and love. That matched in no way with the culture of toughness and rudeness that surrounded me in those days. It seemed that the brash and the bold were the ones who had all the influence, so I would set aside all the soft sentiments and try to be a tough guy.

"I learned in my marriage that toughness got me nowhere good. The brasher and bolder I was, the deeper my relationship holes would become. That doesn't mean I learned my lessons very quickly, because I didn't. I lost a marriage along the way, and more than a few times I've offended people unnecessarily. Once I realized I could create permanent scars in my relationship with my son, I got serious about being different. There had to be more to my emotional makeup than anger."

As Jim contemplated changes in his emotional disposition, he remembered what he had yearned for when he was Patrick's age. He wanted more than anything to be understood and accepted. He also wanted to know that his mistakes would not be held against him forever. And he wanted respect.

"I heard all my life," he told me, "that we need to forgive each other and accept one another despite our imperfections. I'd tell myself that those concepts sounded good, and then I would wonder why no one seemed to give me the forgiveness and acceptance I felt I deserved. Finally, I realized that the priorities of others are none of my business. What others do with their attitude is up to them, but my attitude was another matter. If I believed it would be nice for me to receive acceptance and forgiveness, I had to admit it would also be good for me to extend it to others."

Jim's efforts to get Patrick on the right track could be described as an uneven mixture of success and failure. Sometimes the two were capable of meaningful discussion that resulted in changed priorities. Sometimes his efforts were followed by disappointing regression. Jim acknowledged that he could use a regressive episode as an excuse to go back into his nonproductive style of anger, yet he knew that as he continued to forgive and accept his son even with their differences, he would be a better man. "I can never be certain that my efforts to stand for good beliefs will bring the desired results," he told me, "but I can be certain that my choice to accept him even as I stay the course will keep me in a good place emotionally."

When I work with people like Jim and Carol, I emphasize that attitude is more important than anything else. If the correctly prescribed behavior is coupled with a sour attitude, they can expect to gain little from their efforts. If they approach anger with an attitude of optimism and goodness, they may still fall short of solving all their problems in the desired manner, but they can proceed. Their frustration will never be so strong as to preclude maintaining priorities that ultimately feed a sense of inner contentment.

For Personal Reflection

- How important is your attitude as you grapple with the issue of how to handle your anger? When you seem stuck in your anger, what thoughts are being fed to you by your mental filter system?
- What common indicators show you to be in the mind of distress? How did you learn to think this way?
- How have you been victimized by others? How can you tell if you have carried your victim status too far?
- When do you tend to succumb to an attitude of defeat? What false or self-insulting assumptions are you making as you remain in your mind-set of defeat?
- To you, what does it mean to be an overcomer? How would your approach to anger-producing circumstances change if you thought more consistently like an overcomer?
- How can your negative experiences spur you to make better choices in your use of anger? Specifically, in what recurring conflicts can you choose to apply the lessons learned from past problems?
- In what situations do you need to separate yourself mentally and emotionally from those who might otherwise create great strain within you? How is your sense of separateness a springboard for a mind of optimism?
- Even as you stand firmly for your needs and convictions, how can you tell that you are simultaneously being accepting?

14

HIGHER PRIORITIES

PEOPLE OFTEN ASK ME how I maintain my sanity after listening every day to the many problems of those caught in the throes of anger and other debilitating emotions. They assume I am indeed sane, and for that I am grateful. But their question reflects a basic misunderstanding of the full thrust of my efforts. Yes, I do hear about problems, lots of them; but I also get to witness people who are committed to growth, and I consider it a privilege to be a part of that process.

Once people begin to explore the reasons for their anger, it opens the door for a much fuller exploration of their overall outlook on life. Examining anger promotes a serious look at the needed ingredients for a secure foundation. It forces individuals to question how they can change, so more satisfying qualities can become prominent. It causes them to examine how they would handle life's difficulties in a way that emphasizes goodness, not trouble. It prompts individuals to contemplate true spirituality, and how it can be applied in lifestyle choices. It can turn an impulsive, insensitive person into a considerate, introspective individual who becomes a true joy to know.

After conducting an anger workshop for a local group of managers of a large corporation, I was pulled aside by a man in his midthirties, Judson, who seemed a bit sheepish as he made a confession. "On several occasions," he stated, "you made reference to the healthy way of living. Your teaching emphasized that an ongoing commitment to anger is not consistent with the healthy lifestyle, and I would definitely agree with that. This may sound strange to you, but before today, I never even thought about the healthy life, at least as it pertains to emotions and relationships. I've always been so focused on being a good achiever and impressing others with my business acumen that I've not put two minutes of thought into emotional healthiness."

I could have internally responded to Judson's confession with frustration, as I might lament the fact that too few people take the time to examine personal issues in any depth. Instead, I received his words with great gladness. Though he was a few years late, he was willing to admit that he needed to map out where he wanted to go in his journey of personal growth. He knew he did not want to be defined by anger, so now he had to question what he would substitute for his anger. It was exciting to hear!

As I got to know Judson, I realized that his lack of awareness regarding emotional and relational matters was not due to an inability to understand. His mind was sharp and capable of receiving stimulating thought. Rather, he had little exposure in his childhood and early adult years to concepts about personal issues; they were overlooked almost entirely. In fact, his family history could have been a character study about the effects of anger gone awry.

Judson told me that his father's father was a distant, uninvolved man. Not one to pass out compliments, he was known as a stony, stern person who could strike fear in his family with his disapproving look. Though his grandfather would not have been familiar with the terminology, he was probably a classic passive-aggressive male. He would often give the silent treatment to those in his disfavor, and he was known for stubbornly doing things his own way. If others did not approve or agree with him, that was too bad. He rarely received any input from family or friends, and he made no apology if his timing bothered others or ruined their plans. They simply had to adjust to him because he certainly never budged!

Judson's father carried on the tradition established by his father. Also cold and hard, he was known as an exacting man who had no patience when faced with others' struggles or failings. Most comments from him seemed critical, and he could hardly ever bring himself to join in pleasant or leisurely activity. It was considered frivolous, and being a man who judged others by strict performance standards he always had to be above the fray.

Growing up with these male role models (the rest of the men in his extended family had similar leanings), Judson was a serious achiever who took little time out to enjoy the fun things that often preoccupy a child. He was involved in sports and apparently was quite skilled, but instead of approaching his efforts with the realization that he was playing a game, he was extremely intense and had to win. Like his father, he too learned to be highly critical, toward others and himself. He would lose his temper easily and developed a reputation as someone you never wanted as an enemy. To call him hard-driven was an understatement.

By the time Judson attended my workshop, he was already silently wondering why his life seemed to be so tense. He was taking medicine for high blood pressure, and he regularly heard family and friends talk about how he should settle into a more easy-going manner of life. Such an adjustment appealed to him, but his history had been so completely defined by competition and tension that it hardly seemed possible he could be any other way. Yet there he was, sitting in my office stating that he wanted to get beyond anger as he related with those nearest him. He was primed for change, and I was going to give my best effort to help him succeed.

The misery that Judson's anger created within himself was causing him to examine his emotional alternatives. He told me, "There is one fellow at work that I really admire, and I've silently wished I could be more like him." When I asked what it was that seemed so appealing about this person, he replied: "Well, he's known for having a strong and reliable work ethic, which I respect, yet despite his high standards he's not pushy or impersonal. He seems to get along with most people, and I think he genuinely feels happy a high percentage of the time. That's something I can't say about myself!"

As I counsel people like Judson, not only do I want them to learn how to undo the bad habits they carry, I want them to aim for better alternatives. If they decide to move away from a life defined by anger, they can choose to move toward something that stimulates them, giving them a boost. Let's take the time to examine some of the traits that can offset anger while generating a more stable manner of interacting with others.

Encouragement

When people repeatedly fall into the trap of anger, they seem to become experts at criticism. Being quick to notice what is wrong with the world, they readily think and speak in negative, judgmental tones. Chronically angry people have allowed pessimism to so envelop their minds that they lose the ability to see what in others is good.

Moving away from anger requires the ability to focus on the things in life that are right and uplifting. Healthy people like being in the role of speaking words of support, just as they enjoy giving sincere compliments or commenting about others' successes. They are quite aware that negative things happen, and they are not so superficial as to simply ignore things that are distasteful. At the same time, they realize that life's negatives do not erase the positives. They do not allow their mind to become so jaded that they persistently lead with comments about what they do not like. In fact, they search for what is good even if it is not fully evident.

Examples of positive events abound in most individuals' daily routine. For instance, do you notice when a coworker does something right, making the job just a little easier for everyone else? Say something about it!

When your spouse or roommate takes a moment to listen to you talk about your day's routine, do you appreciate it? Speak openly about your feeling of gratitude. When a family member calls to talk with you about upcoming plans, do you enjoy the fact that you feel included? Make it a matter of open expression. Most people have had numerous experiences of being caught doing something wrong, but it is far less common to be caught doing things that are good and right. You can make this your glad task.

Judson told me, "My dad told me on several occasions that if someone does something right, they shouldn't expect a compliment because they are only doing what should be done in the first place. That always seemed to make sense to me."

"Well, let's look at the logic of that sentiment," I replied. "Such a notion implies that we should only comment on one another's actions when something goes wrong. That leads to each of us being critical and feeling paranoid. That's not exactly my idea of successful living."

I asked Judson to take a challenge for one week. He was to pick five people that he saw daily, whether at home or work, and once a day comment to each person about something that he liked. He agreed to my suggestion, though the look on his face told me he thought it was a corny assignment. The next week, when I saw him again, he was beaming as he told me, "I actually enjoyed my week! At first, it felt plastic when I tried to think of something encouraging to say to each of my five people, but pretty quickly it became easy. After a few days I found myself anticipating that something positive would happen, and sure enough, it did! I felt more at ease, and I know that the people who received my words benefited as well."

It is less easy to remain committed to anger if you honestly choose to focus on the things in others that are good. Openly speaking words of encouragement keeps people from focusing exclusively on the many things that can go wrong. Encouraging words show you to be friendly, and they create an atmosphere of goodwill.

Respect

In my anger workshop sessions, I pose a statement to be answered true or false: "Before respect can be given, it must be earned." A high percentage of participants answer true, and when I ask for an explanation I usually hear something like this: "People can't expect to be treated with respect if they are rude or selfish because that would imply a sense of entitlement, and I'll not participate in that." Of course, this sparks words of debate from the ones who answered the opposite because they claim that a requirement of good behavior turns the quality of respect into nothing more than conditional acceptance.

Trust is a quality that must be earned, but respect can be given whether or not the recipient has earned it. (The correct response to my true-false statement is false.) Whereas the capacity to trust hinges on the character of the recipient, the capacity to respect is a commentary about the character of the giver. The respectful person may not necessarily feel positively toward those who do wrong, yet he or she treats others with regard and dignity, from the belief that each human begins life with innate value, and this is something that merits attention. Even if the recipient acts in a way that is not consistent with innate value, the giver still chooses to offer respect because giving disrespect demeans both the one who receives it and the one who gives it.

Recall that we have linked the emotion of anger with a craving to feel respected. Inevitably, angry people have felt belittled or demeaned, which prompts them to take a stand of self-preservation. Such a response can be good, since it inspires offended people to seek more appropriate treatment. Some angry people, however, rationalize that the act of another person's disrespect permits them to respond with disrespect. "Since you treated me wrong," they reason, "I now have the right to treat you wrong."

In its healthiest forms, anger is an emotion that ideally promotes healing and correction. Well-communicated anger gives notice that indecent or insensitive acts have no place in a constructive, growing relationship. To communicate anger disrespectfully is to contradict the message of healing. By communicating anger respectfully, angry people stand up for what is right and good, and they provide an experiential model for the way they would like to be treated. Respectfulness allows delivery of the message to be consistent with the message itself.

Suppose a family member has been in a foul mood and criticized you unfairly. Your anger is aroused, prompting you to stand up for your need to be appropriately regarded. Your anger is a reasonable reaction, and your desire to seek more respectful treatment is valid. Suppose, though, that you express your anger insultingly. Although you address your legitimate concern, you demean and speak in a haughty manner. What happens to the message? It is lost. The receiver, feeling insulted, inevitably retreats into a defensive posture, and the interaction predictably falls apart.

Givers of respect recognize that it is quite possible to speak forthrightly, without condescension. Even if they believe their perspectives are better than the other person's, they can still operate with the conviction that they have no right to act as if they are of higher value than anyone else. Here are examples of respect in the midst of anger:

- When a wife addresses concerns with her husband about his lack of attentiveness, she does so without resorting to a scolding tone of voice. She speaks her words firmly, yet she maintains an attitude of dignity and knows when to draw her comments to a close.
- As a single man speaks with his friends about a break-up with his girlfriend, he refrains from denouncing her character, recognizing that he need not hold her in contempt even though he has been feeling hurt and disappointed.
- When a businessperson confronts an employee about repeated mistakes, he speaks with an attitude of dignity even as the problems are openly explored.

Maintaining a commitment to respectfulness, even in a moment of anger, demonstrates that you find no satisfaction in maintaining your own personal regard at the expense of another individual. It shows that you so strongly believe in the dignity of humanity that you will not use an incident of another's personal weakness as an opportunity to belittle. Consistency in demonstrating goodness is prioritized.

Patience

I have never met a consistently angry person who also used patience in a steady manner. Hand in hand with troublesome anger is the tendency to respond to others' flaws with a short fuse, being unwilling to allow the needed time for others to make a responsible choice. Many of these people state that they try and try to exercise patience, yet as one frustration piles on top of another willpower erodes, and impatience is communicated through griping, irritability, criticism, or an explosion.

When people attempt to maintain patience, only to have an angry eruption later, I usually learn that what is said to be patience is actually feeble suppression of anger. Because suppression and patience are two entirely separate matters, the angry outburst clearly demonstrates that the suppression was little more than an attempt to mask contempt.

Patience can be defined as the willingness to endure inconvenience, delay, or annoyance. It also is demonstrated by the ability to bear pain or trial without complaint. Because anger is so tied to a history of feeling pain and mistreatment, choosing patience can often seem wrong because of being tantamount to asking for more wrongdoing.

During one discussion with Judson, I mentioned the need for patience, which caused him to shake his head in frustration. He said, "I sure have tried to apply patience at my business and at home, but I find that it just doesn't work. Whenever I act patiently, it seems that other people interpret it as an invitation to take advantage of me, and when they try to do that, I can let my anger fly!"

"Let's look at two thoughts regarding the subject," I responded. "First, patience is not a technique to be tried in difficult circumstances. It's not a behavior to pull out when you are attempting to influence people to act a specific way. Rather, patience is a state of mind. It's a quality that you choose, not for the purpose of changing others but because it is genuinely a part of you. It represents your core beliefs about accepting others for what they are and about the realization that you cannot always expect events to unfold according to your agenda. As you choose to abide in patience, you're fully aware that you have other options at your disposal, such as being pushy, speaking sharply, or rejecting others; yet you know you're choosing patience because it's the better option."

Then continuing, I mentioned, "Secondly, to successfully live with patience, you need to be satisfied that you've made the most of your opportunities to be assertive. Too often, people who practice pseudopatience are actually people pleasers trying too hard to appease others in their bad habits. Sometimes, these people need to be more open about their needs and their personal boundaries—*then* when they decide to apply patience, they do so with the satisfaction that they've also been true to their valid convictions."

Judson had never thought of his failed efforts at patience as being linked to a technique that was little more than suppression of valid anger, but as he contemplated the idea it began to make sense. For instance, he realized that if he were to be more tolerant of the errors made by coworkers, it would be an effort that came from the heart, not the head. He needed to be certain that he was not just biding time in the hope that they would eventually do things his way, but that he was genuinely accepting them, with flaws and all. Likewise, he recognized the need to examine his use of assertiveness. He knew that he tended to operate in extremes, either holding in his anger and quietly begrudging or letting it flow with insensitivity. He was beginning to realize the value of respectful assertiveness, and he came to learn that his efforts to communicate directly clearly made it easier for him to choose a patient spirit. Patience, he realized, could be the byproduct of a balanced manner of managing conflict.

Calm Firmness

A man once heard me speak about the possibility of communicating anger with dignity, and it was clear that he was uncomfortable with my emphasis.

Specifically, I said that it is not necessary to be harsh or abrasive when you are attempting to stand up for your convictions. Forcefully, he blurted out, "You just don't understand how thick-headed people can be. I work with guys who only understand one language: power. If I'm ever going to get through to them, the *only* way I can succeed is to let them know that I'm more powerful than they are. Softness definitely won't work."

I asked him, "When someone is angry with you, and they yell or communicate with great agitation, how willingly do you receive it?"

Pausing a moment and then stammering, he said, "Well, I don't like it one bit, and I usually argue right back." He knew where I was going with my thinking.

I made my point. "In the short term, you may seemingly succeed by forcing compliance via the use of force, but I'm guessing that the recipients have the same feeling about it that you just voiced. They don't like it one bit, and I'm also going to guess that they look for the first opportunity to get away from you. Am I right?" He reluctantly conceded that I *might* be on track, so I finished my thought. "That's not a very powerful way to communicate at all, if power is defined as the ability to wield influence."

There is no rule stating that firmness must be accompanied by oppression if it is to be successful. In fact, to the contrary, such an approach only stirs up strife. If angry people want to remove distastefulness from their emotional disposition, they embrace the notion of calm firmness, the ability to be direct while also emotionally composed. There are many ways this approach can be applied:

- When correcting a child regarding misbehavior (even if it is the tenth time that day), a parent can choose not to belittle, but to explain consequences and follow through in a manner consistent with those consequences. Lecturing and inducing guilt are left out.
- When disagreeing with a family member, words can be spoken without coercion or persuasion. The logic of the words can stand alone without conveying a "What's wrong with you?" attitude.
- When explaining a preference to an argumentative friend, your tone of voice can remain even; you do not need to convince the person that he is wrong and you are right.

When you let others know of your anger, the communication consists of more than the spoken word. Your emotional pitch conveys how confident you are and thus influences others' willingness to receive what you are saying. A stubborn, pleading, or brazen pitch only cues others to receive you poorly because it indicates insecurity and insensitivity on your part. A calm yet firm pitch, however, indicates you are comfortable with your message, and it opens a greater possibility of the message being received. There is no guarantee that the recipient will incorporate your thoughts gladly, but *you* are capable of finding peace more readily since you have chosen to maintain tact rather than contentiousness.

Self-Restraint

Along with the quality of calm firmness goes self-restraint. Angry people can be too forceful with their anger, but they also have difficulty in knowing when to cease. Many people become ensnared by their own anger as they begin with an appropriate message but push it with repetition and longer-than-necessary explanation. These people cannot seem to say what needs to be said and then allow the recipient to digest it in his or her own time.

Accompanying overstatement of an angry message is an insulting covert message. Though the words are not actually spoken, the message is delivered: "I think you're too stupid to process my words on your own, so I'll try to rearrange the thoughts in your brain until you can finally admit how right I am." No recipient of such an approach hears an angry message gladly.

When Judson and I discussed how readily angry people repeat their message to the point of pushiness, he looked at me with a sheepish grin. "I'm glad my wife isn't in here with me right now because she'd be all over my case to make sure I was digesting this." Then in a confessional tone of voice, he said, "I've been known to ramble and rant and rave when I get angry. I'll start out with an idea to express that seems very reasonable, but when it becomes obvious that it's not being immediately received, I turn on the thrusters and try to force agreement."

Asking one of my most common questions, I said, "Does it work?"

Of course, he responded that far from working, his repetitious style only increased the original tension. Judson was recognizing that it was not necessary to sell the goodness of his message. Instead, he could state his case and then restrain himself for the purpose of letting others have the freedom to digest what he had communicated.

As in the case of unnecessary repetition, whenever he used self-restraint he was sending another covert message, only this one was more complimentary. In restraining his anger, he was indicating: "I'm comfortable with what I've just said, and I also affirm your right to receive it in your own timing and manner." This hardly guarantees you will get the results you want every time, but self-restraint keeps you from being too boisterous with your emotion, and it allows you to establish leadership amid conflict.

Timing

Suppose you received a phone call telling you that a longtime friend had just died. Your mind would be awhirl, and surely you would have an immediate surge of emotions as you tried to process what you were hearing. Then suppose that five minutes after the call is finished, a family member approaches you with a confrontation about a minor incident from earlier in the day. Your disposition would not be to receive the confrontation, no matter how valid the complaint was or how cleanly presented. The timing for the confrontation would be atrocious.

When you know that your anger needs to be expressed, factor into the equation for healthiness the matter of timing. People who struggle with imbalanced anger often do themselves no favors as they fail to consider the recipient's ability to receive their words, on the basis of other factors such as surrounding circumstances, people, or experiences. Sometimes, a recipient of anger is so reluctant to be confronted that no time is ever good enough, in which case the anger may need to be expressed regardless of the encumbrance. In many cases, though, anger can be more readily managed if the angry person takes the time to survey the environment before launching into angry expression.

On a deeper level, the matter of timing is tied to empathy and sensitivity. Too often, angry people can be so focused on their own issues that they fail to recognize that it is not a one-dimensional world, with their feelings being all that matters. Healthy people, on the other hand, know that although they have personal matters to address, it is always best to put them into the context of the surrounding world.

A primary goal of healthy anger is promotion of relationship harmony. Healthy people realize that anger can be positive and purposeful, so they look for a way to ensure that their use of anger is as productive as possible. Rather than spewing anger while oblivious to the recipient's state of mind, and rather than using anger passively to make the recipient squirm with speculation, healthy people want their expression of anger to fit within a greater paradigm of cooperation and fairness.

Judson told me about an incident that required him to alter his presentation of anger, as compared to previous episodes that were similar. He was beaming with satisfaction as he said: "Recently, I was very frustrated at work because one of my team members had not completed his portion of a project we were working on. His input was crucial to my efforts, and I was feeling that he had been playing an avoidance game with me. When I walked over to his cubicle to talk with him about this, he was just finishing a phone call, and I could tell that he was upset. In the past, I would have ignored it and launched into my speech. This time, though, I asked him about the situation, and he told me that his father-in-law had been diagnosed as being in the late stages of cancer. For the last several days, he had been trying to juggle his time between working on our deadline and trying to meet his family's needs. I could tell that he was going through a rough time and that he was stressed in ways he had not been before."

Speaking softly, Judson continued, "I took a chair right next to him and we talked for about twenty minutes. He openly acknowledged the need to stay on top of our project, and I realized that he was trying to be conscientious. I strategized with him to determine how we could help ease his burden at work so he could give more attention to the things that mattered most. We had a very affirming conversation, and we parted with the realization that it was not only OK to discuss such personal matters, but essential."

After speaking with Judson, I wondered how many angry people actually pause as he did to determine the circumstances of someone involved in their anger. My musing prompted me to acknowledge that one of the most common complaints registered by recipients of anger is "But you just don't understand." Anger can cause people to be so focused on their needs that they forget others do not exist for the sole purpose of responding to those needs. Most angry people can learn that if they made the effort to determine the needs and concerns of those in conflict with them, the probability of having their feelings heard would rise substantially. Choosing to see their anger as one factor in a multifaceted environment, they can develop a reputation of fairness, and conflict can be reasonably managed.

Kindness

As I speak with people who persistently struggle with anger, I learn that they have become leery regarding the matter of kindness. Many state that they have tried to be kind (perhaps they have tried too hard) and it has backfired. They assume that other people interpret their kindness as an invitation to take advantage of them. Feeling stung by others' willingness to pounce upon soft people, they vow that they cannot afford to be too kind too often.

Almost always, I discover that these people who feel they have been too kind have a deep history of suppressing their legitimate anger for fear that it might be construed as harshness or insensitivity. Operating in a mode of appeasement, their kindness can actually be a form of subtle manipulation, given for the purpose of persuading others to accept them or to respond consistently with their yearnings. To these people, I suggest they continue as kind people, with the added measure of also being more immediate and firm when they recognize that they are feeling used or that others are demonstrating no understanding.

Other angry people determine to swear off kindness, not because they have felt used but because it does not fit their tough, tell-it-like-it-is persona. These people use their anger and their seemingly impenetrable reputation as a means of controlling others; they fear that too many displays of gentleness greatly diminish their power. Of course, their thinking is fueled by great insecurity (though most will never admit it), and over time their commitment to anger costs them heavily as they find themselves having few true intimates.

No one can be considered truly successful without kindness being a major component of personality. Kindness is a cornerstone trait of a person who loves. Kindness can be defined as a commitment to friendliness, generosity, cordiality, and gentleness. Kindness is the outward manifestation of a heart filled with compassion for others. People committed to this trait actively search for a way to help another's life run more smoothly. They experience great delight when others feel welcomed. They are wise enough to recognize that conflict, and its resulting anger, is an unavoidable part of life, yet they desire to handle conflict in the least abrasive manner. They understand that an overall reputation for purity and goodness gives them credibility when the time arrives to use assertiveness. Whether they are in conflict with others or not, they genuinely desire to maintain an uplifting presence in the lives of those surrounding them.

I became acquainted with a man in his midseventies who once had a reputation as hard, mean, and spiteful. "Not only did I not care about the needs and feelings of anyone else, I felt that I was most likely to wield influence if I kept up my tough-as-nails exterior," he told me. At age sixty, he had a massive heart attack and almost died. After complicated surgeries, his cardiologist told him he was lucky to be alive; from that day forward, the surgeon said, he should understand that he was living on borrowed time.

"What struck me the most," this man said, "was how kindly my family and the medical staff treated me during that time. I had been mean to my son all his life, but he helped bathe me and feed me. My wife never left my side, and she was always ready to tend to my needs. The nurses loved to laugh and talk with me in the most pleasant ways. I had to admit right then that up to that point in my life, I had been a sorry person, and I had never once made an effort to treat anyone the way they treated me.

"I told God that if he would let me live just a little longer, I would reform and I would never again swear at people or treat them any way but decent. It's strange how it took an appointment with near-death to wake me up to the reality that my years of anger were a total waste. It's been over fifteen years since my heart attack, and not one day has gone by without me thinking of my vow. I'm committed to it for the rest of my life." Throughout the time he was telling me this, his voice was soft and his face had the look of complete peace. I knew he meant every word he had spoken.

Persistently angry people are not happy people. Although that is not a fact they want to broadcast, deep inside their soul they yearn for something better. Ideally, they do not need a heart attack or some other calamity to bring them to the realization that there is no long-term value in remaining committed to anger. They need only take an honest inventory of the repercussions of their anger to determine that quality of life has not been enhanced by insensitive use of anger. Realizing this, perhaps they can embrace the good that comes from helpfulness, a giving spirit, tolerance, and gestures of support, and they can find gladness in knowing that such effort pays dividends that can last a lifetime. They need not dismiss their feelings of anger altogether, but the anger can be managed within the broader context of making a loving difference toward others.

Joy

Angry people are not usually completely devoid of laughter, joviality, or a winsome spirit. In fact, many are known as cut-ups or comedians, the life of the party. If anger, though, lurks closely beneath the surface of their personality, this lightheartedness is inevitably exposed as the lesser quality. The anger, consistently managed poorly, can be understood as the primary factor in their relating style, while the appearance of happiness is revealed as a mask that covers the pain.

Joy involves the experience of fun, ease, and frivolity, but it is much more than that. Also included in joy is the feeling of contentment, peacefulness, and inner satisfaction. It is possible to be funny and to appear happy, yet without joy. The smiles of joyful people do not represent a mere moment of respite between episodes of aggravation; rather, they are an indication of a deeper sense of satisfaction that comes from knowing they are committed to the things that are good. Their joviality is consistently uplifting, never demeaning.

Joyful people exude a sense of peace within themselves; they are able to join with others in pursuit of contentment. They feel great gain when they witness others as they experience happy emotions, and they typically are able to enhance the gladness felt by others. Not self-absorbed, their joy has an infectious, communal dimension.

As Judson took a long, hard inventory of his life, he concluded that he had indeed succeeded in finding the formula for success as an achiever. He made good money and was known as reliable when he put effort into a task. He recognized, however, that as long as there was a chronic undertow of frustration, criticism, and annoyance, he had not really succeeded at all.

"Looking into my uses of anger," he reflected, "and trying to understand how I perpetuate anger unnecessarily, I have been forced to examine my life as never before. I'm learning that I can possess all sorts of knowledge, and I can achieve many gains in my performances, but if I don't prioritize the loving dimensions of life, it really doesn't matter." In his midthirties, he was just beginning to realize that relational skills, built upon a commitment to inner peace, were where his energy could be most wisely spent.

Every episode of anger indicates there is a longing for something more rewarding, lasting, and affirming. As you turn your efforts away from coercion or condescension, and as you focus instead on contributing to the well-being of others, even while you stand up for your own needs, you will find balance. The net result is inner satisfaction, which is precisely what the angry person needs.

Joyful people have learned that the path toward satisfaction is much more attainable when accompanied by a harmonious spirit.

I consider it a privilege to counsel people who have struggled with the emotion of anger. First, my interaction with them serves an accountability role in my own life, as I too work to maintain balance in my own use of anger. Second, I find great motivation and satisfaction as I get to witness firsthand how individuals who have had personal pain commit themselves to something other than harmful, retaliatory expression. I smile easily when I realize that they have chosen to commit themselves to traits like the ones mentioned in this chapter.

As you consider how you might apply the insights and ideas expressed in these pages, I am hopeful that you too will look for a way to become respectfully involved in the lives of those around you. Though you may not be a psychotherapist, you can find great satisfaction as you illustrate that there are higher priorities in life leading to contentment and relational success. You will never get to a place where you cease to experience anger, yet you can certainly expect to find release from the hold of anger upon personality. Used in a manner that is mindful of the dignity of each person, anger can cease to be a defining feature in your reputation. You can be freed to be the loving person God designed you to be.

❍

For Personal Reflection

- ❍ Why might you choose to remain committed to anger as opposed to more tender qualities? How would your priorities need to change to decrease your commitment to anger while increasing your commitment to goodness?
- ❍ Who in your world would benefit by your encouragement? How can you become a more encouraging presence than you presently are?
- ❍ How do you define respect? In what circumstances could you make a more concerted effort to show positive regard toward others?
- ❍ Calmness and firmness can be experienced simultaneously. How would your communication style change if you gave priority to calmness even as you are firm? How do you suppose others would respond to such an adjustment?
- ❍ What makes self-restraint so difficult when you are feeling angry? How can you remain true to your legitimate anger even as you determine to factor in the needs of others?
- ❍ What causes you to have the keenest sense of timing as you address your anger? How does improved timing affect your overall relational style toward others?
- ❍ Who is the kindest person you know? What is it about this person's kindness that inspires you?
- ❍ Persistently angry people are ultimately not joyful. Why is that? How can a commitment to balanced anger increase the experience of true joy?

THE AUTHOR

LES CARTER has maintained a private practice of psychotherapy at the Minirth Clinic in Richardson, Texas, since 1980, specializing in the treatment of emotional and relational disorders. He is the author of seventeen books, including *The Anger Workbook, The Worry Workbook, The Freedom from Depression Workbook,* and *People Pleasers.* He received his bachelor's degree from Baylor University and has master's and Ph.D. degrees from the University of North Texas.

A popular speaker, Carter leads seminars in cities across America. He can be reached at www.drlescarter.com.

OTHER BOOKS OF INTEREST

The Anger Workbook for Christian Parents

Dr. Les Carter and Dr. Frank Minirth

$16.95 Paperback

ISBN: 0–7879–6903–6

In this practical book, anger experts Dr. Les Carter and Dr. Frank Minirth, coauthors of the best-selling book *The Anger Workbook*, show families how to understand and manage anger in order to create harmony at home. Blending biblical wisdom and psychological research, they show how to distinguish between healthy and unhealthy anger and offer proven techniques for dealing with the root causes of anger. Full of real-life examples, checklists, evaluation tools, and study questions, this is a "must-have" book for those involved with today's youth.

DR. LES CARTER is a nationally known psychotherapist at the Minirth Clinic in Richardson, Texas, where he has practiced since 1980.

DR. FRANK MINIRTH is president of the Minirth Clinic, which he founded in 1975.

[Price subject to change]